BATS
OF THE ROCKY MOUNTAIN WEST

BATS

NATURA

f the Rocky Mountain West

STORY, ECOLOGY, AND CONSERVATION

RICK A. ADAMS

UNIVERSITY PRESS OF COLORADO

Published by the University Press of Colorado
5589 Arapahoe Avenue, Suite 206C
Boulder, Colorado 80303

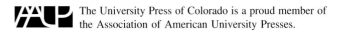 The University Press of Colorado is a proud member of
the Association of American University Presses.

The University Press of Colorado is a cooperative publishing enterprise supported, in part, by Adams State College, Colorado State University, Fort Lewis College, Mesa State College, Metropolitan State College of Denver, University of Colorado, University of Northern Colorado, and Western State College of Colorado.

The paper used in this publication meets the minimum requirements of the American National Standard for Information Sciences—Permanence of Paper for Printed Library Materials. ANSI Z39.48-1992

Library of Congress Cataloging-in-Publication Data

Adams, Rick A. (Rick Alan)
  Bats of the Rocky Mountain West : natural history, ecology, and conservation / Rick A. Adams.
      p. cm.
Includes bibliographical references and index.
  ISBN 0-87081-735-3 (hardcover : alk. paper) — ISBN 0-87081-736-1
(pbk. : alk. paper)
  1. Bats—Rocky Mountains Region. I. Title.
    QL737.C5 A22 2003
    599.4'0978—dc21
                                                                    2003010942

Design by Daniel Pratt

12 11 10 09 08 07 06   10 9 8 7 6 5 4 3 2

In memory of
Henry Lewis Adams III,
1919–2001

Contents

Contents

Acknowledgments

he inspiration for this book was motivated by years of field experiences with bats in the West that have taught me much about biology as well as about myself. When working with "such a mystical beast," patience is the first virtue tested, determination the second, and learning from "defeat" the third. But once taken by the beauty and astounding nature of bats, one is hooked for a lifetime. There really is no turning back.

As for human influences, my parents greatly encouraged my interest in biology as a young child and were almost always supportive of me whenever I dragged some animal home from the woods or pond to keep as a pet, or at least to watch for a few days. To them I owe a loving and wonderful childhood that molded my interest in the natural world. To my partner, Lynne, a relative newcomer on the scene, I thank you for your patience and love (not to mention the editing) during the last two years and throughout the countless hours I've devoted to this project . . . now we can go hiking! And to Jasper, my canine companion, thanks for seventeen years of unwavering friendship, love, and field adventures; you've witnessed it all, man . . . now we can get back to hiking!

Great appreciation goes to the University of Wisconsin-Whitewater, which allowed me sabbatical leave in 2000–2001 to work full-time on this book. In addition, Chancellor Jack Miller, Provost David Pryor, and Dean Howard Ross provided very generous monetary support for the purchase of photographs and original illustrations for this project. Without their support and that of the Department of Biological Sciences, this book would likely never have happened. To the many students who have contributed their hard work, positive attitudes, and courage throughout the many late-night cougar and bear encounters we've had in the field, I greatly appreciate your efforts and wish you the best in your future endeavors, wherever they may take you.

My graduate mentor, Professor David Armstrong, of the University of Colorado, Boulder, has had, and continues to have, the most profound impact on my professional career. His steadfast support and wisdom have paved many rocky roads for me throughout the years (as has all his editing), and by means of many compelling conversations on ecology, zoogeography, and morphology, he has kept me solidly grounded in the theoretical aspects of evolutionary biology. My interest in mammals was piqued by the mind-expanding nature of Professor Armstrong's mammalogy course, and following a year of independent research on bats in Colorado, I was prodded gently but firmly by him and his graduate student Jerry Freeman to give my first talk at the Colorado/Wyoming Academy of Sciences meetings in 1984. Mostly I remember the intense fear of my first attempt at public speaking, but I heard the talk went okay.

Other strong and positive influences were provided by Professors Alex Cruz, Marc Bekoff, Charles Southwick, and Hobart Smith through their captivating courses on biogeography, animal behavior, primatology, and herpetology, as well as their professional advice and encouragement. Professor Dennis Van Gerven engaged me in many pacing, hand-waving conversations on functional morphology during graduate school and provided profound insights with statements such as "Juvenile bats cannot afford to be gangly!" Dr. Scott Pedersen, a colleague and friend with whom I continue to collaborate, has given his blood (via bat bites), sweat (it's very, very hot in eastern Wyoming in summer), and tears (I finished my dissertation before him) in helping me with various research projects in the West, and has provided opportunities for joint research endeavors throughout the Caribbean islands. Since 1990, I have had the great pleasure of being involved with the Colorado Bat Society, whose board and staff have committed immeasurable amounts of time and effort toward public education and the conservation of bats in Colorado. I thank all of you for your dedication and the shared good times throughout the past thirteen years.

Over the past seven years, the City of Boulder Open Space and Mountain Parks (OSMP) Department has consistently provided monetary and staff support for the study of bats in the wildlands around Boulder, Colorado. In particular I would like to thank Jocelyn Hubbell, Clint Miller, Cary Richardson, Burton Stoner, Toni Piaggio, Lynne Sullivan, and Rick Hatfield of OSMP, who have helped with fieldwork and in many cases risked personal injury during technical climbs to place data loggers in bat roosts. A very special thanks to Eric Butler, GIS guru at OSMP, for synthesizing the fabulous distribution maps used in the species accounts. I would also like to thank the Boulder County Parks and Open Space Department and, in particular, Mark Brennan, for providing monetary and field support for bat research on their properties.

I am also indebted to Darrin Pratt, director of the University Press of Colorado, for his enthusiasm, encouragement, and patience with this project. Thanks for the opportunity to publish this book through my alumni institution. Wendy Smith of Brushfire Studios provided many of the awe-inspiring illustrations reproduced herein, and I was very fortunate to be guided to her by Dr. Don Wilson, director of Biodiversity Programs, Smithsonian's National Museum of Natural History. Special thanks to Dr. Scott Altenbach for allowing me the use of his astonishing photographs of bats in this book. I also greatly appreciate the use of photographs submitted by M. Brock Fenton, Paul Faure, and Merlin Tuttle. I thank Dave Armstrong for his several reviews and meaningful comments on this manuscript, and similarly, I thank three anonymous reviewers for their comments on earlier drafts. To anyone I have forgotten to mention, I greatly apologize for this mental lapse. Please feel free to send me a nasty note!

To write a book about such a mystical beast demands a certain degree of detachment and a willingness to turn to the old fairy tales as well as to own oneself defeated

—Loren Eiseley, *The Lost Notebooks of Loren Eiseley*

BATS
OF THE ROCKY MOUNTAIN WEST

1

Introduction

A twitch, a twitter, an elastic shudder in flight
And serrated wings against the sky
Like a glove, black glove thrown up in the light
And falling back

— D. H. Lawrence, "Bat"

Few poets have attempted to portray the nature of bats. Usually glimpsed in fits and moments, bats may appear bigger than life itself, personifying mystery and the unknown. As perceived spawns of Satan, they undoubtedly raise havoc and in their wake disease and destruction follow. Misconceived and shrouded in mystery, these winged shadows of night challenge our senses and cause us to re-evaluate an otherwise seemingly rational natural world.

After centuries of disparaging imagery, many of the intensely negative views of bats are waning somewhat. In many communities bat mythology is slowly being replaced with factual information that proves more astounding and interesting than fabled tales of the crypt and the macabre. With education and outreach, conservation organizations and other groups have begun to reverse many of the age-old, contemptuous attitudes of humans toward bats, and the lives of bats have undoubtedly improved because of those efforts.

With advances in research technology, biologists are able to learn more about the secretive lives of bats, and as a result, many of our preconceived notions about their natural history have proven incorrect. Bats, as it turns out, harbor few diseases contractible by humans and, as mammals go, are exceptionally clean. Despite their generally small body size, bats may live as long as thirty-five years, most species give birth to only a single young per year, maternal care of the young is altogether indulgent, and they appear to be quite intelligent. Furthermore, bats are important to many ecosystems, devouring tons of insects per year, pollinating important plants such as saguaro and organ pipe cactus, and dispersing the seeds of many significant tropical plants. Composing about 20 percent of all living mammalian species, they are one of the most successful groups to have evolved, yet many species are critically endangered.

This book is about the bats of the Rocky Mountain West. More broadly, it is an invitation to better appreciate bats as intriguingly beautiful animals representing part of our diverse world rather than as unresolved mythical creatures of darkness. I anticipate that readers of this book will "pass the word" about the beauty of bats, thereby furthering public education and appreciation. The challenges are great in this task, even in the twenty-first century. I hope this work will provide a welcome contribution to public education about and conservation of bats for years to come.

The intended audience is both the layperson and the specialist. The scope of this book includes bats found in the Rocky Mountain states of Montana, Idaho, Wyoming, Colorado, New Mexico, and Utah, as well as Arizona, which is linked geologically and ecologically to the Southern Rockies via the Colorado Plateau. We begin here with a general discussion about the biology of bats, followed by a description in Chapter 2 of the landscapes of the region and how bats fit into them. In Chapter 3 I discuss the regional evolution of bats, and Chapter 4 covers bat populations and community trends, feeding strategies, and resource use. Chapter 5 explores the strategies, achievements, and future goals for the conservation of bats in the Rocky Mountain West.

A key to species begins the section on species accounts. A picture and distribution map is presented for each of the thirty-one species. The accounts are intended for use by specialists and laypersons alike. For the layperson, information on the natural history of each species is presented, whereas the specialist will find technical information on standard measurements, dental formulae, and subspecies distributions. In addition, sections on ecology and behavior and reproduction and development present data accumulated in the primary literature for the region. A glossary of terms is provided at the back of the book.

Appendix 1 provides short descriptions of worldwide and regional governmental and private conservation groups and their Web site addresses. My hope is that readers will use these as convenient references to stimulate their involvement with organizations promoting conservation of, and educational outreach about, bats. I also provide a table of the current conservation status of each bat species. Although the status of any given species in any given area may change as more data are gathered, these tables at least provide a marker for the various bats at the time of publication of this book. Appendix 2 offers a bibliography of government agency reports and documents, many of which, like bats, rarely see the light of day. I hope this is helpful in disseminating useful information to wildlife enthusiasts and academic biologists alike.

A POWERFUL MISUNDERSTANDING: DECIPHERING THE REALITY OF BATS

The great bat biologist Donald R. Griffin (1958) once stated: "Bats are such unusual creatures that some effort is required to think of them as actual animals living in a world of common sense and concrete reality." Bats are indeed mysterious to humans. Cloaked by the darkness of night, they remain elusive to our senses. Although direct encounters between bats and humans are relatively rare, those that do occur are frequently sudden and unexpected, thus imposing immediate discomfort and distress. On balance, however, bats are gentle, attractive mammals who are simply trying to make a living. Different they are; evil they are not. Intriguingly, bats occupy the extreme edge of "mammalness," being so different from us that our mind struggles against acceptance. As a group, they represent a branch of evolutionary change unmatched in character throughout the six-hundred-million-year history of vertebrates (animals with backbones). Initially drawn to bats by their mystique, people who delve into really knowing them realize quickly that the true-life story of our winged friends is astonishing, easily eclipsing their mythology.

As we begin the twenty-first century, our knowledge of bats has grown considerably since medieval times. Many of the ancient myths vilifying bats, however, infect human impressions still and, in many cases, are all that people know of bats. Continued ignorance is fueled by our own shortcomings in perceiving an elusive mammal whose natural history evolved along a very different "route" than our own. To us they remain ambiguous night shadows whose abilities once suggested possession of supernatural powers. Indeed, human fear of bats dampened even the investigative enthusiasm of naturalists and scientists; consequently, we have only scratched the surface of what we can learn from and about them.

Despite our limited knowledge of bats and their populations, it is abundantly clear that they are important to the health and stability of many ecosystems. Equally clear is the decline in bat numbers worldwide. In fact, on many continents, including North America, if conservation actions are not undertaken, some species may become extinct before much, if any, of their natural history is even documented.

HOW MUCH DO WE KNOW?

Scientific inquiry about bats dates back to antiquity. Nearly twenty-five hundred years ago Aristotle formally described the anatomy of bats, and in 1693 John Ray first categorized bats as mammals instead of birds, although he remained confused about their wings. Carl Linnaeus, who in 1758 began the formal science of classification with the publication of his book *Systema Naturae,* arranged the then known seven species of bats within the order Primates, along with humans, all other known primates, and colugos (flying lemurs). In the mid-1800s the anatomists E. Geoffroy Saint-Hilaire and Georges Cuvier proposed a new order for bats called Chiroptera (whose name is taken from a Greek term meaning "hand-wing"). For the first time, the taxonomic relationship between bats and other groups was finally established. However, the science of taxonomy and systematics typically does not disseminate their findings to the public at large, so misconceptions remained.

For example, outside the scientific community, bats continue to be confused with other animals or misconstrued in character, not only in English but, unfortunately, across many languages. One author writes about the linguistic juggling of the various words used for bats, uncovering the underlying conceptual miscues in the process. He writes:

> The German word for "bat," *Fledermaus,* means "flying mouse," as does the Russian *lyetuchya meesh*. Although certainly the reference to flight is correct, bats are not at all closely related to rodents. In English, bats were referred to as *nattabatta*, "night bat," perhaps of Scandinavian origin. *Aftenbakke* ("evening bat") is Danish for bat, and reference is made using *nattbacka* ("night bat") in Swedish. Possibly, all of these names are traceable to the poetic Icelandic word for bat, *ledurblaka*, meaning literally "leather flutterer." The Italian *pipistrello* (hence the genus *Pipistrellus*) apparently evolved from the Latin *vespertilio*, perhaps from *vesper*, "evening," plus *papilio*, a curious word meaning both "moth" and "the soul of the dead." French gets it all wrong; *chauve souris* translates to "bald bat," mostly untrue, even for the most senior of individuals. Spanish miscues with *murcielago*, a corruption of *murciegalo*, "blind mouse," neither of which is true of bats (Armstrong 1995: 1).

Unfortunately, even today, many people still consider bats to be "flying mice." In reality bats are no more closely related to mice than are humans. We know from several hundred years of anatomical study, especially on teeth, and, more recently, using molecular techniques, that the living group most closely related to bats is the order Insectivora, which includes shrews and moles. As for the evolutionary origin of bats, details of anatomy give insight into ancestry. Although one of the most highly evolved of all mammals, bats retain ancestral anatomical structures that give unequivocal clues as to the origin of the "ledurblaka."

THE ORIGIN OF "BATNESS"

From where did such a spectacular mammal, with wings for cheating gravity and a voice allowing for navigation in complete darkness, originate? As someone once said, "One cannot choose one's ancestors." And as with most compelling evolutionary stories, the origin of flight in mammals stems from quite humble beginnings. But before I describe this one-time-only evolutionary event, perspective is gained by emphasizing the fact that true flight evolved a mere three times throughout the six-hundred-million-year history of vertebrates (Figure 1.1). All three skyward reaches occurred autonomously. Birds, bats, and pterosaurs do not share a common ancestor that had wings, thus their evolution of flight originated independently, in each case stemming from a unique series of momentary interactions between the genotype (within which mutation is the source of innovative form), evolutionary history (which determines who has what genes), and environment (which is the selective influence on gene products, i.e., form).

Pterodactyls (flying reptiles) were the first vertebrates to fly. They witnessed the dawn of birds, but saw their own demise during the Cretaceous extinctions that relinquished the dinosaur's grip on world domination. Only birds and bats

Figure 1.1. The three types of wings evolved in vertebrates; from top to bottom: bat, bird, pterodactyl. Color coding illustrates same bones across types.

winged on into recent times. Evidence for the dawn of birds is inscribed in one-hundred-million-year-old limestone sediment where fossils, such as the famous specimen named *Archaeopteryx* (as well as others), have been found. Having a horny bill while retaining a mouthful of teeth, *Archeopteryx* was built of two worlds, one reptilian, the other avian, marking an important transition in evolutionary history. Curiously, although we associate feathers with birds, the evolution of feathers occurred in a group of theropod dinosaurs that were ancestral to birds. Plumage, it turns out, graced terrestrial species before becoming airborne.

Bats were the most recent vertebrate group to evolve powered flight and the only mammal to venture down that road. Mammals themselves are descended from therapsids, an extinct group that manifested both reptilian and mammalian characteristics and are therefore referred to as "mammal-like reptiles." It is here, in this transitional stage between reptiles and mammals, that hair evolved. Furred forms thus preceded winged forms (as feathers preceded flight in birds) by almost 180 million years, which means that bats have existed for a mere 25 percent of the evolutionary history of mammals. Furthermore, although one might surmise that the ancestor to bats must have been a provocative beast, bats actually descended from a rather nondescript, arboreal, shrewlike mammal that lived inconspicuously among the dinosaurs (Figure 1.2). It was only after an asteroid impact extinguished approximately 60 percent of the Cretaceous flora and fauna, prompting a major resorting of life on earth, that these persistent, furry pioneers prospered. The ensuing mammalian radiations (explosions of species) changed the planet forever, and for the first time in evolutionary history, fur came to dominate scales in terrestrial environments. Within the following thirty million years, all the major orders of mammals evolved, and one of the earliest groups to emerge from a burned and devastated world were bats. From ignoble beginnings, bats came to witness firsthand the coming Age of Mammals, termed the Cenozoic Era. How the first protobat looked, we may never know. Natural selection, however, obviously favored a mammal capable of nocturnal flight, allowing access to an almost completely untapped food resource: night-flying insects. The profits gained from the evolution of night flight propelled one of the greatest mammalian radiations and success stories thus far known.

The success continues today, as illustrated by the more than eleven hundred species of bats living worldwide (there are fifty-two hundred species of mammals alive today, so bats comprise about 20 percent of all living mammalian species). It is sobering to think that all bats share a single ancestral spark ignited long ago perhaps at a time when *Tyrannosaurus rex* and other large dinosaurs thundered across North America, restricting our terrestrial ancestors to their burrows by day and leaving the darkness of night as the only safe time for activity.

THE STRUCTURE OF BATS

The skeletal anatomy of bats is quite unique in form, but is simultaneously composed of easily recognizable bones located in the same relative position as present

Figure 1.2. The hypothetical tree-shrew ancestor that gave rise to bats in Eocene times, fifty million years ago

in all mammals. In fact, the basic anatomy of mammals evolved almost four hundred million years ago at the dawn of the first terrestrial vertebrates, the amphibians. In bats, although the forearm, hand, and finger bones are long relative to body size, the forelimb of bats comprises the ulna, radius, metacarpals, and phalanges found in all vertebrate animals (Figure 1.3), except, of course, for the legless lizards known as snakes and the legless amphibians known as caecilians.

The wings of bats are their most conspicuous trait. Gracile and highly elongated hands and fingers support a thin, elastic membrane (the patagium) that extends from the shoulder, travels between the digits, and reconnects along the body's lateral edge (Figure 1.4). The thumbs appear deceptively small when com-

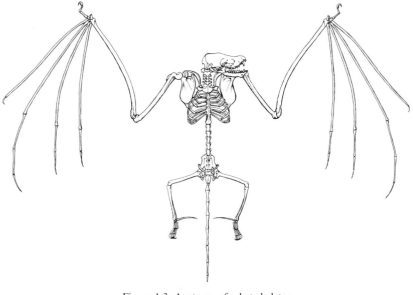

Figure 1.3. Anatomy of a bat skeleton

pared to the other greatly elongated fingers, but they are actually in proportion to body size. Thumbs are not connected to the flight membranes and function well as mechanical hooks for climbing and for manipulating food in carnivorous and fruit-eating bats. The tail in most species is wrapped by a membrane (uropatagium) that stretches outward, meeting the legs at their inner surface. Functioning mostly as a rudder during flight, the uropatagium in some species is highly specialized for use in capturing flying insects. The unique interlacing among supporting bones, membranes, and flight muscles produces a dynamic composite that allows a bat to negotiate a right-angle turn in less than the length of its body, sometimes at flight speeds approaching forty miles per hour. Don't try such a move in your Cessna!

Bats orchestrate flight in a unique manner. To capture and exploit the invisible matrix of air, wing movements are coordinated by using alternating contractions of chest and back muscles. The downstroke provides a force that cheats gravity, whereas the backstroke creates forward speed (Figure 1.5). Contrastingly, birds manage flight by employing a powerful downstroke that both lifts and acceler-ates, whereas the backstroke is passive. And so goes the differing physique between these groups. Birds appear spherical in body shape due to their large chest muscles, whereas bats, which divvy up the task of flight among chest and back muscles, are slender, affording them the ability to squeeze into small cracks

Figure 1.4. The patagium of a bat's wing showing the complex mosaic of meshlike fibers composing the wing membrane

and crevices to hide from predators. In addition, the distinctive ability of bats to flap their wings independently of each other makes them the foremost acrobats of the sky.

At rest, bats hang upside down, remaining that way for up to seven months during hibernation. Unique cavities in the cranium pool blood and other fluids away from the brain. In animals not adapted for upside-down posture, such as humans, death due to brain tissue suffocation from pooling fluids would happen within eight hours. In addition, bats hang passively from a perch while sleeping because of their specialized foot anatomy. The tendons operating the toes are scaly and pass through long cylindrical sheets of roughened tissue called sheaths.

Figure 1.5. Similarities and differences between flapping flight in bats and birds. Both use powerful muscles for flight, but in birds the downstroke is the only power component and the backstroke is passive, generating little or no force as the wing is pulled fully inward to the body. In bats, the wing is fully extended during the downstroke, as in birds. Unlike birds, however, the backstroke in bats creates forward motion because the patagium between the forearm and body remains extended during the backstroke, whereas the patagium associated with the digits is collapsed to help with mechanical leverage during the backstroke as illustrated in the frontal views above.

As the animal's weight pulls against the toes, it causes the scales on the tendons to embed into the sheath, locking the digits in position (Figure 1.6). This "passive-lock system" allows the toes to remain in a gripping posture without the aid of muscle contraction. Disengaging the passive-lock system is achieved simply by contracting the calf muscles that release the tendons from their sheaths. So while roosting, bats hang effortlessly; in fact, the passive system works so well that bats long dead are occasionally found still hanging in their roosts. Curiously, a similar but unrelated passive mechanism has been found in the feet of perching birds.

Bats have large hearts for supplying ample amounts of blood to oxygen-needy flight muscles. Their hearts are also speedy, generating a resting rate of about 450 beats per minute, which is 2.5 times that of a conditioned athlete while running! Although that rate is amazing in and of itself, the magic really begins when bats fly, as their heart rate then approaches 20 beats per second, or 1,200 beats per minute. Perhaps even more impressive is a bat's control over its racing heart, which returns to 450 beats per minute from its speedy 1,200 within a second after landing. Again, even well-conditioned athletes would require ten or more minutes to recover to their basal heart rate of 50–60 beats per minute after a significant run.

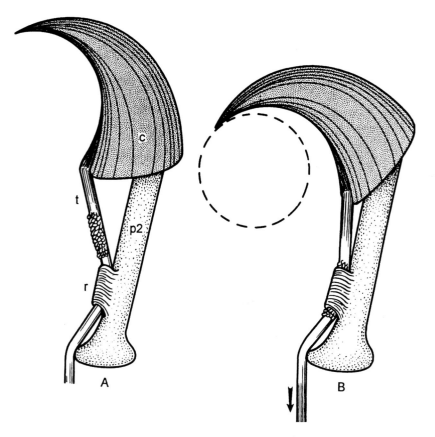

Figure 1.6. The passive-digital-locking mechanism in the foot of bats that allows them to hang passively during roosting (from Schutt 1998)

Because of such accelerated metabolic rates during flight, bats require high-energy food. Consequently, most of today's species consume a calorie-rich diet consisting of insects, fruit, or nectar, and their teeth are adapted for efficient mastication of their primary food source (Figure 1.7). In fact, because the form and function of teeth so clearly depict a mammal's diet, understanding the evolution of bats is enhanced by the study of dental characteristics that allow hindsight back through many millions of years. Furthermore, because teeth are the hardest biological substance and are capable of surviving intact for long expanses of time, they are invaluable materials to paleontologists. The discovery of fossil bat teeth places their ancestry firmly within a group of mammals that witnessed the demise of the dinosaurs and the subsequent explosion of mammalian forms that

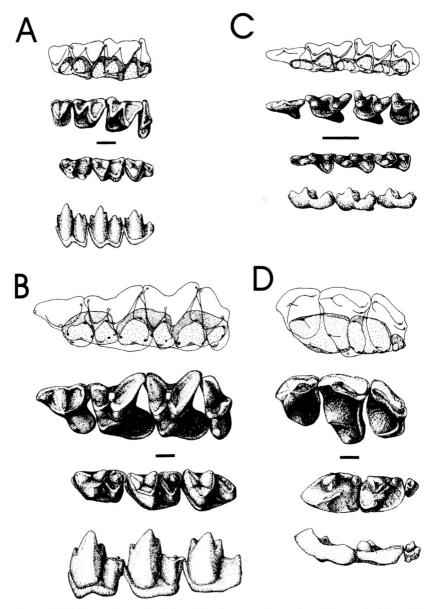

Figure 1.7. Various tooth morphologies of bats that strongly correlate with a species' diet: (A) the insectivorous *Antrozous pallidus*, (B) the carnivorous *Macroderma gigas*, (C) the nectarivore *Monophyllus redmani*, (D) the frugivore *Artibeus jamaicensis* (from Freeman 1998)

radically altered the face of the earth. Indeed, one of the first groups to arise from the original stock of postdinosaur mammals was bats, and through time they have speciated extensively.

BATS TODAY

From their humble beginning, bats have diversified into a tremendous number of species. Bats are classified in the order Chiroptera, which is subdivided into suborders termed the Microchiroptera, meaning "small bats," and the Megachiroptera, meaning "large bats." The megachiropterans occur in Old World regions such as Africa, India, Australia, and Indonesia. They are commonly called flying foxes due to their foxlike facial features (Figure 1.8). With only 150 species in a single family, the Pteropodidae, the megachiropterans are not a particularly diverse group and all are either fruit eaters and/or nectar drinkers. Megachiropterans locate fruiting trees using their excellent sense of smell and color vision as remarkable as our own. No megabats are known to use sonar, but one species in the genus *Rousettus* does use tongue clicks in a primitive attempt at echolocating. The largest of the megachiropterans is the giant Malayan flying fox, with a wingspan reaching six feet. Its scientific name, *Pteropus vampyrus,* falsely indicates a blood-sucking intent; however, in reality this species eats fruit.

The microchiropterans mostly are small-bodied insect- or fruit-eating species. They are much more widespread than are the megachiropterans, occurring on all continents except Antarctica. Ecological diversity among the more than eight hundred species of microbats is phenomenal. Some species are large, having three-foot wingspans, and are carnivorous, consuming mice, rats, other bats, and birds. Some prey upon frogs and lizards, and others are highly specialized, such as the fishing bat, *Noctilio leporinus,* which flies along streams hooking fish at the surface with its huge curved claws (Figure 1.9).

Certainly among the most peculiar bats are vampires. Living only in Neotropical regions, three species coexist. Two species, the hairy-legged vampire *(Diphylla ecaudata)* and the white-winged vampire *(Diaemus youngii)*, hunt the blood of birds, whereas the common vampire bat *(Desmodus rotundus)* lives on the blood of mammals (Figure 1.10). Despite the myths and the revulsion of humans to any animal that feeds on the blood of others, vampire bats represent a pinnacle of natural selection. Biases aside, these bats manifest a suite of characteristics that make them quite extraordinary. Specialized razor-sharp incisor teeth allow vampire bats to nick and penetrate the very thick hide of mammals and birds quickly and efficiently. Once a small incision is made, saliva containing an anticoagulant is drooled onto the cut, keeping the wound open and bleeding. A tubelike structure on the back of the tongue assists in moving blood to the mouth like a straw. Once full of blood, the stomach becomes so distended and heavy that flight becomes difficult due to the excess weight, hence the name of the common vampire, *D. rotundus.* Possessing the shortest gastrointestinal tract of any living mammal

Figure 1.8. The face of a megachiropteran fruit bat (*Epomophorus walhbergi*) illustrating the large primate-like eyes manifesting color vision adapted for crepuscular foraging. Presence of claw on the second finger (arrow) also distinguishes this group from the Microchiroptera. (Photo: M. B. Fenton)

Figure 1.9. A fishing bat (*Noctilio leporinus*) catches a fish from a pond with its specialized hooked claws. (Photo: S. Altenbach)

allows vampire bats to digest blood very quickly, excrete the excess water, and fly off a few minutes later. Furthermore, even though these bats have effective night vision and echolocation, they also use heat pits positioned on each side of their nose that are capable of detecting minute temperature changes from several feet away, helping them locate warm-blooded prey in complete darkness. These heat pits also aid the vampire in choosing where on the skin of the host to make an incision. Before cutting, the bat first slides its heat-sensitive pits along the prey's skin to determine where the blood vessels lie closest to the surface. This ensures that the bat avoids wasted time cutting in areas where blood is not easily available.

"SEEING" IN COMPLETE DARKNESS

The expression "blind as a bat" probably comes from the fact that many species tend to have smallish eyes, and therefore it seems that they would not be able to see well, if at all. In truth, all bats can see, and many have very good vision. As mentioned, the megachiropterans have exceptional human-grade color vision. The microchiropterans utilize black-and-white vision that is adjusted to nighttime lighting. However, for a night-flying mammal, vision is not an optimal sense for

Figure 1.10. A common vampire bat (*Desmodus rotundus*) leaps into the air, showing the powerful ability of its muscles. (Photo: S. Altenbach)

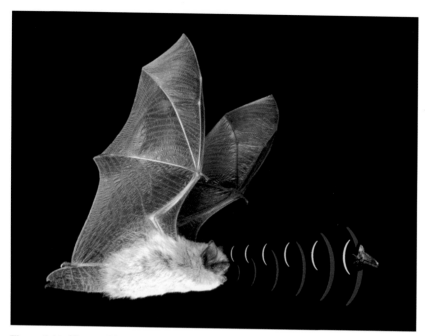

Figure 1.11. The workings of echolocation. Sounds emitted from the bat's mouth (black semicircles) travel away. Upon contact with objects in the environment, the sound waves bounce back to the bat's ears in the form of echoes. The bat's brain interprets these sounds as three-dimensional portraits of the objects present in its flight path (not unlike the human brain interprets light waves). (Photo: S. Altenbach)

reliable perception. After all, even though we humans pride ourselves on having a good sense of sight, most of us would not run through the woods at night without a flashlight, or perhaps even with one. Not too surprisingly, evolution has favored the use of sound for nighttime navigation in bats. Although the use of sonar for navigation is not entirely unique to bats (porpoises, whales, rats, and some birds navigate or hunt by using sound), they do have one of the most complex systems to have evolved (Figure 1.11).

Early investigators were astonished to observe that bats could fly in complete darkness while avoiding collisions with wires as thin as a human hair. The scientific inquiry into bat sonar is an exemplary model of the scientific method at work; it involved dozens of experiments and intense debate over results. Lazaro Spallanzani performed experiments on bats using first hooded and later surgically blinded individuals, and through a series of letters to colleagues, inspired the surgeon Louis Jurine to replicate Spallanzani's experiments and to further explore the phenomenon by plugging the ears of some bats. Jurine found that deafening bats resulted in confused and disoriented individuals when in flight. He sent his results to Spallanzani. Bewildered, both Spallanzani and Jurine were unable to formulate an explanation for their findings. In a flash of insight, Spallanzani in 1799 wrote, "The ear of the bat serves more efficiently for seeing, or at least for measuring distance, than do its eyes, for a blinded animal hurtles against all obstacles only when its ears are covered.... Can it be said then that ... their ears rather than their eyes serve to direct them in flight?" This hypothesis would take almost 150 years to test experimentally. Spallanzani and Jurine predicted that bats oriented primarily using self-generated sounds. Bingo! Unfortunately, their investigations and ideas generated little interest in the scientific community and subsequently fell into the abyss of "unattended concerns." Thus, in spite of Spallanzani and Jurine's carefully controlled experiments and marvelous insights, the concept of "seeing with ears" was simply too mentally challenging for many to accept. Some scientists, such as G. Montague, after reading Spallanzani and Jurine's results, stated: "To assent to the conclusions of Mr. De Jurine ... since bats see with their ears, do they hear with their eyes?" In the nineteenth century, the paleontologist and anatomist Georges Cuvier rather cavalierly decided that bats oriented using a specialized sixth sense (one of Spallanzani's early hypotheses) emitted from their wings and undetectable by humans. Due to Cuvier's fame, this scientifically unsupported idea propagated throughout the world, even spilling over into the next century.

It was not until the 1930s that the puzzle of bat orientation was revisited and subsequently solved. Spallanzani and Jurine's well-reasoned suggestion of ultrasonic orientation aged like a fine wine for nearly two centuries before it was uncorked by biologist Donald Griffin. Griffin, working on a hunch and intrigued by the Spallanzani/Jurine hypothesis, brought some bats to a physicist's laboratory where there was an instrument capable of detecting high-frequency, or ultrasonic, sounds. He writes, "With some trepidation I approached Professor Pierce in the winter of 1938 with the suggestion that we use his apparatus to listen to my bats." Upon entering the room with the bats, the scientists became the first humans to hear a series of sounds that first evolved perhaps when dinosaurs still roamed the earth. Griffin writes, "When I first brought the cage full of bats [*Myotis lucifugus* and *Eptesicus fuscus*] to Pierce's laboratory and held the cage in front of the parabolic horn we were surprised and delighted to hear a medley of rancorous noises from the loudspeaker" (1958: 67). Griffin coined the term *echolocation* to describe this ultrasonic cacophony, and the word is descriptive of how Griffin envisioned bat sonar to function. He hypothesized that bats emit high-frequency sounds from their mouth and utilize their ears to gather the returning echoes to locate objects and to navigate.

Curiously, even before Griffin's discovery, the study of bats led humans to have insights that resulted in inventive technological advances. As early as 1912, the inventor Sir Hiram Maxim proposed that bats navigate by emitting low-frequency sounds (infrasound) and thus hypothesized that humans could construct devices to work similarly for navigating ships in darkness. In 1920 the

English physiologist Henry Hartridge proposed that bats use high-frequency sounds (ultrasound). This, of course, was what was borne out of the Griffin/Pierce experiments.

In a sense, Griffin's discovery of echolocation was the easy part. After all, we humans simply waited for technology to provide the instrument that would allow us to detect what bats have been hearing for millions of years. Deciphering exactly how echolocation works proved to be the real challenge. Despite the involvement of hundreds of biologists conducting thousands of experiments and rigorous investigations since Griffin's discovery, a thorough understanding of how echolocation works and is interpreted by bats remains elusive.

Human radar and sonar systems were developed from a basic understanding of bat, as well as cetacean, biosonar systems, but in comparison, these human devices are quite crude. Yes, you can probably blame, indirectly anyway, that last speeding ticket you received on the study of bats. But the sonar of bats has also given us highly important devices such as ultrasonic orientation systems for the blind and ultrasound imaging to see and investigate our unborn children.

ECHOLOCATION: SEEING WITH EARS IS NOT AS EASY AS IT SOUNDS

The evolution of echolocation is an event that distinguishes bats from most other mammals, and the origin of sonar ability runs deep in bat history. In fact the oldest known fossil bats were capable of interpreting echolocation calls, as illustrated by the extremely refined inner ear structures associated directly with echolocating ability. Fossil teeth tell us that these early bats were insect eaters, and therefore it appears that bats living fifty million years ago hunted insects on the wing using echolocation similar to that used by today's species. We are, of course, lacking in details and therefore whether or not extinct bat species used echolocation in exactly the same way as living species remains unknown. However, the evolution of sonar was evidently an early part of bat natural history and remains integral to their survival. Clearly, bats are a product of integrated evolution among several anatomical systems, including the brain, auditory, cardiopulmonary, vision, vocal, olfactory, and skeletomuscular, that merged in an extraordinarily unique way. It is surmised that the basic integration of anatomy, physiology, and behavior occurred quickly at the dawn of bats. Once the basic integration was established, fine-tuning of what was likely an initially crude system was surely a priority because echolocation requires such a high-energy investment, and species that waste energy are usually doomed to become Darwinian wreckage along the evolutionary landscape—which was positively not the case for bats.

ECHOLOCATION PULSE RATES: SPEED KILLS

A refined aspect of echolocation seen in today's bats concerns phasing the call speed differently in order to help conserve energy while foraging (Figure 1.12).

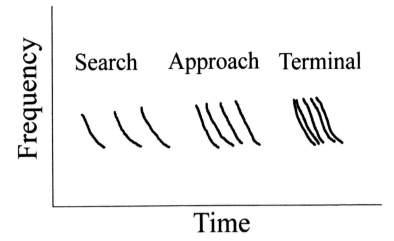

Figure 1.12. Graph of pulse phases labeled *search, approach,* and *terminal* used by bats to lessen the energetic expense of echolocation. Reading this graph from left to right, increased pulse rates are indicated by the more closely packed lines. Vertical axis is energy (kHz), and horizontal axis is time in milliseconds (ms).

When searching for food, the pulse rate is slowest at about 25 pulses per second; upon approaching a potential food source, the pulse rate doubles to about 50 pulses per second; and only when a strike is imminent do bats use their most sensitive call rate, which reaches 250 pulses per second. Referred to as a "feeding buzz" due to the buzzlike qualities of the sound, this terminal phase of echolocation gives bats detailed information about the prey's position, flight speed, and direction of movement. The energy saved by using different call rates is significant when the search phase requires one-tenth the energy of the feeding buzz. Both the search and the approach phases lack discernment, and bats in this phase of echolocation can actually be fooled into approaching a nonfood item (for example, a pebble thrown into the air). However, once the highly discriminatory feeding buzz engages, the pursuit ends as the bat realizes its mistake.

CF VERSUS FM BATS: CHANGING THE CHANNEL IS NOT OPTIONAL

Although the pulse-rate patterns discussed in the previous section are consistent across bat species, there are fundamental differences in the use of tonal frequencies, depending on a species' foraging strategy. Some species are termed CF bats because they use a mostly constant, or relatively invariant, call fre-

Figure 1.13. Graph illustrating two types of echolocation calls. A constant-frequency (CF) call is illustrated by the flat-line call in the upper right-hand corner of the graph. The other three calls illustrate various types of frequency-modulated (FM) calls.

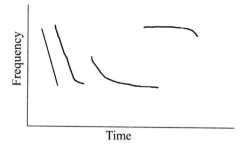

quency (Figure 1.13). Constant-frequency sonar is associated with bats that forage for aerial insects in open areas and at higher flight speeds. Because CF calls have relatively low discriminatory power, CF bats tend to search for insect clouds that they fly through, mouth agape, filtering insects from the air. Free-tailed bats (such as the Brazilian free-tailed bat, *Tadarida brasiliensis*) hunt in this fashion.

Other species of bats use frequency modulation of the sonar call and are referred to as FM bats. These bats vary the frequency throughout the call sequence. Invariably, the call begins as a high-frequency pulse and ends at a lower frequency, sweeping through intermediate values. The big brown bat (*Eptesicus fuscus*) is an example of an FM bat. It begins each echolocation sequence as high as 100 kilohertz (kHz), but each pulse is swept downward to about 20 kHz, thus increasing detail about prey items being hunted. FM bats typically catch insects in flight by isolating individuals, pursuing them, and catching them with their flight membranes. Frequency modulation occurs throughout all phases of echolocation and is typically accompanied by two or three harmonics that give a highly detailed three-dimensional picture of cluttered environments. FM bats are thus well suited for foraging in complex habitats and feeding upon evasive insects. Many bat species use echolocatory pulses that combine the qualities of both CF and FM pulse types, and some species vary their modulation type according to foraging habitat.

Recently is has been suggested that CF versus FM echolocation may not distinguish bats as well as once thought because many species use both types of call strategies under differing conditions, or even integrate the two types normally. The terms therefore serve more to describe calls rather than the bats using them. Some bat biologists, such as M. Brock Fenton, have suggested that "duty cycle" (the proportion of time that a signal is in use) is a more discerning component of echolocation. Some bat species use a low-duty-cycle call in which the signal is on a mere 10 percent of the time because these bats cannot simultaneously broadcast pulses and receive echoes. Other bats emit high-duty-cycle echolocation calls in which the signal is on more than 30 percent of the time. These species are capable of broadcasting signals and receiving echoes simultaneously. Although the duty-cycle dichotomy appears to hold well across bat

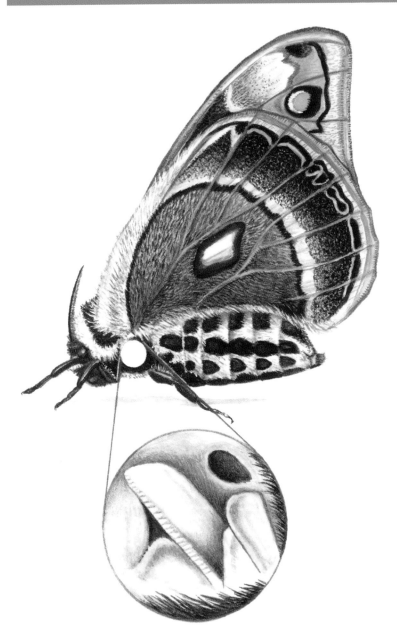

Figure 1.14. The tympanic ear of an arctiid moth is adapted to hear the ultrasonic terminal feeding buzz of bats. Upon stimulation of its ear, the insect changes its flight, making evasive maneuvers to avoid predation.

species, most biologists believe that describing bats solely by their call type is misleading without adding information such as call duration, time between calls, call intensity, and presence or absence of harmonics.

NATURE'S ARMS RACE: THE INSECTS FIGHT BACK

It may seem that bats have all the advantages when hunting insects, but this is not always the case. In fact, the coevolution between insectivorous bats and their prey is a fascinating story that can be characterized as an arms race. In response to the evolution of echolocation in bats, insects have evolved some amazing countermeasures to lessen their chance of becoming prey. In one of the more interesting cases, some moth species have evolved "ears," termed tympanic regions, on their thorax or abdomen that are specially tuned to the echolocation frequencies of foraging bats (Figure 1.14). When an "eared" insect becomes targeted by a bat's feeding buzz, its thorax vibrates, telling the moth to begin evasive maneuvers. In sphinx moths, the tympanic organs not only allow detection of feeding buzzes but actually generate a signal that either warns an approaching bat that the moth tastes bad or, in some species, emits a signal-jamming sound meant to confuse the pursuing bat. The interactions between bats and their insect prey in many ways mimic an aerial "dog fight" (Figure 1.15). As selection favors adaptations that increase the abilities of each species, this escalates adaptive efficiency among the species involved in the "arms race." Evolution has favored fast, maneuverable flight and echolocation in bats, whereas in moths, the ability to eavesdrop on approaching bats and other evasive behaviors have been favored. When all is said and done, the evolution of ears in moths and other insects, such as mantids, results in a 2–5 percent increased success rate in avoiding predation by bats. Although these savings seem minuscule, in reality this increased survivorship ensures that moth populations will persist despite heavy predation by bats.

THE WORLDWIDE IMPORTANCE OF BATS

It is a human tendency to assign importance to other species according to their value to human existence. Because of the increasing practice of humans to use animals for our own needs, many people have lost sight of the importance of all organisms in the function of ecosystems, and some would say that this lack of wisdom will lead to our eventual downfall. We are living in times that many ecologists have labeled "The Sixth Extinction." This is in reference to the fact that there have been five known mass extinction events on earth, and the rate at which we are currently losing species throughout the world due to human environmental destruction equals or exceeds the most extensive extinctions of the past. Bats are a part of this massive loss of biodiversity.

Probably since the beginning of our time, flight has fascinated human beings. Unquestionably, the inspiration for humans to take to the air was a product of

Figure 1.15. Avoidance behavior by a moth having a tympanic ear that has heard the feeding buzz of an approaching bat.

observing the natural world. And with the advent of mechanized flying machines, scientific study of bats, birds, and insects has allowed us to refine our technology. Because bats' wings are replete with extensive arrays of easily observed blood vessels, we have also used bats to study the effects of alcohol and other drugs on veins and arteries. In addition, because they exhibit a very low incidence of infectious diseases, bats are used in medical studies concerning efficiency of immune system responses. We have even employed bats to help us better survive. The anticoagulant available in the saliva of common vampire bats (*Desmodus rotundus*) is used as an anti-clotting agent in human patients. Although in a human-centric worldview the before-mentioned contributions of bats to our endeavors may appear important, their importance to the rest of the natural world far exceeds our narrow-sighted values. Beyond human-centric concerns, bats hold immense importance in many ecosystems worldwide.

In North America, bats are the only "serious" foragers of night-flying insects. Even though some birds, such as poorwills, nighthawks, and others in the goatsucker family, filter-feed insects from the night air, the impact of bats is magnified due to their larger and denser populations. In fact, some bat colonies number in

Figure 1.16. Evening outflight of Brazilian free-tailed bats (*Tadarida brasiliensis*) from the Orient Mine located in the San Luis Valley, Colorado. (Photo: R. Adams)

the millions of individuals, filtering tons of insects from the air nightly. Although in most cases bats don't concentrate their foraging on one particular type of insect, an individual little brown myotis (*Myotis lucifugus*) has been shown to consume as many as six hundred mosquitoes per hour under laboratory conditions and as many as five hundred insects per hour in the wild. Multiplying this consumption rate by a colony containing several hundred "natural insecticides" quickly illustrates how bats affect insect populations. Colonies of Brazilian free-tailed bats (*Tadarida brasiliensis*), such as the one located in the San Luis Valley of Colorado (Figure 1.16), are estimated to consume almost a ton of insects nightly. But even this feeding frenzy pales in comparison to the consumption rate of huge colonies of *T. brasiliensis* in Texas that ingest as much as 150 tons of insects per night. As they forage, bats consume a diversity of species such as moths, beetles, bees, mayflies, midges, flies, wasps, and even surface-dwelling aquatic insects such as water boatmen. From a humancentric perspective, many of the insects consumed by bats are human as well as agricultural pests.

In tropical ecosystems, bats are fundamental to forest health, growth, and stability. Fruit-eating bats are responsible for dispersing more than 90 percent of the seeds of important plants such as figs (*Ficus*) that feed many other animal species. They are justly referred to as "farmers" of the forests because they disperse seeds of their food plants, sometimes over tens of miles. With each dispersal event is included a bit of guano that acts as fertilizer to encourage growth. Consumed seeds are partially digested when passed through the bat's stomach and intestines, and for some plants, this is a necessary first step in initiating seed germination. The essential role of bats in maintaining healthy tropical forests is unequivocal and their importance in helping maintain global biodiversity is well founded. Indeed, studies have shown that in tropical areas where humans have clear-cut forests, plants that grow from bat-dispersed seeds initiate the process of forest regeneration. Bats are vital to this process.

In desert ecosystems, including those of the southwestern United States and Mexico, cross-pollination by bats is critical to successful reproduction of keystone plant species that support hundreds of other species in the harshness of desert environments. For example, nectar-feeding bats such as the lesser long-nosed bat, *Leptonycteris curasoae* (see the Accounts of Species in Chapter 6), cross-pollinate cordon, organ pipe, and saguaro cacti as well as agave and yucca plants (Figure 1.17), all of which are keystone species of southwestern ecosystems. Unfortunately, because long-nosed bats are currently endangered, its feared extinction may precipitate a collapse of the desert ecosystems of the Southwest.

The codependence between bats and their host plants illustrates what biologists term *coevolution*. Coevolution describes complementary evolution between two or more species in a way that makes the fate of one reliant upon the other. The "arms race" between bats and insects described in the previous section is a type of coevolution because as either prey or predator gains an advantage, natural selection favors characteristics in the other that attempt to counter the advantage. Converse to predator/prey attempts to outfox each other, bats and their host plants are driven to cooperate so that both gain from each other through interacting (termed *mutualism*). In this case, natural selection favors characters that enhance the attractiveness of flowers to bats and, for bats, the effectiveness of gaining food and unwittingly cross-pollinating the plants. For example, the lesser long-nosed bat has an elongated snout adapted for fitting efficiently into funnel-like cactus flowers and accessing nectar at the base. The more precisely the snout fits the flower anatomy, the more efficient feeding will be. En suite, bat-pollinated plants are adapted to facilitate and exploit visitation by bats that act as air-worthy transportation for the plant's pollen. It is therefore in a plant's "best interest," so to speak, to have the most bat-attractive flowers to increase bat visitations. In this high-stakes Darwinian drama, those bats best suited for feeding at host plants will gain more energy for reproduction, and those plants whose flowers attract more bats will also reproduce more than other plants. The individuals with the most efficient structure will most likely make the highest and most significant genetic contributions of offspring to the following generations. The reciprocal form and function between flower and bat is a consequence of a timeless waltz that began eons before humans had evolved to hear the symphony; it is only in hindsight that we may marvel at its beauty and magnificence. The coevolution between bats and prey or host plant is readily observed in the Rocky Mountain West.

Figure 1.17. Lesser long-nosed bat (*Leptonycteris curasoae*) visiting a saguaro cactus flower. (Photo: M. Tuttle)

The bat fauna of the Rocky Mountains is diverse and entails a complex natural history of ecologies and behaviors. Almost all species here are insectivorous, but various hunting techniques are employed among them. Some species are adapted to open aerial foraging and pursue their prey, sometimes at speeds approaching 50 mph. Others are forest dwellers that fly at slower speeds, maneuvering through vegetation while feeding on flying insects. Some are specialized to hover, listening for the sounds of fluttering moth wings on vegetation that cue them to approach and pick their prey directly from the surface of plants. Foregoing aerial foraging, some species take to terrestrial pursuit of ground-dwelling beetles, grasshoppers, and even scorpions (Figure 1.18). Although almost all bat species in the Rocky Mountain West are insect eaters, a few are nectar feeders, ecologically equivalent to hummingbirds. Nectar-feeding bats migrate between North and Central America following the flowering progression of their host plants.

Although vampire bats once occurred in the United States (fossils of an extinct species of *Desmodus* have been found in several states), there is only a single record from recent times, and this was a pregnant hairy-legged vampire (*Diphylla ecaudata*) captured twelve miles west of Comstock, Val Verde County, Texas, reported in 1968.

AN UNFORTUNATE LOSS OF BIODIVERSITY

Despite at least sixty-five million years of success, many populations of bats are in serious decline. Bat Conservation International (Austin, Texas) estimates that more than 40 percent of North American bat species are in serious trouble. In addition, because we know so little about most bats, it is impossible to assess the current condition of many populations. This is particularly true in the Rocky Mountain region, where the terrain is rugged and expansive. In a global sense, although bats enjoy high species diversity, which to the casual observer may

Figure 1.18. A pallid bat (Antrozous *pallidus*) in flight carrying a centipede. This bat species forages on the ground for scorpions and large beetles, as well. It has also been known to feed occasionally on fruit. (Photo: S. Altenbach)

suggest ecological stability, the order Chiroptera is in crisis, due to apparent large-scale regional losses of populations for numerous species.

Reasons for declines in bat populations are abundant, but habitat loss over the past two centuries is one prime suspect. For example, logging practices have caused a 99 percent decline of old-growth forests in North America (Figure 1.19), decimating populations of animal species, including bats, that relied on them for survival. In addition, bat populations have been subjected to heavy pesticide contamination, seriously affecting reproduction and survivorship. In particular, the use of DDT in the 1950s and 1960s is thought to be responsible for more than a 90 percent decline (from four million to fewer than two hundred thousand) of Brazilian free-tailed bats (*Tadarida brasiliensis*) at Carlsbad Caverns, New Mexico.

Beyond inadvertent human-caused effects, wanton and intentional destruction of colonies has seriously impacted bat populations. Bats are highly gregarious mammals, sometimes forming colonies in the millions of individuals, and although large colony formation has generally favored the evolutionary success of bats, it also makes intentional eradication of large numbers easy to accomplish. In particular, intentional destruction at hibernation sites by those who have an intense fear or hatred of bats has devastated many populations. Moreover,

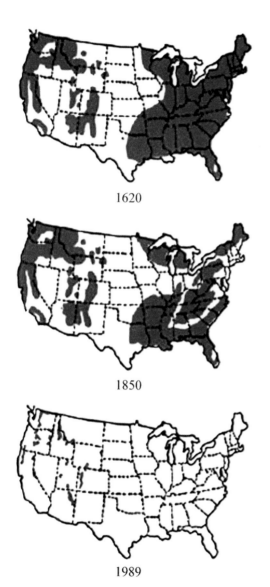

Figure 1.19. Map illustrating the loss of old-growth forest estimated to have occurred in the United States between 1620 and 1989.

1620

1850

1989

some destruction of colonies has occurred unwittingly by humans entering caves in wintertime and disturbing hibernating bats, causing them to awaken and burn large amounts of stored fat needed to survive the hibernation period, thus sealing their fate.

Another natural history trait of bats that magnifies human impacts on populations is their low reproductive rate. Most bats give birth to only a single pup per year, and females invest large amounts of energy and parental care in raising each offspring. Thus, survival rates of preflight young are high, but once the young take to the wing, the likelihood of death soars along with the newly volant young, and many do not survive the first stressful year. A low reproductive potential coupled with low first-year survivorship are natural history traits that are not well adapted to frequent disturbance or catastrophic events. Therefore, the added effect of large-scale human disruptions on bat populations, especially at critical times of the year, leads to dramatic declines from which bat populations may never recover.

The worldwide decline of many bat populations is, in many ways, the inspiration for this book. More and more, people are beginning to realize the importance of all organisms in the complex functioning of planet Earth. It is time for bats to finally be vindicated from the myths, fears, and untruths of the human imagination and for them to be recognized, appreciated, and respected as magnificent products of at least sixty-five million years of evolutionary "tinkering" and as essential components of ecosystems throughout the world. I hope this book will help toward that end.

2

Physiography and Zoogeography of the Rocky Mountain Region

hysiography is the study of land forms, and the Rockies provide a rich, complex canvas for inquiry. They are the dominant landscape feature of western North America, running more than 3,000 miles (4,800 kilometers) from northern British Columbia to northern New Mexico. In some places the Rocky Mountains are more than 300 miles (480 kilometers) wide, and elevations range from 4,900 to 14,430 feet (1,500 to 4,400 meters). The zoogeography of the region is dynamic as well, and for bats, the capacity of flight allows for long-distance traverses across challenging Rocky Mountain landscapes. Bats, like all life-forms, respond to natural barriers rather than the imaginary state borders that humans use for navigation and politics.

The scope of this book covers bats residing in the Rocky Mountain states of Idaho, Montana, Wyoming, Colorado, New Mexico, and Utah. Arizona is also included because it is geologically and ecologically integrated with the Southern Rockies via the Colorado Plateau. The linkage of Utah and Arizona with the Rockies proper is particularly true for bats because of their high mobility and because many of the migrating species that have summer ranges in the Rockies overwinter in Arizona and southern Utah. Furthermore, although some of the rarest bat species in the region currently inhabit only the southern reaches of Arizona and New Mexico, they appear to be extending their ranges northward, and one day may be larger participants in the ecosystems of the West.

NORTHERN, CENTRAL, AND SOUTHERN ROCKIES

The Rocky Mountains proper are conveniently divided into three sections: Northern, Central, and Southern (Figure 2.1). The Northern Rockies are a highly compact group geographically, but are composed of several ranges of distinct origins that encompass Montana, Idaho, and part of Wyoming. Such magnificent places as Glacier National Park, Grand Teton National Park, and the Wind River Range are part and parcel of the Northern Rockies. The Central Rocky Mountains are separated from the Northern Rockies by the Wyoming Basin, consisting mostly of low ridges and gently rolling topography. The Central Rockies reside mostly in Wyoming and include several local ranges such as the Bighorn and Beartooth, which delineate their eastern border. The Yellowstone Plateau of Wyoming and the Teton and Wyoming Ranges unite with the Uinta and Wasatch Mountains in Utah, defining the western edge. The Central Rockies are bisected diagonally by the Wind River and Owl Creek Ranges, which separate the northern Bighorn Basin from the southern Wyoming Basin.

The Southern Rockies consist of mountain ranges running in parallel north-south extensions that stretch from southeastern Wyoming into southern New Mexico and Arizona. The Culebra, Front, Laramie, Snowy, Sacramento, Sangre de Cristo, and Wet Mountains make up their eastern border. Within the Southern Rockies lie some of the most stunning summits of the entire range. In Colorado alone there are fifty-four peaks greater than 14,000 feet (4,300 meters). Alpine tundra is extensive on the highest pinnacles where trees cannot survive, a testament to harsh environmental conditions. The western edge of the Southern Rockies consists of the Elk, Gore, Jemez, La Plata, Park, Sawatch, and San Juan ranges. Five major intermountain basins—North, Middle, and South Parks; the upper Arkansas Valley; and the San Luis Valley—provide large expanses of habitat for specialized animals such as North America's only "native-grown" ungulate, the pronghorn (*Antilocapra americana*). Several minor basins of similar geology and ecology are integrated throughout the range.

GEOLOGY

Various parts of the Rockies formed in different ways throughout time, spanning no less than 1.5 billion years. The foundational rock of the Northern Rockies was deposited in Precambrian times, and rocks of this age are exposed in the Beartooth Mountains of Montana, whose measure once reached heights of 25,000 feet (7,700 meters). Through the actions of thrusting, sliding, exploding, eroding, and flooding, the region convulsed with geologic activity. As mountains go, the current Rockies are relatively young, beginning their formation a mere seventy million years ago. The Rockies had seemingly two pulses. About three hundred million years ago, a chain referred to as the Ancestral Rockies pushed up from a shallow sea and eroded away into sediments compressed into sandstones that "stood up" beginning seventy million years ago. These can be seen today along the eastern flanks of the Rockies. Along the Front Range of

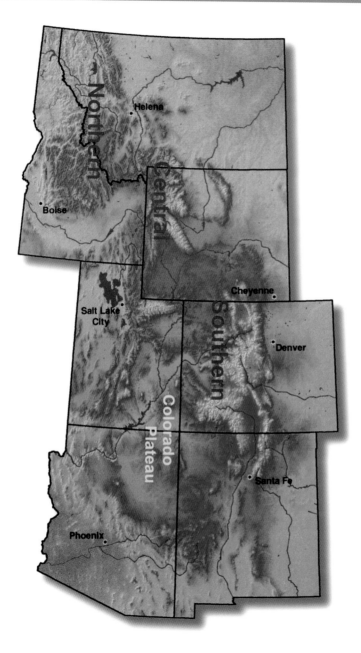

Figure 2.1. Map showing the boundaries between Northern, Central, and Southern Rockies and the location of the Colorado Plateau

Colorado, the red sandstones known as the Fountain Formation are distinctive of the area.

Ranges such as the Wind River Mountains of Wyoming arose via compression fifty million years ago. The Laramide Orogeny, lasting about four million years and followed by volcanism and faulting in Miocene times (35–8 million years ago), constructed much of the present-day Rockies. Some ranges are latecomers, such as the Madison Range in Montana, which faulted upward about seventeen million years ago. The granite Tetons of Wyoming burst skyward a mere nine million years ago, and the Yellowstone region resulted from intensive and cataclysmic megavolcanic eruptions that rocked the land with unprecedented vigor a mere two million years ago.

Today's Rockies, then, are the product of millions of years of dynamic history driven primarily by two forces, uplift and erosion. Precipitation and erosion throughout the Pleistocene (1 million–10,000 years ago), and continuing today, sculpted massive mountains into intricate forms. Thousands of feet of rock have been shaved, chiseled, and scraped from mountaintops, filling valleys below with sediment. An alluvial fan spread to the east creating the High Plains, and as the region faulted and rose, it shifted from a Cretaceous lowland of little relief and warm climate into a place of high relief and climatic variation. Eventually, the region settled into a climate centered around aridity.

Through vast expanses of time, the ebb and flow of the planet's ice sheets resulted in seawater flooding in many areas of the Rockies. The Colorado Plateau, whose endless vistas of naked, unadorned rock are iconic of the desert West, is illustrative of the region's repetitive flooding. The Plateau extends across Utah, Colorado, Arizona, and New Mexico and is the construct of repeated sedimentation events that commenced more than 570 million years ago, at the very dawn of vertebrate evolution. Three oscillations of advancing and retreating seas emanated across 150 million years of time, ending 130 million years ago. Washed-in sediments from the surrounding regions thickened the Plateau, whose contemporary relief and beauty would wait another 100 million years to form. Sediments deposited within large lakes that formed 65 million years ago produced the most colorful rocks of all, and recent exposure of these ancient sediments through erosion spawned such scenic backdrops as Bryce Canyon National Park in Utah.

The exposed geology of the West, in all its unobstructed beauty, provides an easily referenced time frame of events over geologic time. Within stratified rock layers laid down across the ages, entombed ancient life-forms are stored in mineral-hardened graves, as if on display in a museum after a bit of digging. Fascinating to children and adults alike, the strata of the Rocky Mountain region are replete with dinosaur remains of Cretaceous origin, deposited between sixty and one hundred million years ago. But dinosaur bones are not the only fossils found in the area; other buried treasures of the past also abound. In fact, one of the most prized fossils ever found was unearthed in the Rocky Mountain West. Extracted from its sixty-million-year-old Wyoming grave, a fully preserved skeleton of the oldest known bat fossil was uncovered in the early 1960s, telescoping the human

Figure 2.2. West rim of the Grand Canyon, Arizona. (Photo: R. Adams)

mind back to one of the most innovative moments in mammalian evolution. I discuss the details of this discovery in Chapter 3, but first outline how the region itself was shaped through time.

HYDROLOGY

The Continental Divide forms the "spine" of the Rocky Mountain range and separates water flow between the eastern and western halves of North America. Indeed, the headwaters of some of the continent's major rivers have origins in the highest elevations of the Divide. Flowing eastward and emptying into the Gulf of Mexico are the Arkansas, Missouri, North and South Platte, Rio Grande, and Yellowstone rivers, whereas to the west the Colorado, Columbia, Green, Salmon, San Juan, Snake, and Yampa rivers flow to the Pacific Ocean. Together these rivers account for one-quarter of the United States's freshwater supply.

Along the Continental Divide, accumulated winter snow covers the landscape deeply, in some years reaching depths of several hundred inches. Spring temperatures liquefy the snow and ice, creating runoff that begins slowly but eventually gorges winter-sedate drainages with raging torrents. Dislodged boulders, some the size of mid-sized cars, pound and break their way downstream and eventually are reduced to gravel that grades streambeds and provides habitat for myriad life-forms. At peak runoff, erosion of the land is swift and reforming. These annual seasonal events, accumulated over the long expanse of geologic

Figure 2.3. Hoover Dam, Nevada/ Arizona border. (Photo: U.S. Department of Interior—Bureau of Reclamation)

time, are responsible for producing the heavily fissured landscapes of the West, including the mother of them all, the Grand Canyon of Arizona (Figure 2.2). The Colorado Plateau continues to rise, even today, and the Colorado River continuously cuts through its rock like a huge hydraulic saw. On smaller scales, massive thunderstorms arrive unpredictably, bringing torrential downpours of water that cascade through heat-parched creek beds, reworking the soil and rock and surprising the occasional hiker unfortunate enough to camp in the way. Water running over, around, and through rocks weakens their foundations, causing collapses and landslides that change topography abruptly. In other cases, changes are slow, continuous, and persistent, such as wind etching rock into awesome arch systems like those observed in Arches National Park, Utah. Such beauty is at once a spectacular tribute to the laws of physics and to the artist in us all.

In some places, raging rivers that have battered the land over millennia are temporarily halted by the human intervention of dam building (Figure 2.3). Such activity temporarily transforms dynamic rivers into placid reservoirs. In fact, human-made reservoirs submerge and conceal some of the most astonishing panoramas in the Rocky Mountain region. Attempts at "taming" rivers are ephemeral at best in a geologic sense, but nonetheless displace much terrestrial wildlife across human time frames.

Throughout the last 1.8 million years and up until 11,000 years ago, glaciers have molded the deep, U-shaped valleys, steep slopes, and high peaks of the Rockies. Glaciers persist throughout the Rockies at higher elevations, but occur in the highest numbers and greatest extent in the central and northern regions. Some glacial episodes are more recent than others. For example, the Pinedale Glaciation event remained at full scale as recently as 15,000 to 20,000 years ago, covering 90 percent of what is known today as Yellowstone National Park. Remnant glaciers still persist in some places, working rock into talus slopes that provide shelter for many species of lichens, animals, and plants. The Agassiz and Jackson Glaciers in Glacier National Park, for instance, reached their farthest extent as recently as 1860. The Rockies are rich with waterfalls, some of immense scale. Many occur where glaciers are active, but in the springtime, melting snow produces waterfalls at higher elevations around almost every turn. The cascading effects of kinetic energy carried by the water wear away rock, adding further character to the landscape.

CLIMATE

Localized climates vary considerably throughout the Rockies, depending upon elevation and latitude. Incredibly, snowfall may be blanketing the alpine tundra of the highest elevations while surrounding basins are experiencing 100° F (38° C) temperatures. The Rockies themselves make weather as well as receive it. Prevailing westerly winds drive atmospheric water from the Pacific Ocean across the Sierra Nevada and up against the western edge of the Rockies, where it is uplifted and condensed. Thickened clouds, heavily laden with water, stall against high ridges as more clouds push in from behind. The release of water in the form of rain or snow lightens the clouds that are subsequently propelled over the Divide, causing a precipitation gradient to form from higher to lower elevations along the Eastern Slope. Eastern lowlands are typically shrouded by a rain shadow, which makes for locally arid conditions. As clouds move away from the foothills, they begin to regain moisture and move across the Great Plains painting the summer skies in thunderstorms.

The effects of latitude on temperature are not measured as simply and predictably as changes across elevation at a constant latitude. A general rule, however, is that because the sun's energy is more direct at lower latitudes, these regions tend to be warmer than are higher latitudes with less direct sunlight. This is because the earth is spherical and its axis tilted at about a 23° angle to the sun, causing the sun's rays to hit more directly the closer one approaches the equator.

VEGETATION AND LIFE ZONES

Vegetation patterns throughout the Rocky Mountains are the result of elevation, aspect, and precipitation. The uplift that occurred over millions of years immensely impacted life in the region. Vegetation belts across elevations formed, and each is composed of plants sensitive to specific climatic conditions. The transitions between habitat belts can be abrupt and dramatic, forming their own ecosystems, or *ecotones*. The gradient of elevational change is perhaps most evident where the Continental Divide bulges farthest east at the fortieth parallel in Colorado; here the Rockies are compressed so steeply against the plains that a person driving a mere 10 miles (16 kilometers) upward from the plains passes through a climatic transition similar to driving 1,200 miles (1,900 kilometers) northward. In this area, ascending through six distinctive climate/habitat zones is easily achieved in less than forty-five minutes by car. Such striking elevational transitions, where major habitat types are compressed tightly together, concentrate biodiversity. Steep elevational transitions and complex habitat types are integral to the evolution and persistence of the region's indigenous diversity.

Delineated by the abrupt rise and changing climate, the Rockies in profile show obviously distinctive belts of vegetation. The term *life zones* was coined by C. Hart Merriam in 1890 to describe these belts, and he attributed the zonation to altitudinal differences in climate. Many authors have since redefined these zones to apply to specific areas in the Rockies, and herein I integrate the works of D. M. Armstrong (1972), C. F. Mutel and J. C. Emerick (1984), D. F. Hoffmeister (1986), and A. D. Benedict (1991), which readers should reference for any needs of greater detail. In the following descriptions, scientific names of plants are only given the first time each plant is mentioned. Following each life zone definition is a brief description of the importance of each ecosystem to bats.

Desertscrub

Chihuahuan Subdivision: This habitat is contiguous with the Mexican Plateau, which reaches its limits in the southeastern corner of Arizona and southwestern corner of New Mexico between elevations of 3,200 and 5,000 feet (975–1,524 meters). This habitat is extremely xeric (< 10 inches [25 centimeters]/yr.) and supports creosote bush (*Larrea divaricata*), tarbrush (*Flourensia cernua*), whitethorn (*Acacia constricta*), and various cacti.

Sonoran Subdivision (Figure 2.4): This zone pertains to the lower and upland regions of central, southwestern, and northwestern Arizona. It supports creosote bush, saltbush (*Atriplex confertifolia*), desert thorn (*Lycium*), and mesquite (*Prosopis juliflora*) with as little as three inches of rain, and large cacti (*Carnegiea gigantea*) with precipitation amounts between five and thirteen inches annually.

Mohave Subdivision: This is a poorly defined area present mostly in the extreme west-central to northwestern corner of Arizona that is contiguous with the Mohave Desert of California and Nevada. Plant associates are creosote bush and Joshua tree (*Yucca brevifolia*).

Great Basin Subdivision: This region, located in central and northern Arizona and extending into Utah, is known as cold desert and supports sagebrush (*Artemisia tridentata*), rabbitbrush (*Chrysothamnus nauseosus*), and blackbrush (*Coleogyne ramosissima*).

Figure 2.4. Desertscrub, Sonoran Subdivision. (Photo: R. Adams)

Desertscrub and Bats

The various subdivisions of this habitat support the highest diversity of bat species in the region, twenty-six species total. Of critical note, the Chihuahuan and Sonoran Subdivisions support several bat species occurring nowhere else in the region, such as the ghost-faced bat *(Mormoops megalophylla)*, the California leaf-nosed bat *(Macrotus californicus)*, and the endangered nectar-feeding bats: the Mexican long-tongued bat *(Choeronycteris mexicana)* and the lesser long-nosed bat *(Leptonycteris curasoae)*. In addition, several species of free-tailed bats occur only in this habitat, including the greater mastiff bat *(Eumops perotis)*, Underwood's mastiff bat *(E. underwoodi)*, and pocketed free-tailed bat *(Nyctinomops femorosaccus)*.

Semidesert Scrublands

This is a cold desert (4,000–8,000 feet [1,219–2,438 meters]) ecosystem that supports sagebrush, greasewood *(Sarcobatus vermiculatus)*, rabbitbrush, and saltbush (Figure 2.5).

Piñon-Juniper Woodlands

This ecosystem (Figure 2.6) occurs from 5,500 to 8,000 feet (1,676–2,438 meters) and consists of piñon pine *(Pinus edulis)* and Utah juniper *(Juniperus utahensis)*.

Figure 2.5. Semidesert scrub. (Photo: Lynne Sullivan)

Figure 2.6. Piñon-juniper woodland, Colorado National Monument, Colorado. (Photo: R. Adams)

Semidesert Scrublands, Piñon-Juniper Woodlands, and Bats

I place these two ecosystems together because they are contiguous and highly integrated. Occurring extensively throughout the Southern Rockies, these habitats support high bat diversity. Many *Myotis* species take advantage of the myriad roosting opportunities provided by Utah juniper, piñon pine, and deciduous trees such as cottonwoods (*Populus* sp.) that line ephemeral streams. In addition, the steep cliffs and canyons associated with these habitats provide many opportunities for rock- and crevice-roosting bats. Common bats associated with these habitats include almost all *Myotis* species in the region, with the exception of forest specialists such as the long-eared myotis (*Myotis evotis*). Also present are western pipistrelles (*Pipistrellus hesperus*), Allen's big-eared bats (*Idionycteris phyllotis*), pallid bats (*Antrozous pallidus*), and Brazilian free-tailed bats (*Tadarida brasiliensis*).

Chaparral

Chaparral is a relatively diminutive ecosystem that lies mostly in a thin line south of the Mogollon Plateau in Arizona and consists of scrub oak (*Quercus turbinella*), buckthorn (*Rhamnus* sp.), mountain mahogany (*Cercocarpus montanus*), sugar sumac (*Rhus ovata*), and skunkbush (*Rhus trilobata*).

Figure 2.7. High Plains grassland, Pawnee National Grasslands, Colorado. (Photo: R. Adams)

Chaparral and Bats

Bat species diversity in this ecosystem is relatively varied, as in other xeric landscapes. In Arizona, this habitat may be of particular importance to the Yuma myotis (*M. yumanensis*), as it tends to be one of the most dominant bat species in this ecosystem. Other co-occurring species are the western small-footed myotis (*M. ciliolabrum*) and the California myotis (*M. californicus*).

Plains and Desert Grasslands

The plains grasslands occur east of the Continental Divide at the lowest elevations (below 6,000 feet [1,830 meters]). They are characterized today by short-grass prairie species such as blue grama (*Bouteloua gracilis*) and buffalo grass (*Buchloe dactyloides;* Figure 2.7). Extensions of these vegetation types occur well into the Rockies along valleys, dry slopes, and other types of landforms. Typically, animals and plants of the plains grasslands are adapted to a dry climate.

Grasslands and Bats

Grasslands tend to be low in bat diversity due to the few roosting sites available. Bats present are either tree-roosting species, such as hoary bats (*Lasiurus cinereus*) and eastern red bats (*L. borealis*), or those species that easily use human-made structures, such as little brown myotis (*Myotis lucifugus*) or big brown bats (*Eptesicus fuscus*). Bat diversity is increased in grassland ecosystems if cliffs or canyons are directly present or nearby.

Figure 2.8. Montane shrubland in foreground. (Photo: R. Adams)

Montane Shrublands

This zone marks the transition between grassland and mountain forests and is dominated by Gambel's oak *(Quercus gambelli)*, skunkbush, mountain mahogany, and chokecherry *(Prunus virginiana)*. Montane shrubland occurs between 5,500 and 8,500 feet (1,675–2,590 meters), which, west of the Divide, is higher than shrublands and piñon-juniper woodlands but lower than montane forests. East of the Divide, it occurs between grassland or piñon-juniper woodlands and montane forests (Figure 2.8).

Montane Shrublands and Bats

The openness of montane shrubland provides prime foraging habitat for bats and, to some degree, roost sites. This habitat is particularly supportive of fast-flying, open-area foragers such as big brown bats (*E. fuscus*), hoary bats (*L. cinereus*), and silver-haired bats (*Lasionycteris noctivagans*). Several *Myotis* species, including the long-legged myotis (*Myotis volans*), little brown myotis (*M. lucifugus*), small-footed myotis (*M. ciliolabrum*), and Yuma myotis (*M. yumanensis*), also forage in montane shrubland, as do the western pipistrelle *(P. hesperus)* and pallid bat (*A. pallidus*).

Montane Forests

This ecosystem occurs at 5,600–9,000 feet (1,706–2,743 meters) and is represented by ponderosa pine (*Pinus ponderosa*), Douglas-fir (*Pseudotsuga menziesii*), quaking aspen (*Populus tremuliodes*), and white fir (*Abies concolor;*

Figure 2.9. Montane forest. (Photo: R. Adams)

Figure 2.9). Montane forests are bounded by shrublands, piñon-juniper wood-lands, or grasslands below, and subalpine forests at higher elevations. In Arizona, this ecosystem may occur on isolated mountain ranges that form boreal islands surrounded by desertscrub.

Montane Forests and Bats

Montane forest ecosystems are important to many species of bats, especially in providing roost sites for a diversity of tree species. Many montane areas are interdigitated with cliffs and rocky outcroppings that provide sites for crevice-roosting species as well. This ecosystem provides foraging habitats for agile-flying species such as the long-eared myotis (*M. evotis*), the fringed myotis (*M. thysanodes*), and Townsend's big-eared bat (*Corynorhinus townsendii*).

Subalpine Forests

Subalpine forests occur between 9,000 and 11,400 feet (2,740–3,475 meters) and consist of Engelmann spruce (*Picea engelmannii*), subalpine fir (*Abies lasiocarpa*), quaking aspen, bristlecone pine (*Pinus aristata*), limber pine (*P. flexilis*), and lodgepole pine (*P. contorta*). Trees are tightly packed, and the habitat is relatively homogeneous (Figure 2.10). Due to their dense cover, subalpine forests accumulate a high snowpack and tend to "hold" winter late into the year.

Figure 2.10. Subalpine forest. (Photo: R. Adams)

Subalpine Forests and Bats

Because subalpine forests tend toward dense, homogeneous tree stands (very few species of trees can eke out a living at such high altitudes), they are predictably low in bat diversity. However, this habitat may be important to overwintering bats in the region because many species tend to migrate to higher elevations to find suitable hibernacula. In areas where subalpine forests are pocketed with either abandoned mines or natural caves, a higher diversity of bats may be found seasonally. Many bat species undergo "swarming" at hibernacula for about a month before actually entering hibernation. It is during swarming that breeding apparently occurs. Therefore, in many cases, subalpine forests may provide not only hibernacula but also resources for breeding bats.

Alpine Tundra

The alpine tundra ecosystem (Figure 2.11) occurs at elevations above 11,500 feet (3,505 meters) and is represented mostly by small flowering plants such as alpine avens (*Acomastylis rossii*), arctic willow (*Salix arctica*), and marsh marigold (*Caltha leptosenpala*) and a sedge known as kobresia (*Kobresia myosuroides*). Alpine tundra begins at tree line, the uppermost limit where trees, stunted or otherwise, can grow. The environment is open, extremely windy, and thus too harsh to support trees of any species.

Figure 2.11. Alpine tundra, Rocky Mountain National Park. (Photo: R. Adams)

Alpine Tundra and Bats

Providing very little in the form of roosting opportunities for bats, alpine tundra is low in bat diversity. Several high-elevation species, such as the big brown bat (*E. fuscus*), hoary bat (*Lasiurus cinereus*), silver-haired bat (*Lasionycteris noctivagans*), and perhaps the long-legged myotis (*Myotis volans*), are capable of tolerating cooler temperatures and do forage above tree line. In some instances where wet-meadows occur, insect populations may be dense enough to support colonies of bats.

Riparian Systems

The riparian ecosystem tracks valley-bottom corridors along rivers and streams and occurs proximate to lakes and ponds of various sizes (Figure 2.12). Riparian systems thread throughout most life zones and are represented by cottonwoods (*Populus sargentii* and *P. angustifolia*), mountain willow (*Salix monticola*), and broad-leaved cattail (*Typha latifolia*).

Riparian Systems and Bats

Riparian systems often act as hospitable habitat corridors through open and exposed terrain. They provide bats with safe migration routes and roosting opportunities. The diversity of bat species usually increases where riparian systems abut other habitats. Tree-roosting species such as the eastern red bat (*L. borea-*

Figure 2.12. Mountain riparian habitat, Colorado. (Photo: R. Adams)

lis), silver-haired bat (*L. noctivagans*), and hoary bat (*L. cinereus*) use riparian habitat, not only for day roosting but also as safe havens for their young while females forage at night.

Although the organization of habitats from lower to higher elevations is orderly and predictable throughout much of the region, local differences in specific attributes abound. This is because life zones are composed of, and defined by, specific habitats associated with a given temperature/humidity range, length of growing season, form and amount of precipitation, amount and distribution of wind, as well as soil conditions. Slope aspect (discussed in more detail in the next section) also plays a role. Because of their increased solar exposure, south-facing slopes exhibit zonation that is higher in elevation than that of north-facing slopes.

Elevational limits of each life zone are also affected by latitudinal position along the Southern, Central, and Northern Rockies. For example, tree-line (the upper elevational limit at which trees are able to live) decreases in elevation with increased latitude; therefore, alpine tundra occurs at lower elevations in the Northern Rockies than it does in the Central or Southern Rockies. In fact, tree-line drops approximately 360 feet (110 meters) for every degree of latitude as one travels from south to north. Therefore, organisms attempting to eke out a living in the Northern Rockies must contend with not only elevational but also latitudinal climatic effects that influence populations by abbreviating breeding seasons, reducing litter sizes, and possibly decreasing survival of young.

TRANSITION ZONES

Because habitats are compressed vertically across elevational gradients in the Rockies, ecotones, or transition areas, are relatively narrow. They are, however, important to the region's complexity, providing habitat and resources not only for ecotone specialists but also for those species inhabiting adjacent life zones. The most striking ecotone to the human eye lies between subalpine forests and alpine tundra (see Figure 2.11). At approximately 11,500 feet (3,500 meters) in the Southern Rockies, trees are sparse and become dwarfed, eventually giving way to a treeless tundra landscape. Krummholz communities, present in the ecotone between subalpine and alpine ecosystems, are composed of vegetation that has become stunted and deformed by severe winds to the point that it appears recumbent, as if it were crawling across the tundra. At first glance, it seems that the dwarfed trees are some sort of alpine specialist. However, these trees are actually species such as Douglas-fir, limber pine, and Engelmann spruce that are common in subalpine forests, where they reach heights of 20 feet (6 meters) or more. The dwarfing and recumbent nature of such trees at tree-line is the direct result of the severity of high-elevation conditions, where winds can surpass 200 mph (322 kph), literally blowing the limbs from the leeward side of trees, leaving them with a "flagpole" appearance. Other ecotones, although not as obvious to the human eye, are equally dynamic transitions between ecosystems.

NORTH- VERSUS SOUTH-FACING SLOPE EFFECT

Within the Rocky Mountain West, differing degrees of solar gain affect the distributions of life-forms. Due to the drying effects of the sun, vegetation tends to be more desert adapted on south-facing slopes. Even on the east side of the Rockies, south-facing slopes are composed of yucca (*Yucca glauca*) and prickly pear cactus, reminiscent of southwestern desert habitats (Figure 2.13). North-facing slopes, being more shaded from the drying effects of the sun, retain far more moisture in the soil and are therefore capable of supporting coniferous forests. In some locations, vegetative differences between slopes of contrasting aspect are so dramatic that a simple turn of the head catapults a person's mind instantly between Canadian boreal forest and Mexican desertscrub that are usually separated by 1,200 miles (1,935 kilometers).

Figure 2.13. North- and south-aspect slopes (*right and left, respectively*) illustrating vegetation differences, East Slope, Colorado. (Photo: R. Adams)

Cold-blooded (ectothermic) animals such as insects and reptiles are mostly restricted to occupying south-facing slopes, where solar heat energy is highest. Although the distribution of warm-blooded (endothermic) mammals is not similarly affected, fur color differences in mice and other rodents have been observed on north- versus south-facing slopes. North-facing slopes remain relatively cool and wet throughout the day, so their soils are darker than those on drier, south-facing slopes. Selection favors mice and other small mammals whose fur tracks soil coloration because they are more cryptic to predators, making them more likely to survive and reproduce. In this way, the north/south aspect phenomenon adds to the mosaic of selective pressures that enhance populational diversity in the Rocky Mountain region.

For Rocky Mountain bats, nursery roosts in most cases occur on east- or southeast-facing slopes. Females take advantage of higher solar aspect to keep roosts hot during the day, allowing them to enter torpor under conditions that facilitate development of the young. They are essentially roosting in an incubator driven by solar radiation rather than their own body heat and can thereby save energy during gestation. Temperatures in maternity roosts may reach 120° F. Contrastingly, bachelor roosts tend to occur on north-facing slopes, where temperatures are cooler during the day. Not requiring an incubator, male bats can enter the energy-saving torpor state under cooler, and perhaps more comfortable, conditions.

BARRIERS TO DISPERSAL

The elevation of the Rocky Mountains creates a major barrier to organisms attempting to move from east to west or vice versa. In fact, many species reach their limits of distribution on either side of the Continental Divide because they simply cannot move across the inhospitable habitats at higher elevations. For many species, the highest peaks are an impregnable wall to movement, and this is nowhere more apparent than in the Southern Rockies, where many peaks break the 14,000-foot (4,267-meter) mark. This barrier is so formidable, in fact, that even animals capable of flight are turned back in most attempts to breach it. Population communication across the Continental Divide, when it occurs at all, usually happens across the Deming Plain in New Mexico, near the Chihuahuan Desert boundary. There are also intermittent corridors for east-west dispersal across the Divide in central or even northern New Mexico as well as across some of the lower passes in northern and southern Wyoming. However, for many terrestrial organisms, the channels through the barrier are inaccessible, and their world ends at the Divide.

As evidence of the Divide's immense influence, the region of the Rockies made up of Utah and Arizona and some adjacent parts of California, Nevada, and New Mexico contains larger numbers of subspecies than any other continental area of equal size in the world. Apparently, landscape characteristics such as (a) dramatic relief caused by alternating mountain ranges and valleys or closed basins; (b) a great range in elevation resulting in a wide range in temperature and sharply marked zonation; and (c) the high numbers of deeply cut, steep, rock-walled canyons in Arizona, Colorado, and Utah have made the southwestern United States a strong segregator of populations, which, in the long term, may promote the formation of new species. Indeed, this is one way biodiversity is, and has been, generated throughout geologic time.

NORTH–SOUTH CORRIDORS: THE CANADIAN/MEXICAN CONNECTION

Despite the fact that the Rocky Mountain landscape is rugged and discourages long-distance movements, the fauna and flora of the region are not completely isolated. Continual invasions from the north, south, east, and west do occur, and the region shares species with many other areas of North America. Although east-to-west dispersal across the Divide is hindered for many species, north-to-south dispersal is less problematic. Deep, narrow north-south-running canyons in the foothills, and deeper in the mountains, provide channels through which species can disperse without traveling over high mountain passes. To the south, the Rockies are more or less contiguous via the Colorado Plateau, which in southern Arizona merges with the Sierra Madre Occidental and the Sierra Madre Oriental of Mexico, forming a nearly uninterrupted corridor for dispersal and seasonal migrations between temperate and tropical climates. These corridors are likely used by migrating bat species in the region.

Passages extending northward from Mexico split on either side of the Continental Divide and bring with them into the Southern Rockies an assemblage of Mexican species named the Chihuahuan Faunal Element (Figure 2.14). The

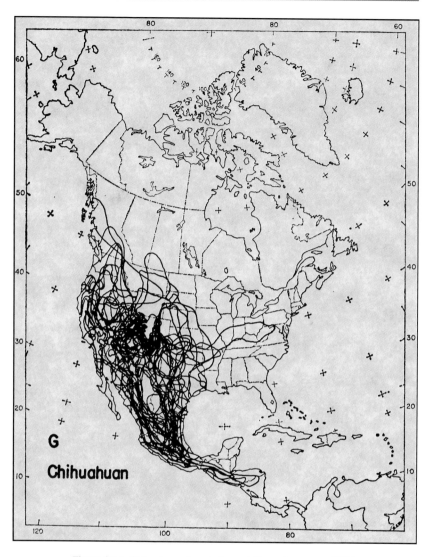

Figure 2.14. Chihuahuan faunal element (from Armstrong 1972)

Chihuahuan intrusion truncates mostly at the northern borders of Colorado and Utah, where seasonal conditions become too extreme for many of the species. The Northern Rockies are influenced by corridors that are contiguous with the most northern expanses of North America and that integrate them with the Cordilleran and Boreo-Cordilleran Faunal Elements. Organisms of these faunal elements reach their northern distributional limits near the Arctic Circle and their southern limits in central Arizona and New Mexico, although a few species occur in more southern parts of both states.

The Rocky Mountain region, then, exhibits a complex mosaic of life. Many species no doubt evolved here, but others are invaders that have persisted, in some cases, in very small populations at the limits of their range. Native species evolved here through the expanse of geologic time, and of these, one evolved wings, raising the stakes of ecological diversity. The Rocky Mountain region was the theater for a high-flying experiment called "batness," and we visit times long past in the following chapter.

3

Evolutionary Origins and Adaptations of Rocky Mountain Bats

old the presses, this just in: *Ancient Bat Fossil Unearthed in Wyoming!* Alright, perhaps it didn't make headlines in major newspapers, but in the world of fossil hunters, this was indeed big news. Even so, uncovering such a relic begged important questions: Did bats evolve first in ancient North America, making this fossil the ancestor of all bats worldwide? Was the first bat to evolve an eater of insects similar to the species we have in North America today? How old are bats as a group, and what ancestor gave rise to this ancient but modern-looking individual? Before we jump into discussing these questions, however, gaining a historical perspective on the evolution of mammals in North America is instructive.

The ancient history of mammals stretches far back in time, and their story is written in rocks buried below our feet. Occasionally we are lucky to discover fossils of our relatives that give insight into past eons. Such finds give momentary glimpses of the past from which a picture is built by employing many of the same forensic techniques used by detectives to solve unwitnessed crimes. Deciphering origins and ancient events is always challenging, but when enough evidence is gathered, patterns begin to emerge, and with mammals, many pieces to the puzzle are available.

Mammals began their existence about 240 million years ago in a world dominated by reptiles. Scurrying about, our ancestors bided their time with patient resolve for more than 100 million years while the most physically dominant vertebrates to have ever lived thundered about. Discovery of huge fossilized bones would stimulate the nineteenth-century anatomist Richard Owen to name this group Dinosauria (meaning "Terrible Lizard"). And as our ancestors likely did, we cower and fade in their shadow (at least I did during the movie *Jurassic Park*).

Consuming insects under the cover of night, the inconspicuous, but big-brained furries were living their lives in unprecedented ways, utilizing teeth, behaviors, and physiology previously unseen on earth. Even with their cleverness, however, early mammals apparently could not outcompete the established monarchy of the dinosaurs without help from the heavens. In an unforeseen event, a rock of extraterrestrial origin, hurled from thousands of miles away, gave mammals the break they needed. The asteroid was approximately six miles wide. Its impact shook the planet to its core, unleashing havoc as mass extinction ripped and gutted the ecosystems of the world. Peaking out from their underground burrows in thick underbrush (Figure 3.1), the furry night-sneakers with large brains and hungry metabolisms were protected from the initial shockwaves of mass destruction. As time passed, they ventured outward from their secluded existence in the undergrowth. For the first time since the dawn of their kind, their world lacked the familiar thundering of giants, and the stage was set for a new world order. Luckily for us, these early mammals had the genetic and behavioral plasticity necessary to survive in a world of new challenges and demands. Astonishingly, almost all of the present-day living orders of mammals evolved relatively quickly over the next twenty-five million years.

The first "new" forms to arise were primates and bats, unprecedented onlookers to a rebuilding earth. Renovation of the planet over the following 55 million years involved fluctuations between extinction and speciation events driven by global changes in climate, deviating ocean levels, monumental volcanic uplifts, and immense reconvergences of some continents that had drifted alone as islands for millions of years. These were dynamic and exciting times as large-scale global and continental events reshuffled newly evolving life.

A major event known as the Great American Interchange brought together two continental assemblages of organisms that had evolved separately for more than 150 million years. The Interchange began three million years ago when South America, which had drifted as an island continent for millions of years, connected to North America via the Isthmus of Panama, facilitating a massive interchange of organisms between continents. It involved thirty-eight genera of South American mammals that migrated into North America, and forty-seven genera that entered South America from North America. The Isthmus of Panama acted as a bridge for "free trade" that quickly altered the biological faces of the two continents. The area of North America known today as the Rocky Mountain region was likely affected by this historic interchange.

Two million years later during the Pleistocene Epoch (1 million to 10,000 years ago), glacial ice flowed and ebbed across the face of North America. At high elevations valley glaciers eventually formed almost to the equator. This so-called

Figure 3.1. Hypothetical Cretaceous mammals peering out from the protection of vegetation after the demise of the dinosaurs that spawned the "Age of Mammals" and facilitated the mammalian radiations of which bats were an early branch

Ice Age sorted the flora and fauna once again, causing extinctions of many species while opening the door for others. Because of significantly lowered sea levels, corridors were exposed between large continents, such as the Bering land bridge between Eurasia and North America (Figure 3.2). The significance of the

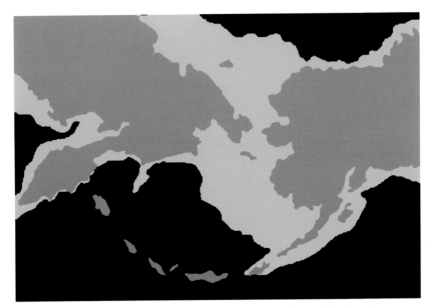

Figure 3.2. Illustration showing the extent of Pleistocene ice sheets (light brown) that connected Eurasia to North America via a landbridge known as Beringia. Beringia allowed for migrations of Old World faunas into the New World.

Bering land bridge to the natural history of North America cannot be overstated, as it allowed for megafaunal migrations, such as that of wooly mammoths, from Eurasia to the Americas. Accordingly, this was the migration route that our own species (*Homo sapiens*) followed into the New World from our evolutionary origin in Africa. The significance of intercontinental migrations for Rocky Mountain bats, however, likely resides mostly in the North/South American connection more than the Bering land bridge. The justification for this is that Old World continents such as Africa, Europe, and Asia share very few species of bats with New World continents, which would most likely not be the case if the Bering land bridge had funneled numerous species of bats between the continents.

Fossils represent history written in stone, indelible imprints marking specific cross-sections in time. Curiously, we know from fossil evidence that fully evolved bats were present in the Rocky Mountain region soon after the dinosaur's reign ended, sixty-five million years ago. Perhaps they were present millions of years earlier, fluttering about the head of *Tyrannosaurus rex* as it settled in for its nighttime slumber. Perhaps bats were witnesses to the cataclysmic events that stirred the pot of biodiversity, allowing mammals to float to the top. We may never know. Few fossils of entire skeletons of bats have thus far been uncovered. What we do know is that bats living in North America fifty-five million years ago already possessed the general characters of today's bat species. The reduced skeleton and elongated hand and finger bones are obvious in fossil remains. Detailed analyses of cochlea of fossil skulls show that the ears were already adapted to receive high-frequency sounds, just as the ears of most bats today. Thus, the ability to echolocate was apparently already present in these ancient bats. In addition, bat fossils found in Germany and dated to about fifty million years ago contained fossilized insects in their stomachs. But how did it all begin?

DIVERGENCE OF TEMPERATE BATS: SOME LIKE IT NOT SO HOT

Fifty-five million years ago, in a dense tropical rainforest, a small insect-eating bat fell into a tropical lake, died, and was covered immediately with sediment. Its entire skeleton would be preserved for millions of years before its discovery by individuals of a species (*Homo sapiens*) whose existence represents the latest eye blink in the evolution of mammals. The specimen (Figure 3.3) is a full-bodied fossil named *Icaronycteris index* (exemplifying the mythical Greek child Icarus, who flew too close to the sun, melted his wings, and fell back to earth) and is the earliest known record of bats in the world. Almost inconceivably, this ancient tropical scene occurred in a place we know today as Wyoming, south of Yellowstone National Park. Because *I. index* manifests many of the advanced physical characteristics of today's species, many believe that the origin of bats runs much deeper in earth's history than represented by this derived individual or other fossil specimens of similar age. This view is supported by the discovery of fossil teeth that date bats to at least eighty million years ago. Yet there have been no discoveries of intermediate forms between volant (flying) and nonvolant mammals. Because bats are typically small in size and have very delicate skeletons, fossilization itself, not to mention recovery by paleontologists, is highly improbable. In fact, it is amazing, and quite lucky, that we have found any full-skeleton fossils of bats at all.

Pinpointing even the continental origin for bats is severely confounded at this moment. The finding of *I. index* in the mid-1960s suggested that bats evolved in North America, or at least in the Americas. In more recent years, however, bat fossils unearthed in Messel, Germany, and dated to be a few millions years younger than *I. index*, have been described. Having well-preserved fossils of bats of approximately the same age found in very different parts of the world did little to help us understand the regional origin of the first bats.

The evolutionary synthesis of today's North American bat fauna remains unclear. Some species did evolve here, but when is uncertain. For populations present fifty-five million years ago, it is unclear if they were driven to extinction along with much of the tropical Eocene period fauna of North America. On the one hand, one would suspect that bat extinction rates in North America were comparable to those of other tropical species present, such as some rodents, monkeys, apes, leopards, and elephants. If so, this would mean that present populations were later re-established via migrating species from Central and South America that adapted over evolutionary time to persist in temperate climates. On

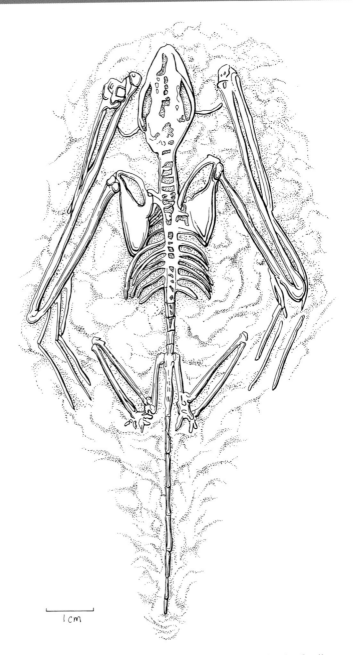

Figure 3.3. Drawing of *Icaronycteris index*, the oldest known complete bat fossil, excavated in the 1960s from an ancient lake bed in Wyoming

the other hand, perhaps bats escaped extinction here, "hiding out" in regional refugia that buffered them from dramatic climatic changes. If so, bats adapted *in situ* to changing climatic conditions and persisted throughout the dramatic climate changes in North America, even the Pleistocene Ice Age.

Whatever scenario of origins eventually proves true, the North American bat fauna has not thus far reached the diversity of bats in Neotropical regions, which in some areas boast more than two hundred species. In the United States there are forty-five species of bats, and the greatest diversity occurs in areas abutting Mexico, including the Colorado Plateau and some areas of the Southern Rockies. But how could a group that evolved under tropical conditions become adapted to live in temperate environments? For bats, much of their success depends upon an amazing physiology.

SPECIAL ADAPTATIONS TO TEMPERATE ENVIRONMENTS: WHEN HEAVEN FREEZES OVER

Torpor

Have you ever tried to awaken a sleeping bat? Upon discovering one, you're likely to question whether the animal is even alive. There are no immediate signs of breathing and no reaction to your cautious prodding with a stick or some other blunt object. If you touch it with your finger (not recommended!), it feels cold and hard. "Yep, no life here—poor little critter," you think. Giving up on your initial anticipation of observing a living bat, you decide to lay it to rest under that old pine tree. Glancing back as you move away, you notice something odd: the bat's ears and nose appear to be twitching. Slightly intrigued, you reinvestigate, and to your amazement, undeniable signs of life begin to appear. You take a closer look and notice a slight pulsing of its lower back that is building momentum, and then a slight movement of its head. It is slightly warmer to the touch now, and its feet begin to move. Perhaps it reminds you of waking up the morning after staying out too late at the local pub. But what's the bat's excuse? Certainly not staying up too late, because night is day to bats. Another minute or two and the bat begins climbing up that old pine tree and disappears from sight. Wow, you think, perhaps I brought it back to life. Then reality sinks in, and you realize the impossibility of that. Still mystified, you return home, eventually forgetting about your little encounter with the world of "bat."

Although one may want to claim responsibility for reviving a fellow being in distress or begin to think that bats have supernatural powers, as it turns out, the bat was just being a bat. In fact, this behavior exemplifies a major energy-saving adaptation that allows bats to persevere in temperate environments. The ability to withstand drops in body temperature to match that of the ambient environment, sometimes 30° below active core temperature, is called *torpor* (Figure 3.4). In torpor a bat's heart rate and breathing are reduced to once or twice a minute, allowing for tremendous savings in metabolic energy. Because most bats are small-bodied and therefore have a large surface area relative to volume, they

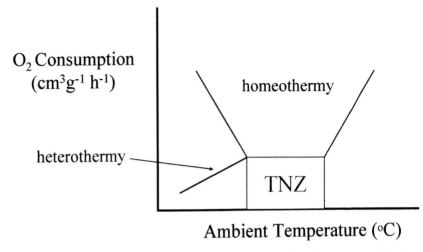

Figure 3.4. Graphic illustration of the highly specialized heterothermic response used by bats and other true endothermic hibernators. TNZ refers to the thermo-neutral zone where basal metabolic rate is maintained. The red lines indicate increased metabolic rate (measured as CO_2 consumption) experienced by homeotherms when ambient temperature is lower or higher than the range supporting TNZ. The blue line indicates the heterothermic response of torpor and hibernation when ambient temperature is below TNZ (see text for further discussion).

readily lose heat to the environment. Consequently, maintaining a constant body temperature requires the burning of large amounts of fuel, which makes fat storage—required for hibernation and migration—difficult. Reducing its metabolic rate to almost zero throughout the majority of its daily cycles allows a bat to store energy for use when environmental conditions degrade.

The idea that a bat can recover after losing almost one-third of its core body temperature is unimaginable to us. Indeed, if a human loses as little as 8 to 10 degrees of core temperature, the result is severe physiological stress, called hypothermia, which can quickly result in death. Initial investigators thought that bats were incapable of maintaining a constant, stable body temperature like most other mammals. They mistakenly considered bats to be primitive, and somewhat crude thermoregulators, essentially akin to a flying lizard with fur. But, as with many first impressions, all is not as it initially seems. As it turns out (and perhaps we are not reminded of this enough in our daily self-involvement), being human is not the only way to be a mammal. This is simply—or not so simply—another example of the diversity of life, replete with myriad adaptations, some of which are astonishingly different from what humans consider "normal."

Torpor is actually a highly specialized physiological adaptation for living in temperate climates. It is an energy-saving measure that allows bats to store enough fat for hibernation or to undertake long migrations. Daily torpor is similar to hibernation, but the physiological response is not as drastic or profound and runs on a daily, rather than a seasonal, cycle. Hibernators that enter some level of stasis during the winter months in temperate regions are also capable of torpor. However, hibernation itself is driven by a seasonal loss of food supply.

Hibernation

Extended periods of torpor in winter are referred to as hibernation, and many species of mammals have evolved this useful trait. Hibernation is particularly adaptive for those species for whom migration is a limited option and whose winter habitat simply cannot supply enough food energy to maintain their metabolic rates. Hibernation in bats is similar to that observed in other mammalian groups. However, because of their small size and their inability to burrow, bats must locate preformed underground caverns that provide the precise microclimate necessary for surviving winter. This is not just a matter of finding a hole in the ground. A hibernaculum (hibernation site) must be suitable within very fine tolerances of temperature and humidity. In many species, such as the smaller brown bats (known as *Myotis* species), hibernation sites need to have a stable temperature of approximately 40° F (4.5° C), with a standing humidity close to 100 percent (saturation). In addition, the amount of air flow in the cavern is important because it replenishes the air supply. However, because air flow can destabilize a cavern's climate, the rate of air movement must be just enough to allow for some circulation and replenishment without impacting the overall cave environment.

Many species of bats may cohabit in the same cavern, but each species will distribute itself throughout various levels and depths depending upon its own specific temperature and humidity requirements. As a general pattern, larger bats prefer a lower hibernation temperature, lower humidity, and higher air flow and therefore tend to roost closer to cavern entrances than do smaller species that prefer more humid and stable, deeper chambers. Length of hibernation varies, depending upon species and locality, but may last up to seven months.

Because bats roost so far underground when hibernating, the sensory cues from the environment that normally maintain daily biorhythms (called circadian rhythms) are not available to them. Typically, day length (sunrise to sunset), which changes seasonally except near the equator, cues an animal's brain to reset its internal clock. Because bats are underground in continual darkness for months during hibernation, their internal clocks should predictably run out of phase and they should lose all sense of time and rhythm. Thus, how bats know when to arouse from hibernation in springtime is a mystery, and biologists have had little success in determining how their internal clock keeps time during months of uninterrupted sleep.

For some bat species, the largest aggregations of the year form at the hibernaculum (Figure 3.5). Typically these gatherings consist of males, females, and that year's juveniles, thereby constituting an entire breeding population. The

Figure 3.5. Hibernating colony of Townsend's big-eared bats (*Corynorhinus townsendii*). (Photo: S. Altenbach)

behavioral dynamics of bats in the hibernaculum are poorly understood. However, clusters of bats, consisting usually of several dozen individuals, form small groups within the colony. Individuals roosting toward the center of these clusters are buffered from the surrounding air by the bodies of their comrades making up the circumference of the cluster. It is assumed that bats somehow vie for position within a cluster, but how they determine who gets the preferred center locations is unknown. The arrangement may simply be by chance, or perhaps it is defined by a dominance hierarchy.

Males and females hibernate together after several weeks of breeding in and around the hibernaculum. In Rocky Mountain bats, females typically store sperm (Figure 3.6) after copulating with one or more males. The sperm is maintained in the uterine lining (endometrium), where it is nourished with glycogen throughout the duration of hibernation. It has been noted that male little brown myotis (*Myotis lucifugus*) will awake during hibernation and copulate with torpid females. Whether or not sperm from these overzealous males are actually stored by the female, or simply represent wasted effort, is not known. Not until awakening from hibernation in spring do females ovulate, and the stored sperm is then released to swim in the competitive race to fertilize the egg. Upon fertilization and implantation, the embryo begins to develop.

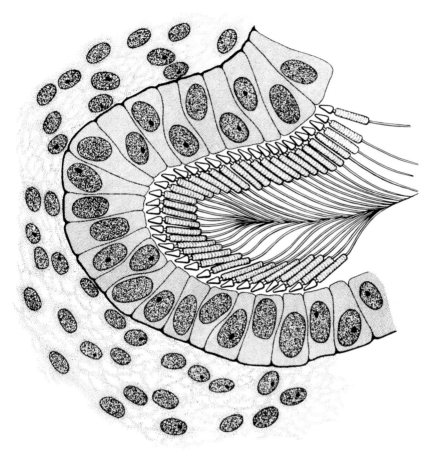

Figure 3.6. Illustration of how sperm align and embed in the uterus of female vespertilionid bats during hibernation (from Hill and Smith 1984)

Bats survive through many months of hibernation by a combination of burning body fat acquired during summer and fall foraging and using the energy-saving effects of daily torpor. During hibernation, their metabolism slows to as little as a single heartbeat and a single breath per minute.

Two types of fat are stored by bats. One type, termed white fat or white adipose tissue, burns slowly during hibernation maintaining basic metabolic functions. Although this fat is obviously important, its slow burning rate precludes its ability to generate enough heat to arouse a bat from hibernation or even torpor. A second type of fat, known as brown fat or brown adipose tissue, is stored solely for this purpose and when oxidized, releases a tremendous amount of energy

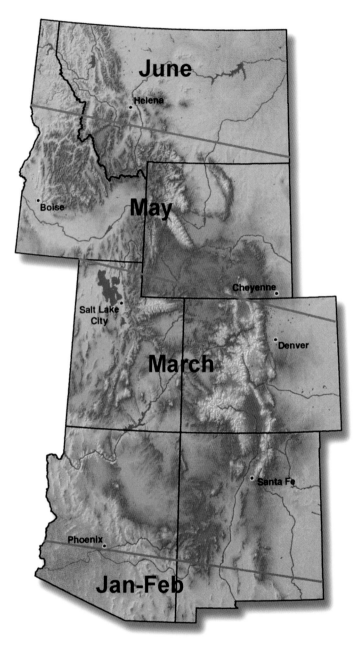

Figure 3.7. Hoary bat (*Lasiurus cinereus*) spring and summer migration patterns across their Rocky Mountain range.

very quickly, raising the bat's body temperature, in some cases more than 60° F (15.6° C) in ten minutes.

Hibernation is the one trait of bats that is probably most responsible for allowing an essentially tropical mammal to live year-round in temperate regions. Temperate species that do not hibernate must migrate to areas where food is available, and these migrations can be long and treacherous.

Migration

Although long-distance migrations are best known as an amazing feat of birds, some bats also undergo lengthy seasonal journeys. Traveling solely at night, they apparently use the stars for navigation. Several Rocky Mountain species, such as the hoary bat (*Lasiurus cinereus;* Figure 3.7), the silver-haired bat (*Lasionycteris noctivagans*), and the Brazilian free-tailed bat (*Tadarida brasiliensis*), migrate north and south seasonally. Although hoary and silver-haired bats are mostly solitary, Brazilian free-tailed bats migrate in groups that may consist of several thousand individuals traveling together over 3,000 miles (4,839 km) or more. Most of the larger colonies of these so-called "guano bats"— for example, those present at Carlsbad Caverns, New Mexico, and Bracken Cave, San Antonio, Texas—are maternity colonies consisting of mostly females and their young. One peculiar bachelor colony consisting of approximately 230,000 males lives in the San Luis Valley of Colorado (see Figure 1.16) during the summer months, arriving north in springtime possibly from somewhere in Mexico. No other bachelor colony of this size is known in North America. How bats navigate during long migrations remains mostly unknown. Experimenters using point-light sources showed that big brown bats (*Eptesicus fuscus*) should be able to see many of the bright stars visible in the northern hemisphere. Colony displacement and controlled planetarium studies using the same species indicate that individuals use post-sunset glow as an orientation clue.

Most of the other bat species in the Rocky Mountain region use relatively short-distance (< 50 miles [80 km]) migrations between hibernacula and summer foraging grounds. Typically males and females segregate as they move away from the hibernation site, returning in mixed-sex groups in the fall to breed (commonly referred to as swarming) and enter hibernation. Species that undergo long-distance seasonal migrations are usually not hibernators, whereas short-distance migrators remain in the region and overwinter in underground caverns.

4

Bats in
Rocky Mountain Ecosystems

he present-day ecosystems of the Rocky Mountain region represent a complex array of interactions between geology, climate, and life spanning millions of years. Populations of organisms respond to changing conditions through a mindless agent called natural selection, which favors certain adaptations. But organisms also manipulate their environments, changing them to fit their immediate needs. The ecosystems of the Rockies are the product of geomorphic changes intertwined with the evolution of life.

Fossil evidence from the region suggests a very different flora and fauna occurring today than any time in the past seventy million years. As discussed in Chapter 2, today's Rockies are a mosaic of habitat types that provide a plethora of opportunities for animals, including bats. Even though possessing wings allows for extensive mobility, bats are still governed by the selective forces of regional landscapes and climates.

BAT DIVERSITY AND ELEVATION:
IT'S LONELY AT THE TOP AND THE BOTTOM

It has long been observed that there is an increasing latitudinal gradient in the numbers of bird and mammal species, especially bats, as one approaches the equator. Curiously, throughout the Rockies the highest diversity of birds and mammals is found at a mid-elevational band known as montane forests. As one moves away from the montane band, species diversity attenuates in a pattern similar to that of latitudinal gradients moving away from the equator.

Grassland habitats of lower elevations tend to lack trees and rock outcrops and therefore allow few opportunities for bats to locate adequate roosting sites. In areas where rivers and streams interdigitate with grasslands, associated riparian habitats provide trees for roost sites that promote increases in bat numbers. Several species of bats roost in the trees of riparian zones and forage over grass-laden fields that produce high densities of insects. But even where riparian zones interface with grasslands, bat diversity remains limited by the lack of habitat complexity.

Habitats that are located at elevations higher than montane forests are similarly low in bat diversity on both the Eastern and Western Slopes. The subalpine zone is a complex of forests, meadows, and rock outcrops that is productive in terms of biomass, but nighttime temperatures at these elevations cut back on nocturnal insect activity, and most bat species are apparently not well adapted to eke out a living under such conditions. Alpine tundra, which is similar to grass-lands in being mostly two-dimensional, supplies little or no roosting habitat for bats, and even though bats are occasionally observed foraging above tree line, this is an exception rather than a rule for most species. Some species such as the big brown bats (*Eptesicus fuscus*), little brown myotis (*Myotis lucifugus*), long-eared myotis (*Myotis evotis*), and long-legged myotis (*Myotis volans*) are known to persist in tree-line populations, but most species do best at lower elevations.

The foothills montane forests of the Eastern Slope and the piñon-juniper montane woodlands of the Western Slope support the highest bat diversity throughout the Rockies proper. Of the thirty-one species ranging from Arizona to Montana, 13, or 42 percent, are found as common inhabitants in those two habitats. It is speculated that the complex nature of the lower slope forests and woodlands provides diversity of roost site opportunities, along with supporting a varied and predictable food base. In Colorado, about 80 percent of the state's bat species are found in piñon-juniper woodlands and desertscrub habitats, which make up less than 8 percent of the state's landscape. Even in the deserts of Arizona, foothills montane areas are highest in bat diversity (Figure 4.1). In the West, the semideserts and deserts of the Colorado Plateau regions of Arizona and New Mexico promote the highest diversity of bat species in the region. Most bats survive best in areas that undergo less dramatic seasonal temperature changes such as in Arizona where twenty-nine species representing four families, or 65 percent of the forty-five species inhabiting the entire United States, occur. As one moves northward, diversity attenuates, dropping to eighteen species of two families in Colorado and Utah, and only seven species of one family present in Montana.

STRUCTURE OF ROCKY MOUNTAIN BAT ASSEMBLAGES

The large diversity of bats living in the Rocky Mountain West coexist because the region's varied habitat allows for tight resource partitioning among species.

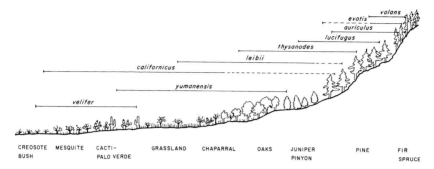

Figure 4.1. Elevational distribution of nine species of *Myotis* in Arizona relative to vegetation type (from Hoffmeister 1986)

Through evolutionary time, bats of the region have diverged in characters, each becoming adapted to exploit different components of the resource base (Table 4.1). Simply put, a diverse resource base favors coexistence rather than exclusion of some species via competition. Interestingly, very subtle differences in anatomy and behavior provide enough ecological separation to allow for coexistence.

The Shapes of Bats: Round Pegs in Round Holes

The generalized body shape of bats is driven for the most part by physics, as opposed to biology. Bats possess an aerodynamic shape required to make flight efficient, and because of this requirement, the diversity of body shapes and sizes available to bats is quite limited relative to that of terrestrial mammals. Therefore, in a general sense, bats all look alike because of the physical demands of flight. Within the overall constraints associated with the ability to fly, the wings of bats manifest different sizes and shapes adapted for foraging in different habitat types (Figure 4.2). Of primary importance is the balance between body size and wing dimensions that is governed by the laws of physics. Nevertheless, several different wing forms and foraging strategies have evolved over the last fifty-five million years.

Shapes and Sizes of Wings: Fitting in With the Crowd

The size and shape of a bat's wings relative to its body mass (weight) is termed *wing loading,* and wing loading determines flight speed and agility. Natural selection has favored wing forms among bat species that adapt them to differing foraging strategies that in turn promote resource partitioning and therefore species coexistence. Bat species that have evolved long, narrow wings are adapted for flying swiftly in open habitats. In fact, because the wing surface area is small,

Table 4.1. Pertinent Ecological Characteristics of Bats of the Rocky Mountain West (in order of species accounts)

Species	Foraging Habitat	Foraging Style	Food	Roost Site	Colony Size
Ghost-faced bat *Mormoops megalophylla*	open areas usually around water	strong, fast fliers, open aerial pursuit	large moths almost exclusively	caves and abandoned mines	may exceed 500,000 individuals
California leaf-nosed bat *Macrotus californicus*	cluttered mixed forests	hovering and gleaning	sphinx moths, butterflies, dragonflies, grasshoppers, cicadas, caterpillars, beetles	caves and abandoned mines	typically 100–200 individuals
Mexican long-tongued bat *Choeronycteris mexicana*	generalist, found in arid thorn scrub, deciduous forests, and mixed oak-conifer forests	hovering at, and landing on, flowers	nectar from predominately *Agave* and cactus flowers	mine tunnels, caves, rock crevices, and, occasionally but rarely, buildings	usually 10 or fewer individuals
Lesser long-nosed bat *Leptonycteris curasoae*	desertscrub and desert grasslands	hovering at, and landing on, flowers	nectar, pollen, insects, and fruits	caves and abandoned mines	may exceed 10,000 individuals
Pallid bat *Antrozous pallidus*	arid scrublands, piñon-juniper woodlands, usually in open habitat	mostly terrestrial gleaning via ground pursuit, but also gleaning from vegetation	ground-dwelling forms such as scarab and carrion beetles, crickets, katydids, praying mantids, moths, and scorpions	usually rock crevices and buildings, but occasionally caves, mines, rock piles, and tree cavities	usually around 20 individuals
Townsend's big-eared bat *Corynorhinus townsendii*	mixed coniferous forests, but also semi-desert scrub, piñon-juniper woodlands, ponderosa pine woodlands	mostly gleaning, some aerial pursuit	moths, lacewings, flies	caves, abandoned mines and buildings	usually 20–30 individuals

Species	Habitat	Flight/Foraging	Diet	Roost	Colony size
Big brown bat *Eptesicus fuscus*	meadows, ponderosa pine woodlands, grasslands	open aerial forager with strong direct flight	mostly a beetle specialist, but also consumes moths, flies, mayflies	mostly buildings, also rock crevices	highly variable, up to several hundred individuals
Spotted bat *Euderma maculatum*	desert specialist, found in desertscrub, semi-desert scrub, piñon-juniper woodlands	aerial pursuit, typically 33–50 feet above ground, using an audible echolocation call	mostly moths	usually rock crevices located on high cliffs	largely unknown, but probably small, 4–10 individuals
Allen's big-eared bat *Idionycteris phyllotis*	usually lower-elevation ponderosa pine woodlands, piñon-juniper woodlands, but has been captured in high-elevation white fir forests	mostly gleaning, but also aerial pursuit in cluttered habitats	primarily small moths, but also soldier and dung beetles, roaches, and flying ants	tree snags, boulders beneath rock shelters, and abandoned mines	up to 100 individuals
Silver-haired bat *Lasionycteris noctivagans*	usually over woodland ponds and streams	slow, maneuverable flier, aerial pursuit	moths, true bugs, flies, mosquitoes, termites, beetles	tree foliage	solitary, but a single tree may host several individuals
Western red bat *Lasiurus blossevillii*	usually over ponds or along waterways bordered by cotton-woods and sycamores	strong, straight pursuit; low maneuverability	mostly moths	tree foliage in deciduous forests along waterways	solitary, but a single tree may host several individuals
Eastern red bat *Lasiurus borealis*	in proximity to riparian habitats	strong, open aerial, straight pursuit; low maneuverability	moths, flies, mosquitoes, true bugs, cicadas	tree foliage in deciduous forest along waterways	solitary, but a single tree may host several individuals

continued on next page

Table 4.1—*Continued*

Species	Foraging Habitat	Foraging Style	Food	Roost Site	Colony Size
Hoary bat *Lasiurus cinereus*	usually high above ground over ponderosa pine habitats	fast, strong, straight pursuit; moderate maneuverability	almost entirely moths	primarily in coniferous trees, but also abandoned woodpecker holes, caves, squirrel nests, buildings, and under driftwood planks	solitary
Western yellow bat *Lasiurus xanthinus*	usually over semi-desert scrub	strong, straight pursuit; moderate maneuverability	mostly beetles	hackberry and sycamore trees, dead fronds of palm trees	solitary
Southwestern myotis *Myotis auriculus*	mesquite and chaparral through oak forests, ponderosa pine woodlands, and piñon-juniper woodlands, usually in proximity to rocky cliffs and water	gleaning, sometimes lands to grab prey	mostly moths	day roosts unknown; night roosts include buildings, abandoned mines, and caves	unknown
California myotis *Myotis californicus*	arid habitats, edge of coniferous woodlands, but also over desert-scrub up to oak woodlands	slow, erratic flight along margins of vegetation clumps in aerial pursuit	primarily flies, moths, beetles	rock crevices, hollow trees, buildings, and under loose bark	small aggregations of a few individuals or solitary

Species	Habitat	Foraging behavior	Diet	Roost sites	Colony size
Western small-footed myotis *Myotis ciliolabrum*	deserts, badlands, semi-arid habitats, oak woodlands, ponderosa pine forests, piñon-juniper woodlands, and chaparral, sometimes over water	slow, maneuverable flight in aerial pursuit	mostly small beetles, but also moths and lacewings	rock crevices, abandoned mines, caves, under rocks on scree slopes	small aggregations of a few individuals or solitary
Western long-eared myotis *Myotis evotis*	cluttered, forested habitats such as Douglas-fir, spruce-fir forests	gleaning	mostly moths, but also beetles, flies, true bugs	hollow trees, under rocks on ground, under loose bark, in abandoned buildings	12–30 individuals
Little brown myotis *Myotis lucifugus*	generalist, uses almost all habitat types equally, but prefers to forage over water when possible	moderate flight speed, aerial pursuit, occasionally gleans insects from water surfaces	moths, flies, lacewings, bees, beetles, mosquitoes	generalist, uses almost any structure with suitable microclimate	up to many thousands of individuals
Northern long-eared myotis *Myotis septentrionalis*	forested hillsides and ridges	gleaning from vegetation and ground	mostly moths	rock crevices	up to 100 individuals
Fringed myotis *Myotis thysanodes*	fir-pine forests, but also ponderosa pine forests and lowland chaparral	slow, maneuverable flight, aerial pursuit proximate to vegetation	beetles, moths, lacewings, bees	rock crevices, abandoned mines, caves, abandoned buildings	up to 40 individuals
Cave myotis *Myotis velifer*	drainage basins	flies low over vegetation	mostly moths, but also flying ants	abandoned mines, caves, bridges	2,000–5,000 individuals

continued on next page

Table 4.1—*Continued*

Species	Foraging Habitat	Foraging Style	Food	Roost Site	Colony Size
Long-legged myotis *Myotis volans*	ponderosa pine woodlands, coniferous forests, piñon-juniper woodlands, aspen woodlands, subalpine forests	direct flier, long-distance pursuit during aerial foraging	mostly moths, but also lacewings, beetles	trees, rock crevices, caves, buildings	up to several hundred individuals
Yuma myotis *Myotis yumanensis*	often occurs in treeless areas, but one constant is open water	low-speed flight in tight circles close to the surface of streams or ponds	beetles, flies, termites, moths, mayflies	rock crevices, abandoned cliff-swallow nests	possibly up to 10,000 individuals
Western pipistrelle *Pipistrellus hesperus*	desert species inhabiting rocky canyons, cliffs, and outcroppings to creosote bush flats	weak, slow fliers staying close to rocky outcrops in canyons, streambeds, water holes	swarming insects, caddis flies, stoneflies, moths, beetles, mosquitoes, flies, ants, wasps	rock crevices, under rocks, in burrows made by other animals	solitary or in small aggregations
Eastern pipistrelle *Pipistrellus subflavus*	forest edges	weak, slow, erratic, fluttery fliers	moths, beetles, mosquitoes, true bugs	trees, rarely buildings	solitary or in small aggregations
Greater mastiff bat *Eumops perotis*	high above ground in open semidesert habitats	high-speed flight lacking maneuverability; uses audible calls in aerial pursuit	mostly large moths, wasps, ants, and bees	rock crevices with large opening allowing for unobstructed approaches, shallow cliff-side caves, buildings	40–100 individuals

Species	Habitat	Flight	Diet	Roost	Population
Underwood's mastiff bat *Eumops underwoodi*	high above ground, known only from mesquite deserts in North America	high-speed flight lacking maneuverability, uses audible calls in aerial pursuit	moths, beetles, grasshoppers, leafhoppers	large, hollow trees and probably rock crevices	probably 40–100 individuals
Pocketed free-tailed bat *Nyctinomops femorosaccus*	arid habitats such as semidesert and desertscrub	swift and direct, using loud audible calls in aerial pursuit	mostly moths, but also beetles, flying ants, leafhoppers, crickets, grasshoppers	rock crevices high on rugged cliffs	up to 100 individuals
Big free-tailed bat *Nyctinomops macrotis*	rocky open country, but also ponderosa pine forests, montane forests, above Douglas-fir forests, Sonoran Desert scrub	swift and direct, using loud audible calls	mostly moths, but also crickets, leaf-hoppers, grasshoppers	rock crevices high on rugged cliffs	up to 150 individuals
Brazilian free-tailed bat *Tadarida brasiliensis*	riparian, desertscrub, and ponderosa pine habitats	open aerial, high-speed flight lacking maneuverability	mostly moths and beetles	abandoned mines, caves, buildings	up to 20 million individuals

these bats experience high wing loading and therefore must fly fast to generate enough lift to stay aloft. Wings of this type are energy efficient for foraging in open areas where high-speed pursuit of insects is adaptive. The trade-off for high flight speeds is limited turning ability, thus species with long, narrow wings exploit open habitats and rarely venture into forests. Other species have evolved shorter, broader wings that are adapted for slower, more agile flight in forests, where higher maneuverability is necessary. Some species possess wings that are intermediate in form and allow for exploitation of both forested and open areas almost equally. Although initially this may appear to be the best strategy, generalist species are outcompeted by those that are better adapted to a particular habitat.

Figure 4.2. Splitting the resources. Rocky Mountain insectivorous bats living together differ in wing shape, foraging strategy, and habitat use. From left to right: The high-flying, high-speed Brazilian free-tailed bat *(Tadarida brasiliensis)* uses its long, narrow wings in aerial pursuit of insects under a crescent moon. Just below, a pallid bat *(Antrozous pallidus)* forages terrestrially incorporating its keen vision to locate and capture a scorpion for dinner. Back into the sky, the larger-bodied hoary bat *(Lasiurus cinereus)* flies above and at higher speeds than the big brown bat *(Eptesicus fuscus)* in ponderosa pine habitat. Both species focus on long-distance aerial pursuit, but the hoary bat concentrates on moths and the big brown bat consumes mostly beetles. A fringed myotis *(Myotis thysanodes)* and a small-footed myotis *(Myotis ciliolabrum)* forage along forest edge, the former darting into and out of the densely cluttered Douglas-fir forest in aerial pursuit of small beetles, moths, and mosquitoes. The long-eared myotis *(Myotis evotis)* hovers within the dense forest, listening for the sound of moth's wings beating against a substrate, and only then does it employ low-frequency echolocation to precisely locate and snatch the prey directly from the limbs, leaves, and bark of trees and bushes. Also foraging in dense vegetation, Townsend's big-eared bat *(Corynorhinus townsendii)* uses aerial pursuit of insects as it flies at slow speeds using low-frequency echolocation and its capacious ears to differentiate prey from the forested background in flight. Utilizing the insect food base in different ways allows various species of bats to coexist without competing directly for food.

Although bats of any wing morphology can potentially forage in any habitat type, they are most efficient at exploiting habitats that match their flight ability. For example, although species adapted to forage in open areas can fly into more cluttered, forested habitats, they would soon become exhausted because their wings are not efficient for moving through such habitat. For bats adapted for foraging in cluttered habitats, flying in open areas where it is typically more windy is inefficient because their broad wings make it a struggle to avoid being blown about; as a result, foraging becomes much more energy intensive. It is fascinating to think that such subtle differences in wing form among bat species have been instrumental in allowing for species coexistence that otherwise would likely not have evolved.

Within the broad categories of open-aerial, inner-forest, and forest-edge foragers, species within each category partition resources more finely. For example, free-tailed bats such as *Tadarida brasiliensis* and *Eumops perotis* are high-speed, open-aerial foragers that target large clusters of insects. Their mouths are large and fleshy, with stiff whiskers around their lips suggesting that they may filter insects from the air using a ram-foraging technique (diving through clouds of insects with their mouths open). Hoary bats (*Lasiurus cinereus*) use high-speed pursuit, zeroing in on individual insects that they catch in their mouths. Other open-habitat foragers such as the big brown bat (*Eptesicus fuscus*) use an acrobatic maneuver to capture mostly slow-moving beetles in flight. As they approach their prey, they sometimes strike it with the leading edge of their wing, knocking it downward and catching the stunned prey in their tail membrane, which they curl forward and reach into with their mouth to grasp the prey (Figure 4.3). The entirety of this maneuver requires a mere two-tenths of a second to perform and is invisible to the human eye except via slow-motion photography. Still other species such as the California leaf-nosed bat (*Macrotus californicus*) and Allen's big-eared bat (*Idionycteris phyllotis*) may forgo aerial pursuit altogether, often dropping to the earth to hunt ground-dwelling insects and, in the case of the pallid bat (*Antrozous pallidus*), even to consume scorpions and centipedes throughout the desert regions of the Rockies (see Figure 1.18).

Forest-dwelling bats use varying styles of foraging as well. Some, such as the fringed myotis (*Myotis thysanodes*), hunt insects aerially through the clutter, using their wing and tail membranes to help in capturing prey. Other species, such as the long-eared myotis (*Myotis evotis;* Figure 4.4) and Townsend's big-eared bat (*Corynorhinus townsendii*), are adapted for flying through cluttered habitat such as Douglas-fir woodlands, and rather than pursue aerial prey, they instead fly in silence listening for the rustling sounds made by an insect's wings against leaves or bark, which they then approach and pluck off. Other insect-eating bats such as the small-footed myotis (*Myotis ciliolabrum*) and western pipistrelles (*Pipistrellus hesperus*) exploit forest or cliff edges, utilizing the interface between habitat types as foraging areas.

Aerial Versus Gleaning Insectivory: How Picky Should One Be?

One of the most extreme foraging tactics involves gleaning insects from substrates while in flight. The characters involved in this foraging strategy are rather unique and deserve a more in-depth commentary. Besides having specialized

Figure 4.3. The three main capture modes used by insectivorous bats in aerial pursuit of an insect. Approaching a prey item, a bat will employ one of the three capture modes depicted here. The center illustration shows the bat capturing prey in its tail membrane (uropatagium) before moving the insect to its mouth. Below, the bat uses its wing membrane as a catcher's mitt, scooping the insect from the air and delivering it to its mouth. Above, the bat captures an insect directly into its mouth. In most cases, the wings of insects are not ingested and fall away as the bat consumes the prey.

wing shapes that allow for hovering flight and the carrying of larger prey loads, gleaning bats also use low-frequency echolocation calls, which their long ears are adapted for hearing efficiently. In addition, these bats listen closely for the low-frequency fluttering of moth wings on vegetation as they maneuver through the dense woods. Once the prey is localized, the bats emit a low-frequency call capable of distinguishing small irregularities on the surfaces of vegetation, rocks, or on the ground. Because many moth species have "ears" sensitive to the approach phase and feeding buzzes of bats, as discussed in Chapter 1, gleaning species avoid using those components of the call.

The evolution of gleaning behavior has effectively segregated use of the food resources among bats using cluttered forest as their hunting grounds. The long-eared myotis (*Myotis evotis*) is a bat of montane forests and forages through dense Douglas-fir habitat. It shares the strategy of gleaning with Townsend's big-eared bat (*Corynorhinus townsendii*), a larger-bodied species that cannot access the spaces that the smaller-bodied long-eared bat can. So even among gleaning species we see segregation of the resource base. In addition, it appears

Figure 4.4. A long-eared myotis (*Myotis evotis*) gleans a moth from a tree stump. In this specialized feeding strategy, the bat hovers through the vegetation listening for the sounds of moths wings beating against a substrate. The bat then uses low-frequency echolocation to discern the insect's exact location before gleaning it away. (Photo: P. Faure and A. Mason, altered by author with permission)

that the exceptional ability of long-eared myotis to hunt moths at rest allows it to live at higher elevations than other gleaning species, where cooler nighttime temperatures drive moths and other insects early to bed. Allen's big-eared bat (*Idionycteris phyllotis*) and pallid bats (*Antrozous pallidus*) are the best-known ground-gleaning foragers in the region. Although capable of picking insects from the ground and vegetation while in flight, these species use also their sturdy legs and wing bones to hunt mostly terrestrially. The pallid bat is finely camouflaged by its whitish, pallid fur that blends well with desert sand, perhaps lessening predation by owls as well as nocturnal carnivores such as foxes. It uses audible calls to communicate with other pallid bats in the area as it flies less than three feet (a meter) above the ground. Using its excellent night vision, especially when moonlight is present, the pallid bat cruises along the terrain, pouncing on ground-dwelling beetles, other insects, and even scorpions. Allen's big-eared bat is known to also forage on the ground, but not to the extent that pallid bats do. One of the more amazing bats in the Rocky Mountain West is the California leaf-nosed bat (*Macrotus californicus*). This species clearly has its origins in the tropics, where populations are mostly fruit-eating. However, populations of the species that have extended their distribution into the southwestern United States are mostly insect eaters. Because their echolocation calls are emitted nasally and are adapted merely for obstacle avoidance, as in most fruit eaters, their ability to aerially pursue insects is very limited. Lacking the sonar ability to facilitate aerial pursuit of insects, this species had adjusted its behavior to become a gleaner that uses vision for much of its hunting technique.

Other species of bats in the region, such as the Yuma myotis (*Myotis yumanensis*) and the little brown myotis (*Myotis lucifugus*), forage commonly over water and have the ability to slow their flight in order to glean insects from the surface of a pond or slow-moving stream. They have no special adaptations for this, but they are medium-speed fliers, which allows them to use a generalist approach to foraging that also includes aerial pursuit. Thus, although gleaning is for the most part a specialist foraging strategy, some species take the jack-of-all-trades, master-of-none approach to survival.

The Shapes and Sizes of Ears: Better Hearing or Just Plain Cooler?

Besides wings, the ears of bats are one of their most conspicuous characteristics. Because bat ears come in such a variety of sizes and shapes, it is likely that each type has adaptive significance, and both hearing and heat exchange are probably involved (Figure 4.5). For example, a quick glance through the species accounts in this book will show that some species have long ears, whereas others have distinctively shorter ones. In other species, ears are either broad or narrow. The spotted bat (*Euderma maculatum*), the pallid bat (*Antrozous pallidus*), and Allen's big-eared bat (*Idionycteris phyllotis*) are desert bats whose large ears may also serve as heat-exchange radiators. In the spotted bat, in particular, the ears are highly vascularized, which suggests a probable cooling function. Because of the large surface area and small volume (thickness) of their ears, these bats can more easily pass heat from their body to the environment. Species as disparate as African elephants and jackrabbits have large ears that function, in part, to facilitate body heat exchange with the environment. Large ears can also facilitate passive hearing ability, and for Allen's big-eared bat and the pallid bat, large ears may help them hear terrestrial insects moving across the landscape at night.

In other cases, long ears have evolved in concert with specialized echolocation, such as the low-frequency calls of the gleaning long-eared myotis (*Myotis evotis*) and Townsend's big-eared bat (*Corynorhinus townsendii*). As described in the previous section, the coevolution of vocalization and hearing characters was likely favored to allow for exploitation of a resource unusable by other bat species.

Bats as Natural Insecticides: Balancing the Diet

Although bat species living in the Rocky Mountain West can be categorized as either moth or beetle specialists, each consumes a wide range of insect species.

Figure 4.5. The ears of bats come in all shapes and sizes. Shown here is the size difference between the ears of Townsend's big-eared bat (*Corynorhinus townsendii*) on the left, and that of the hoary bat (*Lasiurus cinereus*) on the right. See text for further discussion.

Most insects ingested are night flyers, but some bats such as the western pipistrelle (*Pipistrellus hesperus*) are active early enough in the evening to also consume diurnally active wasps and bees. Other species taken by insectivorous bats in the Rockies are flies such as mosquitoes and midges, caddis flies, lacewings, may-flies, and even true bugs such as water boatmen.

Colonies of bats can consume impressive amounts of insects. For example, a colony of 250,000 Mexican free-tailed bats (*Tadarida brasiliensis*) living in the San Luis Valley of Colorado consumes about 1,700 pounds (3,750 kilograms) of insects nightly in this largely agricultural area. Little brown myotis (*Myotis lucifugus*) are capable of consuming five hundred insects in less than an hour, and because they form colonies in the hundreds of individuals, they likely have a significant impact on insect populations. Big brown bats (*Eptesicus fuscus*) are known to attack and consume an insect every three seconds, and this adds up pretty quickly over several hours of nightly foraging. Many of the insect species consumed by bats are known human and agricultural pests, and bats therefore function as natural insecticides whose populations should be promoted in agricultural areas. Instead, we escalate the human/insect war by using insecticides that we ourselves ingest and that insects quickly become immune to. Although we win an occasional battle, clearly we are losing the war. Indeed, we spend more money and energy today on spraying toxic biocides on our food crops, yet there are more strains of destructive insects living in larger populations than ever before. Perhaps we can turn to bats for help in controlling populations of pest insects at a much cheaper cost to the farmer and overall human health.

Other Foraging Modes: Bats That Really Suck

Although most species in the Rocky Mountain West are insectivores, a few are specialized nectarivores. The lesser long-nosed bat (*Leptonycteris curasoae*) and the Mexican long-tongued bat (*Choeronycteris mexicana*) have very broad, short wings that allow them to hover at flowers while feeding. Because of extensive energy demands associated with hovering flight, high-energy foods such as nectar are required. The relationship between nectar-feeding bats and their host plants is a fascinating one. Through time, the facial anatomy of nectar-feeding bats has evolved more and more to fit the shape of their host plants' flowers, and the flowers have likewise evolved to fit the facial shape of nectar-feeding bats. The relationship between plant and bat is mutualistic; that is, each species gains by the relationship. The plants provide nectar and pollen on which the bats feed, and the bats provide a furry face on which pollen is deposited when they insert their face into a flower to drink. Visiting subsequent flowers, the bats cross-pollinate the plants. The bats also have specialized tongues that facilitate the movement of nectar into the mouth. The relationship between nectar-feeding bats and host plants such as saguaro, organ pipe, and cordon cacti as well as agave plants is so tight that the continued existence of one species is highly dependent on the survival of the other. Unfortunately, most nectar-feeding bat populations are in danger of extinction due to human destruction of roost sites and foraging habitats. Their demise would undoubtedly have a negative impact on the survival of these plant species.

Water: Simply a Drink or a Mineral Sink?

Bats drink on the wing. Approaching the surface of a body of water at somewhat reduced speeds, they either dunk their lower jaws or use their tongues to scoop water from the surface (Figure 4.6). Proceeding from north to south along the Rockies, assemblages of bats become increasingly complex and so does their use of standing water sources. In Arizona, as many as twenty-nine species co-occur and all of these species require access to free-standing water, usually on a

Figure 4.6. The long-legged myotis (*Myotis volans*) scoops water into its mouth as it skims a pool for a drink. Bats drink on the wing. Some species use their entire mouth to gulp water, as shown here, whereas others will drag just their tongue to scoop a drink. (Photo: S. Altenbach)

daily basis. In fact, as many as nineteen species of bats have been observed using the same watering hole. Because much of the Rocky Mountain West is semidesert or desert environment, usable water resources may be limited in many areas. Indeed, water in desert environments, when it occurs, is commonly found as ephemeral streams that run periodically in unpredictable fashion. Thunderstorm-induced flash flooding within otherwise dry drainages brings much-needed water to the region. Subsequent rapid evaporation leaves behind discrete and randomly dispersed puddles available for use by bats and other wildlife that find them. How bats locate water is unknown, but they apparently utilize only certain types of water holes that allow them to approach safely, skimming the surface while in flight.

It is possible that in areas where water is scarce, competition for use at water holes has resulted in different times of visitation among species. Researchers discovered discrete visitation times among nine species of bats using small water holes in Boulder County, Colorado. Typically, little brown myotis *(Myotis lucifugus)* arrive first en masse at water holes, drink for about five to ten minutes, and then leave the site for that night. Even though they are first to leave their roost sites to forage in the evenings, big brown bats (*Eptesicus fuscus*) visit water holes last, usually after all other species have already drunk. The long-legged myotis (*Myotis volans*) is intermediate between the little and big brown bats in its timing of visitation at drinking sites. Some species such as the long-eared myotis (*Myotis evotis*), which has a gleaning foraging strategy, tend to come to watering sites in pairs or foursomes rather than in large groups. In addition, the same individuals may make several visitations throughout the night.

Water holes may provide important resources beyond just the water itself. Data collected on Colorado bats show that females and juveniles tend to visit water holes that have the highest content of dissolved calcium in the water. Both female and juvenile bats need extra calcium during the reproductive and development season, and water holes may provide an added source they can exploit. More work is needed to understand water holes as potential mineral sources, because the importance for conservation may be profound.

Potential Competitors: Poorwills, Rich Bats, and Sneaky Mice

Most competition for resources among bats comes from other bat species, but other animals may under some circumstances compete with bats for food or roosting habitat. Although many species of birds forage on the wing for insects, almost all of them are active diurnally, and therefore direct competition with bats is avoided. In fact, it is reasoned that insectivory is so popular among the 1,100-plus species of bats in the world because little competition exists for the flying, nocturnal insects. Almost all small mammals are nocturnal, so the fact that the vast majority of bats maintain an "after-hours" job description is not surprising. In the Rocky Mountain region, birds in the goatsucker family (poorwills and nighthawks; Figure 4.7) forage on nocturnal insects, making them likely competitors with bats. In fact bats and nighthawks use very similar attack rates and strategies when foraging for insects, but little is known about how these birds and bats interact when active in the same foraging areas. Observations I have made at a small pond in Boulder County, Colorado, suggest that bat-bird interactions at water holes may be more intense than those observed away from water.

In some cases there is little or no overlap in foraging times between bats and birds living in the same area. For example, cliff swallows in the canyons of the Colorado Plateau, and probably in other areas as well, tend to retire when bats begin to forage. Although later in the summer, when foraging time for birds is decreasing due to less daylight and is increasing for bats due to earlier sunsets, I have observed big brown bats and cliff swallows foraging practically wing to wing along the canyon walls of Colorado National Monument, in both the early evening and early morning hours. Although they seem mostly to avoid each other, occasional close encounters do occur, and it is interesting to fathom what they must think of one another.

There is also the possibility of interactions between ground-foraging bats, such as the desert-adapted pallid bat (*Antrozous pallidus*), and insect-eating mice, such as the deer mouse (*Peromyscus maniculatus*) and grasshopper mouse (*Onychomys leucogaster;* Figure 4.8). Grasshopper mice, in particular, consume grasshoppers, crickets, and ground-dwelling beetles, much as pallid bats do. In

Figure 4.7. Common nighthawk (*Chordeiles acutipennis*). (Photo: Wendy Shattil/Bob Rozinski)

Figure 4.8. Northern grasshopper mouse (*Onychomys leucogaster*). (Photo: Wendy Shattil/Bob Rozinski)

fact, mammalogists working in desert habitats have reported catching pallid bats in their mousetraps. Except for these encounters between pallid bats and field scientists studying mice, however, observations of interactions between mice and bats competing for insects have thus far escaped notice, if they do indeed occur. For crevice-roosting bats, wood rats (*Neotoma mexicana* and *N. cinereus*) may be competitors for cliff-face crevices. Each prefers deep crevices that protect them from predation, and it is at least reasonable to hypothesize that competition for space may occur under some circumstances. In addition, I have observed *N. mexicana* preying upon juvenile bats that had fallen from their roost site in a Brazilian free-tailed bat (*T. brasiliensis*) colony in the San Luis Valley of Colorado. In those species of bats that roost in narrow rock crevices, the risk of predation by co-habitating wood rats may result in their avoidance by bats.

Understanding the structure of Rocky Mountain bat assemblages is the first step in understanding what methods should be employed to conserve their populations. In the next chapter we explore the relationship between the ecology of the Rockies and how this comes into play with efforts to conserve bats in the region.

5

Rocky Mountain
Bat Conservation Strategies

 espite the diversity of today's Rocky Mountain landscapes, only a
few habitats support the majority of bat species. What does this
mean in terms of conservation of bats throughout the Rocky Mountain region? First, it is important to identify which habitats are most
significant as reservoirs of bat biodiversity. Baseline studies of
foraging habitats as well as the location of summer and winter roosts are important for conservation management. Finally, areas deemed important to the long-
term survival of bat populations should be preserved from human development,
recreational impacts, and other disturbances that may jeopardize bat population
stability. Habitats of greatest value to bats in the Rocky Mountain West appear to
be desert, semidesert, piñon-juniper woodlands, and riparian systems.

Wetlands are also important for sustaining bat diversity. Unfortunately, these
areas have been greatly reduced in the continental United States (Figure 5.1).
More than 53 percent of total wetlands in the lower forty-eight states were for-
feited between 1780 and 1990, with most losses occurring in the midwestern
states for cropland conversion. Wetland areas include marshes, swamps, flood
plains, peat bogs, and prairie potholes (formed from the retreat of the last glacier),
all of which are important to ecosystem health because they filter out pollutants
from surface water and act as reservoirs for rainfall and runoff. In addition, wetlands help extend stream flow during droughts and aid in preventing devastating
floods. They also provide refuge for more than 50 percent of fish species, one-
third of bird species, and one-sixth of mammal species presently listed as federally threatened or endangered in the United States.

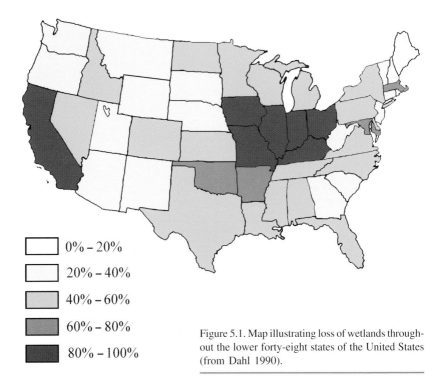

0% – 20%

20% – 40%

40% – 60%

60% – 80%

80% – 100%

Figure 5.1. Map illustrating loss of wetlands throughout the lower forty-eight states of the United States (from Dahl 1990).

Wetlands that remain in the Rockies and the surrounding regions are important breeding areas for insects that serve as food for bats and other wildlife. Wetlands also provide dependable sources of drinking water for bats. Historically, the Rocky Mountain region had modest amounts of wetlands, estimated at less than 5 percent of the landscape for 1780. Today, however, more than 50 percent of these wetlands have been lost. Perhaps just as important, regions east of, but contiguous with, the Rocky Mountains have also undergone massive reductions in wetland habitats. In some cases these areas have dwindled from 35 percent of the landscape to less than 5 percent. The effects of these losses on the maintenance of biodiversity in the Rockies is uncertain and will probably remain untestable. However, strong conservation actions associated with preservation, conservation, and rebuilding can stop the decline and can even reverse the trend of wetland extinction. Strong federal laws concerning the protection of wetlands are currently in place and are of paramount importance in protecting these unique habitats that are constantly under threat of development and conversion. Our votes to continue such protections are more important than ever as more land becomes threatened by development.

MOUNTAINS: THEIR EFFECT ON AND IMPORTANCE TO CONSERVATION EFFORTS

Not surprisingly, mountains are both a blessing and curse for bat conservation. On the positive side, steep elevational gradients make many areas difficult for humans to develop or even to access. These topographical limitations don't restrict bats, however, as they can get just about anywhere on their wings. Therefore, bats are protected to some degree by the intrinsic structure of the Rocky Mountain landscape. But the same steep, inaccessible mountains and canyons also hamper the gathering of information on species abundances and distributions, and thus knowledge of most populations in the region remains unclear. In places where good information has been gathered, the overall trends for bat populations are disturbing. Some areas do indeed support high bat numbers and species richness, but other areas of seemingly similar, or even identical, habitats and conditions are surprisingly low in population numbers or richness.

One would expect the overall distribution of bat populations to be clumped, that is, to occur in highest numbers and greatest richness in areas that contain the most adequate resources, rather than equally distributed across the landscape. Due to their high mobility and general lack of competitors, one would expect bats to occur in most areas with adequate water, roosts, and food. This, however, is not the case. For example, an annual bat trend survey conducted by members of the Colorado Bat Society over the past ten years has shown that many areas with apparently resource-rich habitats contain surprisingly low or nonexistent numbers of bats.

The Colorado survey, conducted by volunteers and based on pass data (numbers of times that bats fly past a fixed point), gives insight into the presence or absence of bats over a wide area. These data can be used to guide the activities of bat biologists and wildlife managers to further investigate the initial findings using the scientific method. Although the science of bat conservation is in its infancy, through the hard work of many field biologists and dedicated volunteer observers, some general understanding has developed concerning population trends for some species. In addition, we are beginning to better understand possible causes of population decline in some species, such as disturbances at roost sites as well as losses of foraging habitats and old-growth forests and alteration of water resources. In addition, accumulations of pesticides and other toxins in the environment are amplified as they travel through the food chains of bats. In the conservation of bats, as with most species, protection of the resource base is an important first step.

PROTECTING ROOST SITES

With the development of radio transmitters weighing less than half a gram (Figure 5.2), biologists are able to conduct unprecedented field projects to locate bat roosts. These small radio tags are attached to the fur on a bat's back with surgical

Figure 5.2. Radio transmitter glued to the dorsal fur of the fringed myotis *(Myotis thysanodes)*. (Photo: R. Adams)

glue that decays after a few days, allowing the tag to fall away. Each tag transmits a signal over a distinct frequency that the researcher receives using a telemetry receiver. Once the signal is acquired, researchers traverse the landscape (which in canyon country or mountainous areas can be quite challenging) to determine the exact location of a roost (Figure 5.3). This practice can be very similar to trying to find the proverbial needle in a haystack.

What biologists have deduced is that locations and types of roost sites vary seasonally for many species of bats. In summer months, known to be the reproductive season, bats use a diversity of roost sites such as rock crevices, caves, scree slopes, tree snags, and living trees, as well as unoccupied and occupied buildings, undersides of bridges, and even utility poles. However, each species typically inhabits only one or two types of roosts. In addition, males and females choose different types of roosts. Because males tend to be solitary and not as picky about temperature, moving among many different types and locations of roosts is common for them. Females, however, seek out roost sites that provide the temperature and humidity conditions that facilitate rearing their young, as well as affording protection against predators and inclement weather. Females of

Figure 5.3. The Flatirons in the foothills outside of Boulder, Colorado, illustrating typical bat habitat and the difficulty faced by researchers in radio-tracking bats in these areas. (Photo: R. Adams)

some species move among a variety of roost sites of similar characteristics during the summer if there are several in an area that provide the conditions required for successfully raising young.

Little is known concerning choice of hibernation sites by bats (see Chapter 3 for a discussion of hibernation). However, some basic principles appear to link all species. The need to hibernate is driven mostly by the seasonal loss of food supply—namely, insects—as fall progresses into winter. The conditions for hibernation require underground caverns where temperatures do not drop below $32°$ F ($0°$ C) to avoid a freezing death. Of great importance to Rocky Mountain bats are deep limestone caverns. In many cases, though, these caverns are disturbed by human activities that may arouse bats during hibernation. Abandoned mine shafts, which typically are not impacted by humans, have become important hibernacula for bats, perhaps in response to disturbances at natural caves in some areas.

Human activities have directly threatened roost sites. Winter spelunking, or caving, can be particularly devastating to overwintering bats because an awakened individual may burn thirty days of vital fat reserves in a single minute. If a human simply stands below a bat roosting ten feet (three meters) above on a cave ceiling, the person's body warmth may be enough to stimulate the bat's arousal.

Figure 5.4. Cliff-face, rock-crevice roost of a maternity colony of big brown bats (*Eptesicus fuscus*) outside Boulder, Colorado. Arrow points to opening of the roost that more than eighty females and pups call home. (Photo: R. Adams)

In most cases these unfortunate bats burn so much stored fat during such disturbances that they die of starvation during hibernal sleep. Thousands of bats are
thought to have been killed by humans' inadvertent act of disturbing hibernating
colonies.

Summer maternity colonies are also highly susceptible to disturbance. Because females choose maternity sites that protect them from natural predators,
human impacts at these sites, unwittingly or not, can be devastating. For many of
the cave-roosting species, humans entering into these sites during the maternity
season can cause adults to abandon their newborn young. Because many bat
species in the Rocky Mountain region use rock crevices for maternity sites (Figure 5.4), rock climbing in some areas may be taking a toll on nursery colonies, and
conservation plans should consider safeguarding such sites in areas used by
large numbers of climbers.

Although colonies of bats may be good educational tools to teach about the
biology of bats in field workshops, such situations can lead to disturbance of the
very animals you are attempting to protect via education of the general public.
Cave tours in Arizona have been shown to adversely affect the breeding behavior of
the cave myotis (*Myotis velifer*). Thus, special care should be taken when exposing
bat colonies in caves and in human-made structures to disturbance, and educators
need to account for the effects of human groups visiting large colonies of bats,
especially at certain times of the breeding cycle such as when young are present.

Mining activity in the West has unintentionally provided roost sites for bats,
and twenty-eight of forty-five (62%) species in the continental United States are
known to use underground mines. When mines are abandoned, bats will often
move in, and abandoned mines now provide important maternity roosts and hibernacula in many areas. Because of the danger posed to the public by leaving
open the entrances to abandoned mines, mining companies typically backfill
shafts and adits with dirt and concrete. Unfortunately, if bats are present when
this occurs, they become entombed. In response to the potentially devastating
effects on bat populations in areas where mining is or has been present, conservation groups have worked with welders to design grates to be placed on abandoned mine entrances. Rather than backfilling abandoned mines, mining companies
and the U.S. Bureau of Reclamation are encouraged to install bat-friendly gates
designed to deny humans access to the mines but to allow bats their continued
use (Figure 5.5).

Bat gates at abandoned mines have been used extensively in the Rocky Mountain West to protect roosting sites. However, recent studies on the effects of
gates as obstacles to bat movements into and out of a shaft or cave have raised
some serous concerns. In one study, removal of gates from selected caves showed
that bat activity increased significantly at the mines with cleared openings. In
others, comparisons of gated versus nongated mine shafts have shown higher
use of the latter, suggesting that gates themselves can adversely impact bat
usage patterns. Where possible, erecting perimeter fencing rather than gating
may be more appropriate and effective as well as less costly. Perimeter fencing

Figure 5.5. Roosevelt Mine located at about 11,000 ft. near Pitkin, Colorado. This shaft has been gated to keep humans out but to allow continued access for up to seven species of bats that use it as a hibernaculum. (Photo: R. Adams)

also has the advantage of keeping people farther from the roost site than do gates erected at the cave or mine entrance. The down side, however, is that unlike gates that seal the entrance from human entry, perimeter fencing can easily be breached by those intent on reaching the site.

For protection of rock crevices, gating is usually not an option; however, seasonal closures on climbing rocks that house maternity colonies can be effective. In areas outside of Boulder, Colorado, seasonal closures are in effect for several rocks and caverns known to house colonies of imperiled bat species (Figure 5.6). Following a model enacted to protect nesting raptors, seasonal closures for bat sites are announced with signs posted at trailheads and along hiking routes, alerting hikers to areas closed for protection. Breaching a closure can result in a mandatory court summons and fines of up to $1,000 or ninety days in jail.

PROTECTING FORAGING HABITAT

When bats are on the wing, they are secure from most threats. Despite the fact that owls and other raptors prey upon flying bats, and that some snake species prey on individuals as they leave the roost site, when bats are foraging they are typically too aware, evasive, and fast to be at risk. For this reason, most conservation effort has been directed toward protection of roosting sites, where bats

Figure 5.6. Base of rocks leading to Mallory Cave outside Boulder, Colorado. Photo taken at perimeter of seasonal close, marked by educational and warning signs instructing people to stay out of the closure area from 1 April until 30 October to protect a maternity colony of Townsend's big-eared bats (*Corynorhinus townsendii*) from human disturbance. (Photo: R. Adams)

tend to be most vulnerable. However, on a grander scale, loss of critical foraging habitats can affect the stability and survival of entire bat populations as well.

Protecting critical foraging habitats for bats is of great importance, and several critical factors need to be considered. For example, all things being equal, foraging in less cluttered habitats is most energy efficient for bats because they do not have to evade as many obstacles while they hunt. However, foraging in open areas has its own risks, such as predation from owls at night or other raptors before darkness, and bats appear sensitive to such risks, often foraging in shadows during times of full moon. Perhaps more important, open areas tend to be windy, and this affects both the anticipated flight path of insect prey as well as the flight performance of the bats themselves, possibly wasting valuable energy. Because of these factors, many bat species forage along forest edges, which allows them some protection from wind and predators. Complex, or heterogeneous, habitats composed of open, brushy, and forested areas tend to have extensive edge where one habitat abuts another, providing optimal foraging opportunities.

Human impacts on foraging habitats usually come in the form of forest cutting and various other degradations. Clear-cutting practices have likely caused the loss of or declines in some bat populations. Studies in the West have indicated that bats, with the exception of open aerial specialists, tend to avoid large open habitats when possible, and thus bat activity was low where clear-cutting occurred. On the other hand, the less severe practice of forest thinning may enhance foraging habitat for some bats.

Paradoxically, in terms of forest structure, what appears to be good foraging habitat tends to be bad for roost opportunities and vice versa. This is because many tree-roosting bats prefer tall, thick, older trees for roost sites, exactly the kinds of trees that have high economic value, and therefore the ones usually harvested by timber companies. In addition, dead tree snags of larger diameter are preferred by bats, and these are typically removed in areas where logging occurs.

Riparian systems associated with water tend to be rich in bat activity because the trees provide shelter and the water provides a breeding ground for insect prey. Human impacts on riparian systems are high in some areas and range from large-scale developments for recreational opportunities and extensive, well-used trail systems to less obvious problems associated with pollution. Herds of cattle can have large-scale effects on riparian systems that course through grazing areas. The size and weight of cows alone can cause landscape damage leading to erosion that degrades water quality and changes the flow dynamics of streams. Such damage probably does not directly affect bats, but it can have the indirect effects of suppressing the growth of vegetation and lowering the diversity of insect prey.

IMPORTANCE OF OLD-GROWTH FORESTS

Another factor affecting bat biodiversity is forest age. The controversy over preserving spotted owls (*Strix occidentalis*) in the Pacific Northwest raised awareness of the importance of old-growth forests to many wildlife species and to biodiversity worldwide (Figure 5.7). In particular, old-growth forests provide cover and protection for many species of animals, especially those that use tree cavities. Although younger forests contain trees capable of housing cavities, ancient forests have trees of large diameter that provide a specific microclimate within the cavity. Many wildlife species utilize such cavities and cannot survive outside these ancient forests. Unfortunately, in areas of the United States where clearcutting techniques are used, old-growth forests have disappeared at an astonishing rate (99% over the last 250 years). Although the spotted owl became symbolic of the fight to save what remains of old-growth forest in the United States, many other species similarly depend upon these ancient forests.

Several studies indicate that higher densities of roosting bats occur in older forests. In Oregon and Washington the activity of tree-roosting bats was highest in old-growth forests due to the abundant old trees and large snags that provide a larger diversity of roost sites absent in younger forests. In many cases bats do

Figure 5.7. Examples of old growth rain forest in Olympia National Park, Washington. Such forests consist of large-diameter trees that provide important day-roosts for many bat species. (Photo: National Park Service)

not seek living trees, but instead select tall, large-diameter dead trees in the early stages of decay. Apparently, the microclimate created within the trunk (accessed sometimes by using abandoned woodpecker holes) of such trees is perfect for housing maternity colonies of many bat species. In the past, foresters often removed older trees and decaying tree snags because they were considered dangerous to humans or a threat to forest health. However, these types of living and dead, decaying trees are of considerable importance for maintaining bat diversity in forests. With the advent of controlled burns used to reduce deadwood fuel from forests, more attention to these factors is needed when deciding what areas are to be burned, and tree snags should first be checked for use by bats before prescribed burns are employed.

Furthermore, because older open stands (those with more space between individual trees) tend to be higher in bat activity than younger open stands, conservation biologists should consider forest age when they design forest management plans. In addition, radio-tracking data have shown that some bat species, such as the long-eared myotis (*Myotis evotis*), establish maternity colonies in short stumps and even downed logs, and therefore these should be checked for bats prior to any burning programs.

PROTECTING WATER RESOURCES

Beyond the obvious tenet that most bats require free-standing water to survive, almost no studies have discerned the importance of available water resources to bats. In the Rocky Mountain West, the highest diversity of bats occurs in desert and semidesert habitats where water resources may be limited. This might suggest that bats require little in the way of free-standing water sources, but bats are actually highly susceptible to water loss during roosting because of their small size and extensive wing membranes, which make for large evaporative surfaces. In fact, bats may lose as much as 30 percent of their body weight in one eight-hour period. Although this amount of weight loss is unthinkable by human standards, bats can survive such high daily losses if they have an opportunity to replenish themselves. Three ways of doing this are by (a) visiting water holes, (b) gaining water from their food, and (c) producing metabolic water, a cellular by-product of metabolizing fat and carbohydrates.

Water availability in proximity to roosting sites is suspected to be an important factor for bats, even for those species adapted to living in desert environments. Typically, myotis bats that live in the foothills outside Boulder, Colorado, arrive at water holes shortly after emergence. One would predict that the smaller-bodied bats would be the first to arrive at water holes because they are more prone to dehydration during diurnal roosting (Figure 5.8), and this appears to be the case. More research is needed to learn if the association between water and bats observed in the Colorado study is ubiquitous. If so, such information may prove important in the conservation of bats in xeric regions of the West.

Another compelling aspect of the Boulder study is that females and young tended to preferentially visit water holes with the highest concentrations of dissolved calcium (Figure 5.9), whereas males showed no such preference. Surprisingly, a diet of insects does not provide reproductive females and their offspring enough calcium to meet daily needs, so it appears that there must be other calcium sources in the environment besides food that bats can utilize. If the calcium link holds true, then water holes provide not only an obvious water resource but also a mineral source for ingesting calcium. In support of this notion is the fact that biologists have observed bats licking wet limestone in caves, presumably to

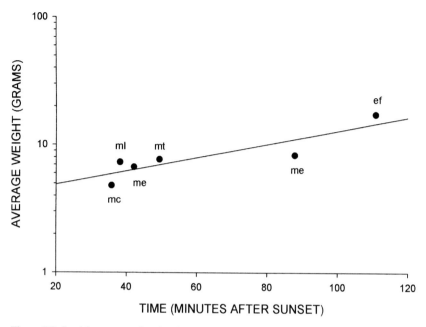

Figure 5.8. Semi-log scatter plot showing average arrival times of bats at water holes relative to body size. The correlation is significant ($r = 0.87$, $p = 0.02$). See text for further discussion.

ingest calcium leaching directly from rock. Much more needs to be done to clarify the role and importance of water resources in maintaining bat diversity throughout the Rockies, but preliminary evidence suggests a compelling relationship between bat species abundance and richness and types and availability of water in the xeric West. Knowledge of such relationships may have significant importance in the management and conservation of bat populations, as degradation of water sources could have detrimental effects on local bat populations.

ENVIRONMENTAL CONTAMINANTS AND BATS

Artificial ponds and reservoirs may provide water for bats in arid areas, but the by-products of human activities that create some artificial ponds are major hazards to bats and other wildlife. Particularly hazardous are oil-field waste pits located throughout the West. Besides the two million migratory birds that die in such pits yearly, bats also become entrapped and killed. The numbers of bats killed in oil waste pits is unknown because counts have not been as rigorously conducted for bats as they have been for birds. Bats are small-bodied and therefore difficult to see and discover once covered with oil. In addition, as with all carcasses, dead bats may sink below the surface, thereby going undetected, and

Figure 5.9. Bat visiting a calcium-rich water hole to drink near Boulder, Colorado. (Photo: R. Adams)

even if found, their condition may be too poor to allow for species identification. Solving the deadly consequences of wildlife and oil-pit interactions can be relatively easy and inexpensive. For example, exclusionary devices, such as netting placed above the pond or even plastic balls floating on the surface, deter visitations by bats and other wildlife. Even so, redesigning contamination systems so that either open pits are eliminated altogether or surface oil is kept off open pits or ponds is perhaps the best long-term strategy.

Other death traps for bats and birds are associated with open exhaust stacks on gas production equipment. In one study, a total of 252 birds and bats were found killed inside fired units of 2,500 gas wells throughout the San Juan Basin in Colorado and in southeastern New Mexico. The Bureau of Land Management now requires that exhaust stacks be covered with screen and other excluder devices to discourage bats and birds from entering them. Again, this is a relatively inexpensive solution that can save hundreds of animal lives.

Toxins associated with mining operations have potential direct and indirect effects on bats, and the adverse effects of gold mining are well documented. In particular, cyanide used to extract gold from ore is typically stored in open ponds, some of which are more than two hundred acres in size. Ingestion of cyanide by vertebrates can cause rapid asphyxiation. Although some bats are found dead in cyanide-laced ponds in the Rockies, true numbers of deaths are unknown because no studies have rigorously quantified deaths, and bats may die from exposure after they have flown away from the site. However, in Nevada it was reported that among fifteen mines, 158 bats died in cyanide-solution ponds between 1986 and 1989. In southeastern United States large numbers of bats, including many eastern red bats (*Lasiurus borealis*), were found dead in tailings ponds. Suggested measures for correcting this problem include net exclosures, floating plastic balls, or plastic sheeting, and decreasing or eliminating cyanide concentrations in water before releasing it into open ponds. Conscientious mine operators are beginning to employ these simple measures, with good success.

Exposure to heavy metals is also a danger for bats living near mining operations. Little is known about the impact of metals on individual health and populations of bats. However, the presence of arsenic, cadmium, chromium, copper, lead, mercury, methyl mercury, nickel, and zinc in bat carcasses verifies that they do ingest these toxins. Furthermore, guano collected from a colony of Mexican free-tailed bats (*Tadarida brasiliensis*) living five miles (eight kilometers) from a major copper smelter mine near Morenci, Arizona, showed that uptake by bats had occurred by accumulating atmospheric mercury in the terrestrial food chain. In another study conducted in Arizona, pallid bats (*Antrozous pallidus*), big brown bats (*Eptesicus fuscus*), western pipistrelles (*Pipistrellus hesperus*), and Brazilian free-tailed bats (*Tadarida brasiliensis*) had elevated levels of mercury in their liver and muscles. In the eastern United States, bats with elevated levels of cadmium, chromium, copper, lead, mercury, and zinc are linked with environmental exposure.

Terrestrial insects that forage on contaminated plants in mining areas eventually make it into the diet of bats. In addition, because the nymph stage of many insects is aquatic, pollutants from ponds, streams, and lakes may be ingested disproportionately by those species that forage mostly over water, such as the little brown myotis (*Myotis lucifugus*) and the Yuma myotis (*M. yumanensis*).

Radiation associated with underground caverns of abandoned mines where bats roost could potentially have health risks. Of particular concern is Townsend's big-eared bat *(Corynorhinus townsendii)*, an imperiled species that tends to roost in abandoned mines in the Rockies. Additionally, although the use of DDT was banned in the United States, species such as the Brazilian free-tailed bat (*Tadarida brasiliensis*) that migrate between North and Central America may ingest DDT-laced insects in Mexico and then transport this contaminant into the United States upon their return. DDT is bioamplified throughout food webs, accumulating in large amounts in the tissues of animals that eat at higher levels in a food chain.

WIND TURBINES AND COMMUNICATION TOWERS

The devastating effect of wind turbines and communication towers on migrating bird populations is well documented. Historically, few studies have sought to examine casualties among migrating bats that come into contact with these structures, but some data are known. Five eastern red bats (*Lasiurus borealis*) were killed in collisions with television towers in Kansas, and fifty-four bats of seven species were reported killed in collisions with television towers in Florida over a twenty-five-year period. In Ontario, several bats were killed in collisions with a lighthouse on Long Point. In California, bat collisions with wind turbines do occur, but the numbers have been low (one dead individual over a twelve-month period at one site, and two dead individuals over a twenty-four-month period at another). In a survey conducted from April 1994 until December 1995 in southwestern Minnesota, 2,941 turbine plots were searched for dead bats. Thirteen carcasses of five bat species (*Eptesicus fuscus, Lasionycteris noctivagans, Lasiurus cinereus, Lasiurus borealis*, and *Pipistrellus subflavus*) were found, along with twelve bird carcasses. Because of new wind turbine farms being planned in California, Texas, and Wyoming as well as in some eastern states, the effects of such technology on bat populations may become more significant in the near future.

OTHER HUMAN-MADE STRUCTURES AND BATS

For many bat species, the loss of natural habitats has encouraged them to use human-made structures such as houses, bridges, and outbuildings. In particular, two species, the little brown myotis (*Myotis lucifugus*) and the big brown bat (*Eptesicus fuscus*), have habituated well to human-made structures (Figure 5.10) and will even roost in human-occupied buildings. In fact, the attractiveness of human houses to bats is historic, and during the Dark Ages in Europe, many people were accused of witchcraft if bats were found roosting in their homes. Some of these unfortunate people were burned at the stake.

In the Rocky Mountain West, bats use buildings as summer roosts, but because of low humidity and low temperatures, individuals do not hibernate in such structures. In the eastern United States, big brown bats (*Eptesicus fuscus*) will sometimes overwinter in heated buildings, but in the West, not even this hardy species attempts this, as apparently the humidity is too low for their survival. Some summer colonies in buildings can be large and have histories dating back decades. For example, the historical buildings of Fort Laramie National Historical Site, Wyoming, are home to several thousand little brown myotis (*Myotis lucifugus*), resident there for more than one hundred years (Figure 5.11). At emergence, the night skies become so thick with bats that the late evening light quickly turns to darkness. Outside of Boulder, Colorado, a one-hundred-year-old farmhouse accommodates a maternity colony of more than 250 big brown bats (*Eptesicus fuscus*) that have used this structure for decades, even at times when humans occupied the residence. In the evening, these house-dwelling bats leave their roosts and fill the sky, feeding on insects by the thousands. Although no longer occupied by humans, the house has been set aside as a bat sanctuary to protect the colony.

Figure 5.10. Big brown bat (*Eptesicus fuscus*) roosting in the attic of a house. (Photo: R. Adams)

Figure 5.11. Fort Laramie National Historical Site, Fort Laramie, Wyoming. (Photo: R. Adams)

Other bat species avoid human-occupied buildings but are willing to use abandoned or otherwise little-used structures such as barns, storage units, and stables that are less likely to place them in direct contact with people. Bat Conservation International estimates that human-made structures provide important roost sites for about one-half of the forty-five species of bats in North America. Of recent discovery is the affinity of bats for using bridges and culverts. Thus far, twenty-four North American species are documented using bridges and thirteen others likely do. For example, 93 percent of the rare species of bats in California use, or probably use, bridges. It has been estimated that 4,250,000 bats of twenty-four species are currently known to be living in 211 highway structures. In some areas, understanding the parameters associated with bridges and culverts that are used by bats is important to conservation efforts, and many of these structures are used to promote and facilitate public education about bats.

The most famous human-made bat roost in North America may be the Congress Avenue Bridge located in downtown Austin, Texas (Figure 5.12). This structure is home to approximately 1.5 million Brazilian free-tailed bats (*Tadarida brasiliensis*) every summer. The site is a major tourist attraction where visitors watch evening outflights and are educated about facts such as how these bats consume between 48,000 and 1,450,000 pounds (22,175 and 657,000 kilograms) of insects each night. Such educational outreach can be highly productive. Today,

Figure 5.12. Crowd gathering to watch the outflight of Brazilian free-tailed bats from the Congress Avenue Bridge, Austin, TX. (Photo: M. Tuttle)

the locals in Austin overwhelmingly support the bats, a far cry from earlier years when the city was considering exterminating them.

Because of the success of the Congress Avenue Bridge bats, biologists have begun to check bridges in cities and remote areas throughout the country to ascertain patterns of use by bats. They have determined that many bridges in remote areas support resident bat colonies. In terms of conservation, this is an important discovery, not only in recognizing the importance of bridges to bats but in understanding how bridges can be designed, or retrofitted, to accommodate colonies of bats, especially in rural areas (Box 5.1). A downside of bats using bridges may be that they are exposed to vehicle exhaust and other pollutants. Most species apparently choose concrete crevices of specific design, and retrofitted existing bridges and culverts that meet these criteria are highly successful in attracting bats. Many of the initial surveys of highway structures were done in Oregon, where seventy-seven bridges and two culverts were surveyed in July 1998. Of the seventy-nine structures, sixty-six bridges were considered suitable as roost sites for bats, and of these, 96 percent (63 of 66 structures) were occupied during the night. In the Rocky Mountain West, several species of bats, including the Brazilian free-tailed bat (*Tadarida brasiliensis*), the California myotis (*Myotis californicus*), and the small-footed myotis (*Myotis ciliolabrum*), were discovered using the drive-through rock tunnels along the main access road into Colorado National Monument.

One reason bats use human-made structures may be the loss or disturbance of natural roost sites resulting from human impacts. Paradoxically, throughout history humans have destroyed bat habitats in the process of development and resource gathering such as mining, but have simultaneously and unwittingly provided some roosting opportunities with the construction of buildings, bridges, and culverts. With a little ingenuity and willingness, humans can give something

Box 5.1. BATS IN AMERICAN BRIDGES
Brian W. Keeley and Merlin D. Tuttle

Ideal day-roost characteristics for crevice-dwelling bat species that use high-way structures include (in descending priority):

BRIDGES:
location in relatively warm geographic regions, primarily in southern half of
    United States
construction material: concrete
width of vertical crevices: 0.5–1.25 inches (0.25–3 cm)
depth of vertical crevices: 12 inches (30 cm) or greater
roosting height: 10 feet (3 m) or more above the ground
full sun exposure of structure
not situated over busy roadways

CULVERTS:
location in relatively warm geographic regions
concrete box culverts
between 5 and 10 feet (1.5 and 3 m) tall and 300 feet (100 m) long
openings protected from high winds
not susceptible to flooding
inner areas relatively dark, with roughened walls or ceiling
crevices, imperfections, or swallow nests

back to bats in the form of "affordable housing" by engineering structures for human purposes that can also support colonies of bats.

BAT HOUSES: DO THEY WORK?

One of the most important conservation efforts for bats was the invention of the bat house. The impetus for building structures as bat roosts began at the turn of the twentieth century, when Dr. Charles A. Campbell, a physician and bacteriologist working in San Antonio, Texas, initiated a series of experiments meant to attract bats to roost sites. His motivation was twofold: (1) he thought bat guano could be used as an excellent fertilizer, and (2) he assumed that bats eat mosquitoes and thus could potentially help in the fight against malaria. "Can bats, like bees, be colonized and made to multiply where we want them?" asked Campbell. The biggest obstacle faced by Campbell, and unbeknown to him as he began his project, was that bats do not inhabit any old ramshackle structure presented as a roost. Undaunted by his initial failures to attract bats, Campbell built what he called a "Malaria-Eradicating, Guano-Producing Bat Roost" near San Antonio in

1907. The structure was thirty feet tall, and inside Campbell built inclined shelves for bats to roost on. In fits of inspired determination, he even lined the walls of the house with twenty yards of guano-saturated cheesecloth and added a collecting hopper that he seeded with one hundred pounds of guano. It was with his next idea that Dr. Campbell displayed his unqualified ignorance of bats. He laid out food for his intended mosquito-eating guests in the form of "three perfectly good hams with a slice cut out of each." To say the least, this attracted no bats. After more failure, desperation struck in 1910 and Campbell captured five hundred bats and entrapped them in his self-declared "monument," hoping they would, by their squeaking, attract other bats passing by. This also failed. After six years of effort, Campbell's bat house was home only to hundreds of English sparrows. It was subsequently dismantled and sold for scrap lumber.

Dr. Campbell, mostly undaunted, did eventually prevail. After taking some time away to study cave roosts, he felt he finally knew enough about bats to succeed in his endeavor. He chose a new site at Mitchell's Lake, ten miles south of San Antonio, and completed a bat tower there in 1911. Building the roost near water was an important decision on Campbell's part. His tower worked this time, and he returned over the following years to watch the colony grow. The guano harvest from the Mitchell Lake roost was 22,000 pounds (10,000 kilograms) in 1921, and even as late as 1948 his last heir, Mrs. Milton Campbell, received $500 a year from the annual guano crop. All told, sixteen of Campbell's towers were built in the United States from Texas to Florida, the last one erected in 1929 (Figure 5.13). In areas where the towers were assembled, the occurrence of malaria in the local residents significantly declined. Dr. Campbell was nominated for the Nobel Prize in 1919 for his attempts to eradicate malaria in the United States.

Not until the early 1980s were bat houses again popularized when Bat Conservation International (BCI, http://www.batcon.org/) began efforts to educate people about bats and to propose the use of bat houses to aid in countering the loss of bat biodiversity in North America (Figure 5.14). Since then, the effectiveness of bat houses has been questioned. However, in 1993, BCI made public the results of a study on bat house occupancy in the United States in its publication *Bats* (Vol. 11, No. 1, pg. 3). The most encouraging news is that 52 percent of the houses surveyed (BCI called 420 people in twenty-six states) were occupied. This was much higher than many had expected. Unfortunately, in the Rocky Mountain West, only four sites (Colorado: Denver and Grand Junction, and Arizona: Phoenix and Tucson) were included in the survey, so little can be discerned from this survey about the effectiveness of bat houses in this area.

Data were also compiled on the positioning of houses relative to occupancy success rates and on the types of houses (from six different basic models) that bats tended to occupy. Typically, houses placed in live trees attracted the fewest bats. This is probably a result of too much shade, preventing the house from reaching and maintaining an appropriately high temperature. Species that use bat houses for maternity roosts, such as the little brown myotis (*Myotis lucifugus*), prefer sites with temperatures exceeding 110° F during the day. BCI found the best

Fig, 5.13. Perky bat tower, Sugarloaf Key, Florida. It is 50 ft. tall and was ordered built in the 1920s by Richter Clyde Perky, a real estate investor from Denver, using plans he purportedly attained from Campbell. Rumor has it that Perky brought in one thousand bats from New Jersey that subsequently flew off and never returned. The house remains vacant of bats to this day. (Photo: D. Sable)

Figure 5.14. Bat house mounted on a chimney of a private residence in Lafayette, Colorado, containing a maternity colony of about thirty big brown bats (*Eptesicus fuscus*). (Photo: R. Adams)

Box 5.2. WHAT BATS LIKE (See *Bats* vol. 11, No. 1, for Model Types)

Percentage of Bat House Occupancy by Variable

SIZE AND MODEL:
Small (Models 1–3) = 32%
Medium (Model 4) = 58%
Medium (Model 5) = 46%
Large (Model 6) = 71%

TIME FROM INSTALLMENT:
< 1 month = 24%
1–6 months = 46%
1 year = 15%
2 years = 11%
3 years = 2%
4 years = 1%
5 years = 1%

WOOD TYPE:
Cedar = 54%
Pine = 53%
Cypress = 29%
Exterior Plywood = 74%

PLACEMENT HEIGHT:
< 10 ft. = 40%
11–15 ft. = 50%
16–20 ft. = 63%
21–30 ft. = 70%

results occurred in houses placed in the open, either in a dead tree, on a pole, or on the side of a house. In addition, bat houses positioned with an eastern exposure were the most occupied. Apparently, not only do bats like their houses hot, they like them heated by the first rays of the morning sun. BCI published a second article (*Bats,* Vol. 11, No. 1, pg. 16) concerning new-style bat houses that are expected to be more effective at attracting bats (Box 5.2). Before buying a bat house you should be sure that it is of an approved model by groups such as Bat Conservation International, as there are many poorly designed houses on the market. BCI sells and promotes the latest designs and also provides information on how to construct your own bat house in a book titled *The Bat House Builder's Handbook,* which is also available on videocassette.

THE FUTURE OF BATS

We live in a world of diminishing biodiversity. Bats, which comprise about 20 percent of all living mammalian species, are in decline worldwide. Ultimately, conservation of natural resources is an individual decision that must first be focused on educating the public, especially children, who will inherit what previous generations leave behind. But we must also be proactive because knowledge is power in the conservation arena, and power, political and otherwise, is paramount in facilitating meaningful conservation measures where needed. Fortunately, many nonprofit, governmental, and environmental organizations have come forward to help conserve bats (see Appendix 1).

The future health of bat populations in the West and elsewhere depends upon a strong commitment to management plans and conservation efforts on the part of humans. The status of most species populations is speculative because few data exist to support strong conclusions. Because bats fly, can move long distances, and are active at night, they are among the most challenging mammals on which to gather data. In addition, the mountainous terrain of the Rocky Mountains requires great human effort for even the smallest bit of data. As a result, efforts to conserve bats need to include the help of people from all walks of life willing to contribute to the task.

Data on known colonies and other aggregations of bats are sorely needed. With these data, specialists can eventually analyze population trends and make knowledgeable recommendations to governmental agencies responsible for protecting wildlife populations. Even though the number of bat biologists has more than tripled in the last decade, their numbers still fall far short of being adequate to monitor and collect data from most wild populations of bats. More and more the public is volunteering to be the eyes and ears of biologists, and there is no greater contribution to the study and conservation of bats than the involvement of local people in the process. Appendix 1 includes lists, brief descriptions, and web-site addresses of conservation organizations that work with bats. I encourage readers to use this information as a resource for getting involved in the conservation of bats in your area. Together we can make a huge difference in reversing the precipitous decline of some bat species and in helping ensure that populations of those species that are now apparently stable remain that way for future generations. If not now, when?

6

Accounts of Species

he species accounts listed here provide scientific and common names; physical descriptions; and information on the distribution, ecology and behavior, reproduction, and conservation status of bats found in the Rocky Mountain West. A dichotomous key precedes the species accounts. The order of individual accounts follows Koopman (1993). A photograph of each species is included as well as a map of its distribution. The relief maps depict the landscape and vegetation of the region to provide the reader with some feel for the terrain and habitat used by each species, as well as a visual image of potential natural barriers to distribution. The reader should keep in mind that distribution patterns are fluid and ever changing, and they are constructed upon incomplete data for most species.

When available, a representative spectrograph is presented for each species. Spectrographs are graphic illustrations of the echolocation call patterns of each species recorded using the sonar device ANABAT II and displayed using Analook software (Titley Electronics, Australia: www.titley.com.au/). The y axis plots a kilohertz scale and the x axis plots time in milliseconds. These spectrographs illustrate a visual image of the general call pattern for each species. The reader should be aware that, as with the photographs, which cannot illustrate regional variation in pelage color, the call patterns are only representative of each species and will likely vary depending upon specific areas, habitats, and prey types under pursuit. Because of this, establishing a call library of species in a given study area is required for scientific analyses of echolocation calls. What is presented here are basic graphical illustrations of the call patterns of each species recorded somewhere in the West. (These and other spectrographs may be viewed online at the *Bat Call Library* [http://talpa.unm.edu/batcall/html/introduction.html] maintained by William Gannon, Museum of Southwestern Biology, University of New Mexico, Albuquerque.) All spectrographs shown herein were provided to the Bat Call Library by Dr. Michael J. O'Farrell and are used with permission from Dr. Gannon.

Abbreviations for the standard measurements for each species are: TL = Total Length, TAL = Length of Tail, HFL = Length of Hind Foot, EL = Length of Ear, FA = Length of Forearm. Dental formulas are based on the number of teeth in one upper and one lower quadrant for each type of tooth, abbreviated as follows: I = Incisors, C = Canines, PM = Premolars, M = Molars. Conservation status is based on the Western Bat Working Group's Priority Matrix, provided in Appendix 1. High threat refers to species that are either imperiled or at high risk of imperilment; medium threat refers to species that warrant closer evaluation, more research, and conservation actions; and low threat refers to species that occur in apparently stable populations in the region.

FIELD KEY TO BATS OF THE ROCKY MOUNTAINS

1a. Nose leaf present.   2

1b. Nose leaf absent.   3

2a. Ear length greater than 17 mm.   *Macrotus californicus*

2b. Ear length less than 17 mm.   4

3a. Distinctive leaflike folds and grooves in the chin region, tail
     measuring one-half the length of tail membrane and protruding   *Mormoops*
     from dorsal surface of tail membrane for approximately 13 mm.   *megalophylla*

3b. Leaflike folds and grooves on chin absent.   6

4a. Tail obvious but short, extending about 10 mm from dorsal side
     of tail membrane, distance from nose to eyes about twice   *Choeronycteris*
     distance from eyes to ears, forearm less than 48 mm.   *mexicana*

4b. No apparent tail, eye about midway between nose and ear,
     forearm greater than 48 mm, fur length less than 5 mm, third   *Leptonycteris*
     finger less than 104 mm.   *curasoae*

5a. Tail extends beyond tail membrane a full one-third its length
     or more.   27

5b. Tail extends beyond tail membrane less than half its length or
     not at all.   6

6a. Pink ears 44 mm or greater, dorsal fur jet black with two white   *Euderma*
     spots on shoulders and one on rump.   *maculatum*

6b. Ears not pink, no distinctive dorsal spots.   7

7a. Ear length greater than or equal to 25 mm.   8

7b. Ear length less than or equal to 22 mm.   10

8a. Forearm 50 mm or greater, fur pale yellow and lighter at base
     than at tips, piglike snout with forward-facing nostrils, no   *Antrozous*
     lappets or distinctive glands lateral to nose.   *pallidus*

8b. Forearm 49 mm or less, fur various but darker at base than at tips.   9

9a. Ventral hairs with pinkish buff tips, prominent lumps above   *Corynorhinus*
     nose, no lappets in ear region, calcar not keeled.   *townsendii*

9b. Lumps on nose absent, prominent lappets at the base of ears   *Idionycteris*
     projecting over snout, calcar keeled.   *phyllotis*

10a. At least anterior half of dorsal surface of tail membrane well
     furred.   11

10b. Dorsal surface of tail membrane naked, scantily haired, or at
     most anterior third lightly furred.   15

11a. Color of dorsal hair black with many hairs distinctively silver   *Lasionycteris*
     tipped, ears short and rounded.   *noctivagans*

11b. Color various but never uniformly black.   12

12a. Color yellowish, total length less than 120 mm.   *Lasiurus xanthinus*

12b. Color reddish, brownish, or grayish, but never yellowish.   13

13a. Color brownish or grayish with heavily frosted fur, yellow ring
     of fur surrounding throat, ears edged with black, forearm more   *Lasiurus*
     than 45 mm.   *cinereus*

13b. Color reddish, might be lightly tipped in white.   14

14a. Tail membrane fully furred.   *Lasiurus borealis*

14b. Posterior third of tail membrane bare or scantily haired.   *Lasiurus*
                                                                         blossevillii

15a. Forearm length greater than 33 mm.   17

15b. Forearm length less than 33 mm.   16

16a. Tragus short (less than 5 mm), blunt, and club-shaped, black
     mask present, tail membrane sparsely furred on anterior third   *Pipistrellus*
     of dorsal surface.   *hesperus*

16b. Tragus short, black mask not present, leading edge of wing
     noticeably paler than rest of membrane, distinctively tricolor   *Pipistrellus*
     hairs, cark at base   *subflavus*

17a. Conspicuous fringe of hairs on trailing edge of tail membrane.   *Myotis*
                                                                         thysanodes

17b. Fringe absent or inconspicuous on trailing edge of tail membrane.   18

18a. Distinct keel on calcar.   19

18b.	Keel absent or rudimentary.	22
19a.	Forearm length greater than 42 mm.	*Eptesicus fuscus*
19b.	Forearm length less than 42 mm.	20
20a.	Forearm length greater than 37 mm, underside of wing furred from body to elbow, rostrum markedly shortened, braincase distinctively elevated from rostrum.	*Myotis volans*
20b.	Forearm length less than 37 mm, underside of wing not furred.	21
21a.	Thumb length greater than 4.2 mm, long shiny hair appears to be tricolored when viewed from above, fur does not extend down from rostrum.	*Myotis ciliolabrum*
21b.	Thumb length less than 4.2 mm, fur dull and bicolored when viewed from above, fur extends midway down on rostrum.	*Myotis californicus*
22a.	Ear length is greater than or equal to 19 mm.	23
22b.	Ear length is less than or equal to 18 mm.	24
23a.	Ears 21 to 24 mm, extending past end of nose when laid down, wing and tail membranes blackish and opaque.	*Myotis evotis*
23b.	Ears 18 to 20 mm, wing and tail membranes brownish and translucent.	*Myotis auriculus*
24a.	Dorsal fur usually lacking a sheen, forearm length less than or equal to 36 mm, total length less than 80 mm.	*Myotis yumanensis*
24b.	Forearm length greater than 36 mm.	25
25a.	Dorsal fur with a slight sheen, no fur between body and elbow on underside of wing, no keel on calcar, ear length 10 to 11 mm, tragus not pointed.	*Myotis lucifugus*
25b.	Ear length greater than 14 mm, tragus long, sharply pointed.	26
26a.	Color dull grayish to gray brown, usually bare patch between shoulder blades, ears usually light colored, forearm length 40 to 45 mm.	*Myotis velifer*
26b.	Color light brown, no bare patches, ears brown, forearm length 36 to 40 mm.	*Myotis septentrionalis*

27a. Forearm length greater than or equal to 66 mm, no deep
      vertical grooves in upper lip.   27

27b. Forearm length less than or equal to 66 mm, lips with vertical
      grooves.   28

28a. Forearm greater than or equal to 70 mm, ear length between
      36 and 47 mm.   *Eumops perotis*

28b. Forearm length less than 70 mm, ear length between 28 and   *Eumops*
      32 mm.   *underwoodi*

29a. Ears united at base, leading edge of ear closest to eye broad,
      rounded.   29

29b. Ears not united at base, leading edge of ear closest to eye fine,   *Tadarida*
      not rounded.   *brasiliensis*

30a. Forearm length less than 52 mm.   *Nyctinomops*
                                                                  femorosaccus

30b. Forearm length greater than or equal to 52 mm.   *Nyctinomops*
                                                                     macrotis

FAMILY MORMOOPIDAE

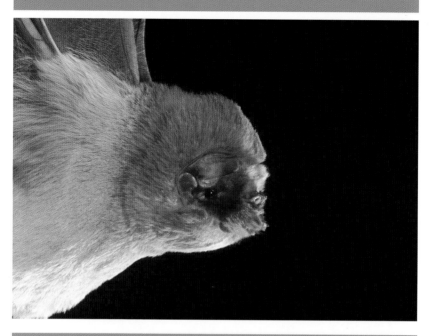

GHOST-FACED BAT
Mormoops megalophylla Peters (1864)

Description. This bat weighs 13–19 grams (0.5–0.6 ounce) and has a wingspan of 35–40 centimeters (14–16 inches). One of the strangest-looking bats in the world, this species has a strongly reduced snout (rostrum) and distinctly domed cranium. The face is so reduced that the eyes appear to be located within the ear cavity. It is a relatively large bat, with long, lax, dorsal fur that is deep cinnamon red in color. In North America, however, this species lacks the iridescent purplish frost over the shoulders formed by long, stiff hairs that is observed in South American populations. The underside (ventrum) is pinkish to reddish in color.

Standard Measurements [sex (*n*) mean (range)]: **Mexico** (Smith 1972), Jalisco: TL = **M** (18) 88.9 (85.0–97.0), **F** (13) 90.9 (87.0–95.0); TAL = **M** 24.9 (22.0–28.0), **F** 25.1 (23.0–27.0); HFL = **M** 13.0 (12.0–14.0), **F** 13.0 (all 13.0); EL = **M** 14.3 (13.0–15.0), **F** 14.5 (14.0–15.0). **North America** (Smith 1972): FA = **M** (18), **F** (3) 54.5.

Dental Formula: I 2/2, C 1/1, PM 2/3, M 3/3 = 34 teeth.

Echolocation. This species produces a long-duration call in which the initial component of its constant frequency ends in a short and swift modulated component used for aerial pursuit of large-bodied moths in mixed boreal forests. The call begins around 55 kHz and sweeps gradually to about 45 kHz. The depicted spectrograph was recorded from an individual on 5/30/96 at Agua Adentro, Big Bend Ranch State Park, Texas.

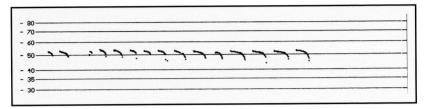

Distribution. Ghost-faced bats occur in the southwestern United States, throughout most of Mexico, and into South America. Their distribution in the Rocky Mountain West is limited to southern Arizona and the southern tip of the Santa Rita Mountains in the southwestern corner of New Mexico.

Subspecies Distribution: M. m. megalophylla: Arizona and New Mexico.

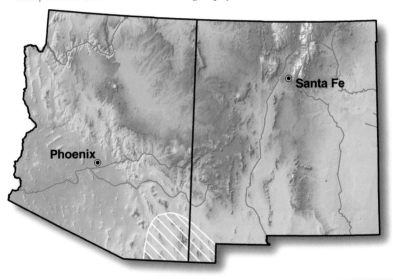

Ecology and Behavior. Little is known of this species' ecology and behavior. It tends to inhabit humid, semiarid, and arid regions below 300 meters (980 feet) in elevation from southwestern Texas to southern Arizona (Hoffmeister 1986). A June capture of two females in Arizona occurred among cottonwoods, sycamores, and willows. They were active at about 1,400 meters (4,600 feet), flying over a water hole near Patagonia (Beatty 1955). Ghost-faced bats eat large moths almost exclusively and inhabit mixed forests (the transition zone between pine-oak forests and tropical deciduous forests); tropical rain forests; and in Arizona and

New Mexico they are found in riparian areas with mature cottonwoods, sycamores, and willows in oak-woodland habitat. These bats are strong, fast fliers that forage in open areas, usually around standing water. Little is known of this species' ecology in North America (Hoffmeister 1986). Ghost-faced bats use caves or abandoned mines as day roosts and emerge shortly after dark to feed, preferably along arroyos and canyons. Colonies may exceed 500,000 individuals.

Reproduction and Development. Currently, there is very limited knowledge of this species' reproductive biology. Pregnant females carry a single embryo and give birth throughout June in Santa Cruz County, Arizona (Hoffmeister 1986). Nursing females roost separately from males and nonreproductive females, choosing areas within a cavern that has minimal ventilation and maximal heat retention. Maternity roost temperature is usually around 36° C (96.8° F).

Conservation Status. **Threat Medium** throughout Rocky Mountain range.

FAMILY PHYLLOSTOMIDAE

CALIFORNIA LEAF-NOSED BAT
Macrotus californicus Baird (1858)

Description. California leaf-nosed bats weigh 8–16 grams (0.3–0.6 ounce) and have wingspans of 33–38 centimeters (13–15 inches). With their large pinnae, large eyes, and prominent nose leaf, they are one of the most distinctive bats in the region. Ears are joined to each other at the base, and the tail extends freely beyond the end of the tail membrane for 5–10 millimeters (0.2–0.4 inches).

Standard Measurements [sex (*n*) mean (range)] : **Arizona** (Hoffmeister 1986), 27 mi. SW of Casa Grande, Pinal County: TL = **M** (10) 98.0 (94–102), **F** (10) 98.9 (95–102); TAL = **M** 36.7 (33–41), F 38.8 (35–43); HFL = **M** 12.9 (12–14), **F** 13.5 (12–15); EL = **M** 33.1 (29–38), **F** 32.4 (31–35); FA = **M** 50.07 (49.1–51.2), **F** 50.29 (48.4–53.1).

Dental Formula: I 2/2, C 1/1, PM 2/3, M 3/3 = 34 teeth.

Distribution. This species is the northernmost representative of its family, and it lives in the southwestern United States, western and southern Mexico, and northern Central America. In the Rocky Mountain West, it occurs in central to southern Arizona, stated below (Hoffmeister 1986).

Subspecies Distribution: M. c. stephensi: Arizona.

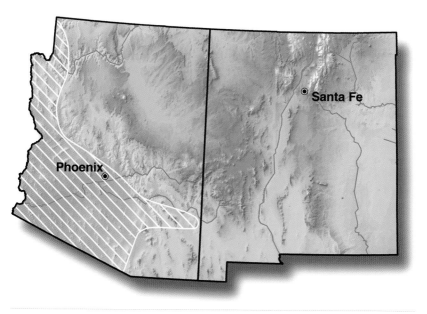

Ecology and Behavior. This rather large bat prefers abandoned mines as retreats from the drying effects of the desert day. At rest, it hangs pendant from the ceiling of its roost using either one or both feet. When hanging from a single foot, the other foot may be used in grooming. Night roosts may form in open buildings, cellars, porches, bridges, rock shelters, or shallow mines and caves.

In Arizona, this species dwells mostly in caves or mines and, depending upon the season, roosts either singly or in groups (Hoffmeister 1986). They do not cluster in the roost even when colony sizes exceed hundreds of individuals. They typically leave the day roost one hour after sunset, and emergence of the entire colony may take several hours, with small groups leaving in unison. California leaf-nosed bats eat grasshoppers, cicadas, moths, caterpillars, and beetles that they take from the ground. In addition, the wings of sphinx moths, butterflies, and dragonflies have been found beneath their roost (Huey 1925; Ross 1967). Vaughan (1959) noted that this species exhibits exceptional hovering ability that aids in gleaning food from substrates. *Macrotus californicus* is a year-round resident in Arizona and apparently does not migrate or hibernate. In fact, at temperatures as low as 9°–12° C (48°–53° F), individuals regulated their body temperature but apparently could only survive a few hours under such conditions (Krutzsch et al. 1976).

Reproduction and Development. Females congregate in colonies of 100–200 individuals. Although some males are found at maternity sites, bachelor colonies also exist (Bradshaw 1962). Insemination, ovulation, and fertilization take place from September to November. However, embryonic development is slowed or delayed until March (Bradshaw 1962). Bleier (1975) found that among the females he examined in southern Arizona, all were pregnant and, in most, implantation had started by the end of October. Typically, one young is born per female each year; however, twinning does occasionally occur. Parturition ensues between mid-May and mid-June. In Arizona, lactating females are captured in June and July, and juveniles are volant as early as June (Hoffmeister 1986). Males become reproductively active in July and August. By flapping their wings and vocalizing while in the roost, males attract females, with whom they breed in September.

Conservation Status. **Threat High** throughout Rocky Mountain range.

MEXICAN LONG-TONGUED BAT
Choeronycteris mexicana Tschudi (1844)

Description. Mexican long-tongued bats weigh 10–25 grams (0.4–0.9 ounce) and have a wingspan of 33–38 centimeters (13–15 inches). This is a small- to medium-sized bat with grayish to brownish pelage and an elongated muzzle. The dorsal pelage can vary from buffy brown to a darker grayish brown, whereas the ventrum is paler. It has a long muzzle that houses an extensive, slender tongue for drawing nectar from flowers. Protruding from the nose is a pointed nose leaf. The ears are medium sized, and the eyes are large. The tail is reduced in size, but evident in the tail membrane.

Standard Measurements [sex (*n*) mean (range)]: **Arizona** (Hoffmeister 1986), Huachuca Mountains: TL = **M** (4) 81.75 (76–88), **F** (13) 81.31 (75–89); TAL = **M** 10.5 (10–12), **F** 9.77 (7–12); HFL = **M** 13.0 (12–14), **F** 12.8 (11–14); EL = **M** 17.25 (16–18), **F** 17.1 (15–19); FA = **M** 44.50 (44.1–44.9), **F** 45.02 (42.7–47.1). **New Mexico** (Findley et al. 1975): TL = **F** (12) 84.6 (78–96); TAL = **F** 10.3 (7–11); HFL = **F** 11.4 (11–12); EL = **F** 15.7 (15–17).

Dental Formula: I 2/0, C 1/1, PM 2/3, M 3/3 = 30 teeth.

Distribution. This species occurs southward through Mexico to El Salvador and Honduras. The northern margin of its distribution is as far east as southern New Mexico through southern Arizona westward to southern California (Arroyo-Cabrales et al. 1987). The usual elevational range of *C. mexicana* is between 299 and 2,408 meters (980 and 7,900 feet). In Arizona it specifically occurs south of the Mogollon Plateau, and has also been captured in southern and northwestern Mohave County (Hoffmeister 1986). This species leaves New Mexico in August, and Arizona in October, migrating southward (Arroyo-Cabrales et al. 1987).

Subspecies Distribution: Monotypic species.

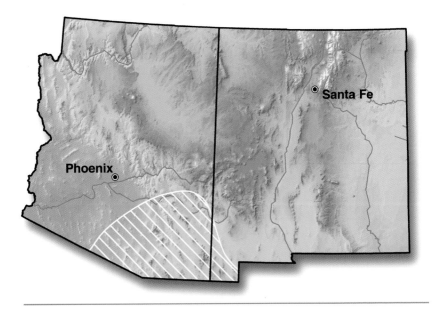

Ecology and Behavior. The Mexican long-tongued bat is a generalist and has been captured in a variety of habitats, including arid, thorn scrub, tropical deciduous forests, and mixed oak-conifer forests (Davis and Russell 1954; Barbour and Davis 1969). This species is known to roost in caves and abandoned mines where it hangs in dim light near the entrance (Arroyo-Cabrales et al. 1987). The Mexican long-tongued bat appears to be less gregarious than other bats, forming smaller colonies in which individuals hang several centimeters apart from each other. They also occupy human-made structures on occasion, but are extremely wary, easily disturbed, and will readily flee their roost if disturbed. This species eats fruits, pollen, nectar (Gardner 1977) and probably insects (Arroyo-Cabrales et al. 1987).

In Arizona it roosts in mine tunnels, caves, rock fissures, and, occasionally but rarely, buildings, and this species shows high site fidelity (repeated yearly and seasonal occupation of the same roosts). *Choeronycteris mexicana* is found inhabiting foothills and higher elevations on forested slopes in Arizona, where it feeds predominately on cactus and *Agave* flowers (Van de Water and Peachey 1997). In addition, pollen from flowers apparently provides an important protein source to reproductive females (Howell 1974).

In New Mexico, very little is known about this species. It is captured flying through dry-wash canyons surrounded by evergreen oak, juniper, manzanita, and other shrubs. As in Arizona, high levels of roost-site fidelity are evident in New Mexico (Mumford et al. 1964). In an unpublished census of historical sites in New Mexico and Arizona, *C. mexicana* was reported to still occupy eighteen of twenty-four (75%) previously known sites (Cryan and Bogan 2000).

Reproduction and Development. Females are known to carry their young in flight. Births occur in September in Mexico. A female giving birth in Arizona was observed to labor for approximately fifteen minutes. She hung head down and gave birth to a well-furred, well-developed youngster (Arroyo-Cabrales et al. 1987). Apparently females become pregnant in Mexico in early spring, and those that migrate to Arizona and New Mexico give birth in June. Maternity colonies in Arizona consisted of ten or fewer individuals (Hoffmeister 1986) that gave birth to a single young each in June or July.

Conservation Status. **Threat High** throughout Rocky Mountain range.

LESSER LONG-NOSED BAT
Leptonycteris curasoae Hoffmeister (1957)

Description. Lesser long-nosed bats weigh 21–23 grams (0.7–0.8 ounce) and have wingspans of 36–40 centimeters (14–16 inches). This leaf-nosed bat has an elongated snout, and the tail appears to be absent. It is light brown on the dorsum and lighter brown to white on the ventrum. The pelage is short and dense, and the tail membrane does not show a fringe of hairs, as in the greater long-nosed bat (*Leptonycteris nivalis*).

Standard Measurements [sex (*n*) mean (range)]: **Arizona** (Hoffmeister 1986, as *Leptonycteris sanborni*), Miller Canyon, Huachuca Mountains, Cochise County: TL = **F** (12) 77.33 (71–84); TAL = none; HFL = 15.4 (14–17); EL = 16.4 (14–18); FA = 53.03 (51.3–54.5).

Dental Formula: I 2/3, C 1/1, PM 2/3, M 3/3 = 36 teeth.

Distribution. Its distributional range is from southwestern United States to southern Mexico. In the Rocky Mountain states, it occurs in south-central Arizona, from near Phoenix on the north and the Agua Dulce Mountains on the west and southward (Hoffmeister 1986), as well as in the southwestern corner of New Mexico (Findley et al. 1975).

Subspecies Distribution: L. c. yerbabuenae: Arizona and New Mexico.

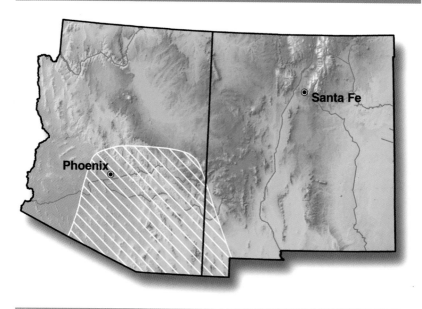

Ecology and Behavior. Day roosts include caves and abandoned mines, where colony sizes may be more than 10,000 individuals. Night roosts include small caves and older structures. This species prefers desertscrub habitat as well as desert grasslands in southern Arizona. It is highly colonial and sets up residence in mines and caves at the base of mountains that support agaves, yuccas, saguaro, and organ pipe cacti. Lesser long-nosed bats are easily disturbed by humans and readily take flight if threatened. They form foraging flocks that descend on flowering trees, remaining there to feed for about twenty minutes. Strong wing beats elevate the body to near horizontal before they release for flight. Foraging activity begins about one-half hour after sunset, and as the lesser long-nosed bat approaches the flowers of its host plant, it uses its long, protrusible tongue to gather nectar. In the process, its face and neck fur become covered with pollen that it unwittingly transports to other flowers it visits, resulting in cross-pollination. Like other nectar feeders, lesser long-nosed bats may either hover at, or land on, flowering stalks to feed. Although nectar, pollen, and insects are consumed, fruits are also eaten after the flowering season. This species is known to travel as far as 30 kilometers (19 miles) from its roost site to its feeding grounds. The sexes roost separately during the summer months, and little is known about bachelor colonies.

In Arizona, roost sites are found in mine tunnels and caves, including a limestone cave near Tucson that houses a maternity colony. Other maternity roosts are known from the Slate Mountains southwest of Casa Grande, Pinal County (Hoffmeister 1986). In New Mexico, the southern long-nosed bat was captured in the Animas Mountains and Guadalupe Canyon, Hidalgo County (Findley et al.

1975; Baltosser 1980; Cook 1986; Hoyt et al. 1994). This species was listed as threatened by the New Mexico Department of Game and Fish in 1996 and has been listed as endangered by the U.S. Fish and Wildlife Service since 30 November 1990 (Jones and Schmitt 1997).

Reproduction and Development. Females form maternity colonies from May to August in caves and tunnels in Sonora and Arizona, whereas males spend the summer in small bachelor groups (Hoffmeister 1986). Parturition occurs from May to June, resulting in a single offspring. In Arizona, a single young is born between early May and late June, and in a cave site near Tucson, newborn young were present on 5 and 26 May, although some females still were pregnant (Hoffmeister 1986). Young are born with eyes closed, and the forearm is about one-half the length of that of adult bats. Sizes of maternity colonies vary, but may harbor several thousand individuals. When mothers leave the roost to feed, the young are left hanging on the ceiling of the maternity site. Females allow only their own young to suckle from them (Hayward and Cockrum 1971). Colonies in the Slate Mountains consisted of both naked and furred youngsters on 24 June, but the age groups were not intermixed (Hoffmeister 1986). Juveniles begin flying at about one month postpartum and venture freely outside the refuge of the colony within another two weeks.

Conservation Status. **Threat High** throughout Rocky Mountain range.

FAMILY VESPERTILIONIDAE

PALLID BAT
Antrozous pallidus Le Conte (1856)

Description. Pallid bats weigh 20–35 grams (0.7–1.2 ounces) and have wing-spans of 37–41 centimeters (15–16 inches). They are distinguishable from other vespertilionid bats by their large eyes; prominent, separate ears; large, bare muzzle; and pale coloration. The head and body are pale brown, with the ventrum tending toward white. The muzzle is square and truncated, with a horseshoe-shaped ridge dorsally. Several wartlike bumps are present on the face. These glands produce a musky odor and are thought to have a defensive function, but the exact signifi-cance is unknown. The tragus is long, more than half the length of the pinna.

Standard Measurements [sex (*n*) mean (range)]: **Arizona** (Hoffmeister 1986), Cochise, Santa Cruz, and Pima counties: TL = **M** (11) 110.6 (105–115), **F** (11) 116.2 (109–125); TAL = **M** 44.1 (40–48), **F** 44.9 (39–49); HFL = **M** 11.7 (11–13), **F** 11.9 (10–13); EL = **M** 28.2 (27–31), **F** 29.1 (25–33); FA = **M** 52.63 (50.4–55.6), **F** 52.67 (50.85–54.7). **Colorado** (Armstrong 1972): **F** (2), TL = 119, 116; TAL = 52, 53; HFL = 11, 10; EL = 36, 36; FA = 56.2, 57.8. **Utah** (Durrant 1952): TL = **M** (1) 119, **F** (2) 109, 106; TAL = **M** 45, **F** 41, 40; HFL = **M** 12, **F** 12, 12; EL = **M** none given, **F** 35, 33; FA = **M** 52.3, **F** 52.7, 52.5. **Wyoming** (Clark and Stromberg 1987), no localities, ranges only: TL = 92–135; TAL = 40–45; HFL = 11.5–16; EL = 23–37, FA = 48–60. **Montana** (Foresman

2001): TL = **M** (1) 104.0, **F** (1) 110.0; TAL = **M** 45.0, **F** 42.0; HFL = **M** 12.0, **F** 13.0; EL = **M** 58.0, **F** 55.1.

Dental Formula: I 1/2, C 1/1, PM 1/2, M 3/3 = 28 teeth.

Echolocation. Pallid bats emit short-duration, steeply sweeping, frequency-modulated calls of relatively low frequency that begin at about 60 kHz and end at about 30 kHz. These calls are used as it flies within a meter of the terrain searching for ground-dwelling insects and scorpions. The depicted spectrograph was generated from a tape recording of an individual on 10/17/97 at Lime Canyon, Mohave County, Arizona.

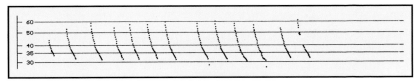

Distribution. Pallid bats are common throughout arid desert regions and grasslands of the southwestern United States, and are abundant mostly in the Sonoran Desert. In New Mexico, pallid bats are most common in arid country around rock outcrops (Findley et al. 1975). In Colorado, they are most common in the dry canyon country of the southwestern and southeastern portions of the state below 3,100 meters (10,000 feet) (Armstrong et al. 1996). They are also present sparingly in Wyoming (Stromberg 1982; Clark and Stromberg 1987) and Idaho (Hall 1981). Records in Utah are sporadic and are currently lacking from the Wasatch and Uinta Mountains and most of the high plateaus of the central part of the state. The literature is contradictory in terms of the extent of this species' distribution in Utah (Hermanson and O'Shea 1983), and I therefore believe that their distribution will eventually be

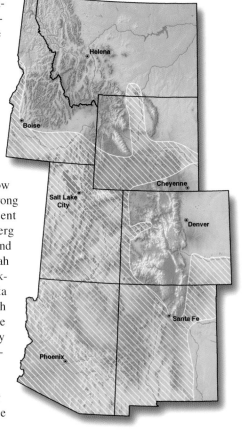

shown to be statewide in suitable habitats. Pallid bats have been captured in Carbon County, Montana, only since 1980 (Shryer and Flath 1980; Worthington 1991).

Subspecies Distribution: A. p. pallidus: Rocky Mountain region.

Ecology and Behavior. This is a gregarious and locally common bat. Pallid bats usually roost in small colonies of twenty or more individuals in rock crevices and buildings, but they also use caves, mines, rock piles, and tree cavities. Relative to other bats, they leave their roost later at night, but the time of emergence varies seasonally. Roost-site fidelity is low, as females switch roosts frequently (Lewis 1987, 1995). Mothers and offspring may emerge and forage in unison. Individuals commonly alight on overhangs to manipulate prey, typically using the tail membrane to help. Foraging occurs in two bouts, one at the beginning and the other at the end of the nocturnal cycle. After an initial foraging period, bats with full stomachs gather at night roosts by directing each other with vocalizations. Often individuals will enter torpor at the night roost. Echolocation is the primary sensory modality used in hunting, although vision and hearing are important. Directive calls, consisting of one to six loud, high-pitched notes given in rapid succession and sweeping through a range of 30 kHz to 5 kHz, function to orient bats to each other in flight. Individuals entering night roosts use directive calls to assess the presence of others in the roost, and those present alert passersby to their location.

Pallid bats feed mostly on large (2–7 centimeters [0.8–2.8 inches]) prey captured as they forage along the ground. These include flightless arthropods such as scorpions, ground crickets, and darkling ground beetles, as well as flighted but largely ground-dwelling forms such as scarab beetles, carrion beetles, and short-horned grasshoppers. They also glean from vegetation cicadas, katydids, praying mantids, and sphingid moths, and they are known to eat lizards and rodents (Hermanson and O'Shea 1983).

In Arizona, the diet of this species is similar to that consumed by pallid bats elsewhere, consisting of large, night-flying insects (body lengths 20–70 millimeters), flightless insects (20–40 millimeters), and scorpions and water bugs that venture onto the ground (Ross 1961). In Pima County, Arizona, as much as 25 percent of the diet consisted of organ pipe cactus fruit and seeds (Howell 1980). This type of foraging apparently leads to a high incidence of injury. Davis (1968) found wing defects in 28 of 63 (~ 45%) individuals examined in Arizona.

The homing ability of pallid bats is particularly impressive. In Arizona, individuals displaced by more than 97 kilometers (60 miles) have returned to their roost sites (Davis and Cockrum 1962). Pallid bats are gregarious and 95 percent of roosting individuals counted over an annual cycle in Arizona occurred in groups greater than twenty individuals. The pallid bat is active throughout winter in southern Arizona. Banding reports of captures are available for February and March in Graham County, and for November from Wupatki National Monument and east of the Southwestern Research Station (Hoffmeister 1986). Working near Camp Verde, Vaughan and O'Shea (1976) noted individuals returning to their roosts in mid-March and vacating by late October. In the Mogollon Mountains of Arizona and New Mexico, most captures of *A. pallidus* occurred in xeric scrub grasslands (45.2%), whereas 37.4 percent of captures happened in deciduous woodlands. This species foraged in evergreen forests rarely (17.4%; Jones 1965). In Colorado, Freeman (1984) found *A. pallidus* foraged exclusively in open areas, consuming mostly beetles (Coleoptera, 45.7%) and grasshoppers (Orthoptera, 37.1%), but did ingest some scorpions (Scorpionidae).

A hibernaculum of *A. pallidus* in Utah was found by Hardy (1941) in Millard County and revisited by Twente (1960). The hibernating colony consisted of ten males and was located near the cave entrance. In Washington County, near the Arizona border, pallid bats were mist-netted in December and January (Ruffner et al. 1979). A search of caves in the Pryor Mountains of Montana failed to locate colonies of this species (Worthington 1991).

Reproduction and Development. Copulation, which occurs on horizontal surfaces or when hanging upside down, generally happens from October through December and perhaps even into February. Timing of parturition appears to coincide with, and may in fact be determined by, local climate. Gestation lengths are highly variable but probably average about nine weeks. In the southwestern United States, birth occurs in May and June. The ears and eyes of newborns are closed for 2–5 days. Pups begin to take short flights within 4–5 weeks after birth. Young emit isolation calls that direct the mother to the infant when they become separated. Females answer isolation calls with directive calls, but young do not respond until they are 7–9 days old (Hermanson and O'Shea 1983). In Colorado, pregnant females are captured in June, July, and August in about equal ratios (Adams 1988). Females may give birth to 1–3 young, with yearling females having only a single offspring. Findley et al. (1975) reported an average of 1.8 newborns per litter in New Mexico. Young are born in an altricial (dependent) state, and remain attached to the mother's teat while in the roost, enveloped by her uropatagium. In Arizona, females leave the young behind when foraging, but return to the roost often throughout the night (Vaughan and O'Shea 1976).

Conservation Status. **Threat Medium** in southern Idaho, south-central Wyoming, central Utah, and western Colorado. **Threat Low** in Montana, northern Idaho, northwestern Wyoming, southeastern Colorado, northeastern Utah, New Mexico, and Arizona.

TOWNSEND'S BIG-EARED BAT
Corynorhinus townsendii Cooper (1837)

Description. This species is easily distinguishable from other bats in the Rocky Mountain region. The dorsal hairs are slate or gray, with tips varying in color from pale cinnamon brown to blackish brown. This species is also known as the "ram-eared" bat because when individuals are sleeping, the pinnae are often rolled down and back across the head, mimicking ram horns. Glands of unknown function are located on the muzzle on each side of the nostrils. Body weight is 8–14 grams (0.3–0.4 ounce), and wingspan is 30–34 centimeters (12–13 inches). The exceptionally long ears are often directed forward during flight, suggesting that they may contribute to lift.

Standard Measurements [sex (*n*) mean (range)]: **Arizona** (Hoffmeister 1986), **M** Coconino, Yavapai, Mohave, Maricopa counties; **F** South Rim of Grand Canyon: TL = **M** (9) 100.8 (92–106), **F** (12) 105.2 (100–107); TAL = **M** 48.4 (45–55), **F** 49.5 (47–52); HFL = **M** 10.3 (10–11), **F** 10.2 (9–11.5); EL = **M** 35.2 (33–37), **F** 35.9 (34–38); FA = **M** 41.32 (40.1–42.8), **F** 42.88 (41.2–44.9). **Colorado** (Armstrong 1972): TL = **M** (5) 91.8 (82–100), **F** (6) 96.5 (87–102); TAL = **M** 43.6 (35–50), **F** 45.0 (38–51); HFL = **M** 10.2 (9–12), **F** 11.0 (10–12); EL = **M** 33.6 (30–37), **F** 35.8 (34–38); FA = **M** 42.83 (39.0–44.5), **F** 43.58 (42.4–44.7). **Utah** (Durrant 1952): TL = **M** (1) 100, **F** (7) 96 (93–100); TAL = **M** 49, **F** 45 (41–47); HFL = **M** 9, **F** 10 (7–12); EL = **M** 32, **F** 34 (33–36); FA = **M** 43.5, **F** 43.1 (41–45). **Wyoming** (Long 1965), Sand Creek, Crook County: TL

= **F** (8) 105 (100–107); TAL = 49.3 (45–52); HFL = 11.6 (11–12). Clark and Stromberg (1987), no locality given, ranges only: EL = 30–39; FA = 39.2–47.6. **Idaho** (Davis 1939), means only, as *Corynorhinus rafinesquii:* TL = 97.6; TAL = 46.1; HFL = 9.3; EL = 35.3; FA = 43.5. **Montana** (Foresman 2001): TL = **M** (10) 95.7, **F** (3) 96.7; TAL = **M** 45.5, **F** 48.0; HFL = **M** 10.3, **F** 10.7; EL = **M** (8) 35.5, **F** (2) 29.5.

     Dental Formula: I 2/3, C 1/1, PM 2/3, M 3/3 = 36 teeth.

Echolocation. Townsend's big-eared bats emit short-duration, steeply sweeping, broken, frequency-modulated calls that begin at about 60 kHz and end at about 20–30 kHz. The calls are used to forage for small-bodied moths and other insects along forest edges, using both gleaning and aerial-pursuit strategies. The depicted spectrograph was generated from a tape recording of an individual exiting a cave on 8/23/97 at Whipple Cave, Lincoln County, Nevada.

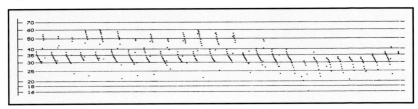

Distribution. *Corynorhinus townsendii* occurs throughout much of western North America, with some isolated populations in the eastern United States. It occurs in all of the Rocky Mountain states, but does not occur in north-central and northeastern Montana. In Colorado, populations are restricted to the western, central, and southeastern parts of the state (Armstrong et al. 1994) and along the foothills of the Front Range (Adams, unpubl. data). In Utah's Henry Mountains, Mollhagen and Bogan (1997) captured sixteen individuals at six locations along an elevational gradient from 1,295 to 2,396 meters (4,250 to 7,860 feet). This species is especially rare in Montana, where, until recently, it was known from only a single population in the Lewis and Clark Caverns, Jefferson County. Other colonies were found more recently in abandoned coal mines in the Bull Mountains, Musselshell County (Swenson 1970; Foresman 2001).

     Subspecies Distribution: (Handley 1959) *P. t. pallescens:* Arizona, New Mexico, Colorado, Utah (except NW corner), Wyoming, Montana (except SW portion). *P. t. townsendii:* Montana (SW corner). Probable intergradation zone between subspecies: Utah (NW corner) and Montana (SW portion).

Ecology and Behavior. In spring and summer, females form maternity colonies in caves, mines, and buildings, whereas males are typically solitary. Maternity colonies break up in August. In winter, most Townsend's big-eared bats roost singly, although some form clusters up to several dozen individuals. A cluster of 420 was found hibernating in Kentucky, but such large colonies are not known from the Rocky Mountain states. Hibernation sites in caves are usually near entrances in well-ventilated areas. Individuals sometimes awaken during the winter to change location within and between caves. During hibernation, individuals curl the ears across the back and shoulder, imitating ram's horns. No long-distance migrations are known for this species, and individuals tend to return to the same roosting locations year after year (Kunz and Martin 1982).

In Arizona this species is found in desertscrub, piñon-juniper woodlands, oak woodlands, and coniferous forests. Hoffmeister (1986) reported no known hibernacula in the state; however, Cockrum et al. (1996) reported hibernation colonies located in Mohave County, where this species is very common. In New Mexico, specimens were collected from caves, rock shelters, and mines ranging from low, arid desert to the Canadian Zone, and hibernacula were not uncommon (Findley et al. 1975). It is most commonly captured in evergreen forests and least commonly captured in xeric shrub grasslands. A male *C. townsendii* was found using an equipment barn in the Bosque del Apache National Wildlife Refuge, Socorro County, marking the first record of this species in the refuge (Valdez, Stuart et al. 1999). In Colorado, this species is known predominately from abandoned mines,

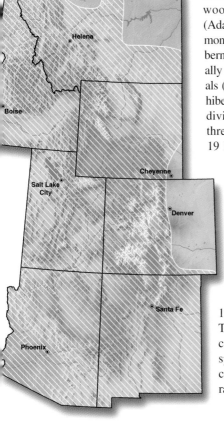
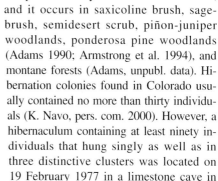

and it occurs in saxicoline brush, sagebrush, semidesert scrub, piñon-juniper woodlands, ponderosa pine woodlands (Adams 1990; Armstrong et al. 1994), and montane forests (Adams, unpubl. data). Hibernation colonies found in Colorado usually contained no more than thirty individuals (K. Navo, pers. com. 2000). However, a hibernaculum containing at least ninety individuals that hung singly as well as in three distinctive clusters was located on 19 February 1977 in a limestone cave in the White River National Forest, Rio Blanco County (Finley et al. 1983). Freeman (1984) found that lacewings (Trichoptera) were a primary component (45.4%) of the diet for *C. townsendii* near Elk Springs, Moffat County.

Hibernacula are known to occur throughout Utah (Hardy 1941; Durrant 1952; Twente 1960; Stock 1965; Hasenyager 1980). Although Townsend's big-eared bat was once considered the second most common species in the state (Hardy 1941), recent work has found it to be much more rare (Hasenyager 1980). Sherwin et al.

(2000) found that although maternity colony movements among sites was common, roost fidelity was higher in colonies using caves than in those using abandoned mines. Wyoming records for Townsend's big-eared bat are scant but are dispersed throughout the state. Adams (1989, 1992) found a single male individual roosting in a historic building at Fort Laramie National Historical Site, Goshen County, and Wyoming State Veterinary Laboratory collections contained specimens from Yellowstone National Park and Albany, Big Horn, Converse, Crook, Hot Springs, Platte, and Sweetwater counties (Bogan and Cryan 2000) as well as Carbon, Fremont, Johnson, Park, Sheridan, and Washakie counties (Priday and Luce 1996). Some of these records are from hibernating colonies of up to forty-nine individuals (Priday and Luce 1996).

Major reductions, up to 59 percent, in colony sizes of this species occurred between 1987 and 1994 at hibernacula on the Shoshone BLM District in south-central Idaho (Wackenhut 1990; Lewis 1994). This species occupies habitats ranging from western mesic Douglas-fir forests to more arid juniper/limber pine/curl-leaf mountain mahogany vegetative type in Montana. Localities of captures include Lewis and Clark Caverns and forested parts of the Pryor Mountains in juniper–black sagebrush communities (Foresman 2000).

Reproduction and Development. Generally, mating begins in autumn and continues into winter, as sperm is stored during hibernation, with fertilization taking place in spring. Females form maternity colonies in mid-March in caves and sometimes in buildings, especially in the West, and colony sizes range from several hundred to a thousand or more individuals. Gestation is between 56 and 100 days, after which a single young is born in June. Individuals are known to live up to sixteen years (Kunz and Martin 1982).

In Cochise County, Arizona, some females collected on 24 June were nearly full term, and pregnant females were collected throughout April and June (Hoffmeister 1986). In addition, nursery colonies were located at Crystal Cave in the Chiricahua Mountains and in Sycamore Canyon in the Baboquivari Mountains, as well as near Union Pass in Mohave County (Hoffmeister 1986). In Colorado, all twelve females captured in Chaffee County on 19 June were pregnant or lactating, whereas on 29 July, all nine females captured at the same site were lactating. One of eight females captured there on 26 August was lactating (Freeman and Adams 1992). Similarly, four of six females captured in La Plata County in mid-July were pregnant (Freeman and Adams 1992). Only eleven maternity roosts have been identified in Colorado (K. Navo, pers. com. 2000), with two of these colonies being discovered in Boulder County in 1995 and 1999 (Adams, unpubl. data).

Unlike most vespertilionid bats, *C. townsendii* prefers cool microclimates within which to establish maternity colonies. Average July temperature recorded from a maternity roost in Colorado was 15.2° C (59.36° F). A single maternity site, containing forty to fifty individuals, is known from Craters of the Moon National Monument in Idaho (Keller and Saathoff 1995).

Conservation Status. **Threat High** throughout Rocky Mountain range.

BIG BROWN BAT
Eptesicus fuscus Young (1908)

Description. The big brown bat weighs 14–21 grams (0.5–0.7 ounce) and has a wingspan of 32–40 centimeters (13–16 inches). It differs from other North American bat species according to this combination of characters: overall brown color, naked membranes, tail vertebrae mostly enclosed by tail membrane, length of ear less than 21 millimeters, keeled calcar, and length of forearm greater than 40 millimeters.

Standard Measurements [sex (*n*) mean (range)]: **Arizona** (Hoffmeister 1986), Graham Mountains: TL = **M** (11) 110.3 (103–116) , **F** (11) 114.2 (109–125); TAL = **M** 43.7 (40–49), **F** 47.5 (41–55); HFL = **M** 10.3 (8–10), **F** 11.0 (10–13); EL = **M** 16.9 (15–18), **F** 17.45 (15–19); FA = **M** 47.04 (44.7–48.6), **F** 47.68 (44.5–50.0). **Colorado** (Armstrong 1972), from southwest of Fort Collins: TL = **M** (2) 105, 116; **F** (10) 115 (108–123); TAL = **M** 40, 40; **F** 48.7 (45–52); HFL = **M** 10, 12; **F** 11.4 (11–13); EL = **M** 16, 14; **F** 16.9 (15–18); FA = **M** 47.0, 47.4; **F** 47.5 (45–50). **Utah** (Durrant 1952): TL = **M** (4) 122 (125–120), **F** (3) 119 (110–125); TAL = **M** 47 (42–52), **F** 46 (41–49); HFL = **M** 12 (9–14), **F** 9 (9–11); EL = **M** 16 (14–17), **F** 15 (13–16); FA = **M** 47 (47–48), **F** 49 (45–52). **Wyoming** (Long 1965), two miles south of Rockypoint, Campbell County: TL = **F** (9) 113.9 (109–118); TAL = 44.9 (41–48); HFL = 11.4 (10–13); EL = 16.2 (14–19). Clark and Stromberg (1987), no localities, range only: FA = 42–51. **Idaho** (Davis 1939), means only: TL = 115; TAL = 44; HFL = 11.5. **Montana** (Foresman 2001): TL = **M** (4) 101.5, **F** (2) 111.5; TAL = **M** 44.0, **F** 42.0; HFL = **M** (3) 13.0, **F** (2) 13.0; EL = **M** (4) 14.3, **F** (1) 16.0.

Dental Formula: I 2/3, C 1/1, PM 1/2 , M 3/3 = 32 teeth.

Echolocation. Big brown bats use steeply sweeping, frequency-modulated calls that begin at greater than 60 kHz and end at about 30 kHz; they serve well as a generalist forager throughout many habitat types. The depicted spectrograph was generated from a tape recording of an individual on 10/17/97 at Lime Kiln Canyon, Mohave County, Arizona.

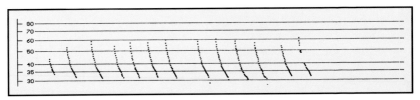

Distribution. This species occurs from southern Canada through middle America into South America, including several of the Caribbean islands. It is distributed widely throughout the Rocky Mountain West. It has been captured at elevations as high as 2,860 meters (9,400 feet). In Arizona, it ranges from the Virgin Mountains and Grand Canyon in the north to the Huachuca Mountains in the south (Hoffmeister 1986). This species remains active in southern parts of its range and has been captured in flight from November through March. In New Mexico, it is thought to occur at lower elevations only when migrating to hibernacula (Findley et al. 1975). I have witnessed colonies of *E. fuscus* foraging as high as 3,800 meters (12,500 feet) in the Collegiate Mountains of Colorado. A maternity colony was located east of Penrose, Fremont County, which extended this species' range

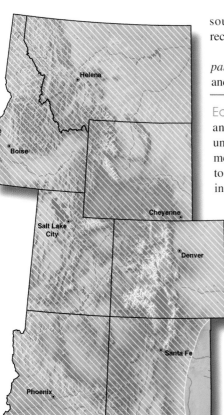

southwest from the previous nearest record in Teller County (Valdez 1998).

Subspecies Distribution: E. f. *pallidus:* Rocky Mountain region (Kurta and Baker 1990).

Ecology and Behavior. The ecology and behavior of this species are well understood because it tends to be commensal with humans and therefore easier to observe. Summer roosts are common in buildings, barns, bridges, or other human-made structures. Females form maternity colonies of up to several hundred individuals. Males form small colonies of a few individuals or roost solitarily. In flight, this species is readily recognizable because of its strong and direct flying style. They also tend to form large figure-eight patterns in flight. Big brown bats are beetle specialists but may also eat ants, flies, mosquitoes, mayflies, stoneflies, and other insects (Agosta 2002). Vegetation and nonflying prey may compose up to 4 percent of stomach contents (Whitaker 1972). Emerging at dusk, big brown bats forage 6–10 meters (20–33 feet) above the ground. Night roosts are commonly used. These bats are hibernators utilizing caves and mines during the coldest weather. Big brown bats apparently hibernate alone or in small clusters of fewer than twenty individuals. They will hibernate in buildings in the eastern United States, but few natural hibernacula are known for this species (Kurta and Baker 1990). Big brown bats roosting in rock crevices in Alberta, Canada, roost-switched frequently and rarely returned to previously used sites. In addition, roosts used during lactation had different physical attributes (deeper and larger openings) than those used during pregnancy and postlactation (Lausen and Barclay 2002).

In Arizona, big brown bats occur in deciduous and coniferous woodlands, as well as desertscrub with creosote bush, mesquite, bursage, palo verde, and cacti. In New Mexico, and likely throughout the rest of its range, this species leaves the roost early and forages before visiting water holes to drink (Findley et al. 1975). In Colorado, big brown bats occur in deciduous riparian woodlands, saxicoline brush, piñon-juniper woodlands, ponderosa pine woodlands, montane forests, montane meadows, subalpine forests, aspen woodlands (Armstrong et al. 1994), and sagebrush (Finley et al. 1983) and have been observed foraging over alpine tundra (Adams, unpubl. data). Analysis of individuals captured near Elk Springs, Moffat County, showed that beetles (Coleoptera) compose 48 percent of its diet (Freeman 1984). In Utah, *E. fuscus* was observed hibernating in March in caves and mines in Washington County (Hardy 1941). This bat is one of the most abundant in most of Utah (Durrant 1952; Shuster 1957, Stock 1965; Hasenyager 1980), although it was the least abundant bat captured in the Henry Mountains, Wayne and Garfield counties (Mollhagen and Bogan 1997). Habitat use was largely associated with riparian areas in Grand Staircase-Escalante National Monument and Dixie National Forest (Day and Peterson 1999a, 1999b). Davis (1939) observed *E. fuscus* at Double Springs, Idaho, and reported it to be an early forager that prefers open areas. The big brown bat is a common resident of Montana, and maternity colonies are known to occur throughout the state (Swenson and Shanks 1979).

Reproduction and Development. Breeding occurs in autumn, and females store sperm throughout hibernation. Curiously, in the eastern United States, females typically give birth to twins. However, in the Rocky Mountain states and throughout the West, big brown bats produce a single young per year. Pups are pink and hairless at birth, weighing around 3.5 grams. Lactation lasts 32–40 days (Kunz 1974). Youngsters learn to fly in 18–35 days. Females leave their pups in the roost when foraging. Maternity colonies disband in August and September, after which short migrations to hibernacula and reuniting with males occur (Kurta and Baker 1990).

Hoffmeister (1986) reports no known maternity colony from Arizona, although some must surely occur. Although previously known to occupy only human structures, Adams (unpubl. data) has found rock-crevice roost sites in the Boulder area to contain as many as eighty individuals. Lactating females are captured in June, July, and August, with the highest percentage in July. No females captured in April, May, and September were lactating (Adams 1988; Armstrong et al. 1994). Lactating and pregnant females were present in Colorado National Monument in mid-June and early July (Adams 1990, 1993), and lactating females were captured in early July at the Peacock Mine, La Plata County (Freeman and Adams 1992). Maternity colonies in buildings shared roosts with nursery colonies of Brazilian free-tailed bats (*Tadarida brasiliensis*) in Utah (Long 1940). In Idaho, females gave birth in mid-July in the Monitor Range, Nye County (Davis 1939).

Conservation Status. **Threat Low** throughout Rocky Mountain range.

SPOTTED BAT
Euderma maculatum Allen (1891)

Description. The spotted bat weighs 16–20 grams (0.6–0.7 ounce) and has a wingspan of 34–38 centimeters (13–15 inches). This species is one of the most distinctive bats in the world. It has black dorsal fur with three prominent white spots, one on each shoulder and one on its rump. Its ventrum is white, and the ears are long, wide, and pinkish.

Standard Measurements [sex (*n*) mean (range)]: **Arizona** (Hoffmeister 1986), 1 mile north of Littlefield, Mohave County: TL = **M** (1) 113, **F** (1) 116; TAL = **M** 52, **F** 53; HFL = **M** 10, **F** 9; EL = **M** 44, **F** 42; FA = **M** 48.1, **F** 49.9. Ft. Pearce Wash, Utah-Arizona boundary: TL = **F** 115; TAL = **F** 54; HFL = 9; EL = 42; FA = 50.7. **Colorado**

(Fitzgerald et al. 1994), no sex or number given: TL = 107–119; HFL = 10–12; EL = 37–47; FA = 48–52. **Utah** (Durrant 1952), Salt Lake County: TL = **F** (1) 115; TAL = **F** 47; HFL = **F** 12; EL = **F** 47; FA = **F** 51. **Wyoming** (Clark and Stromberg 1987), no localities, ranges only: TL = 107–115; TAL = 47–50; HFL = 9–10; EL = 45–50; FA = 48–51. **Montana** (Foresman 2001, from Warner 1981): TL = **M** (1) 114.0, **F** (1) 132.0; TAL = **M** 48.0, **F** 58.0; HFL = **M** 9.0, **F** 12.0, EL = **M** 39.0, **F** 39.0.
Dental Formula: I 2/3, C 1/1, PM 2/2, M 3/3 = 34 teeth.

Echolocation. Spotted bat calls are relatively low-frequency, choppy, frequency-modulated sweeps that begin at about 12–14 kHz and end around 6–7 kHz. Its call has been described as a "soft," extremely high-pitched, metallic squeak, which is emitted as individuals forage for moths, mostly along cliffs in open, rough terrain. Such low-frequency calls are readily audible to humans. The depicted spectrograph was generated from a tape recording of an individual flying over a calm river on 6/13/95 at Lees Ferry Landing, Coconino County, Arizona.

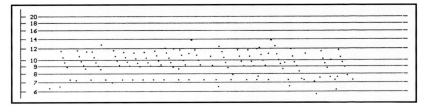

Distribution. This species occurs from south-central British Columbia to southern Mexico. It has been documented sparingly throughout desert regions. Although widespread, it is apparently not common. Few records have been verified in the northern part of its distribution. In Arizona, the few specimens that are known are from Yuma, Maricopa, and Mohave counties. In New Mexico, Findley et al. (1975) captured individuals apparently migrating to hibernacula through lowland valleys, and though it is considered to be a species of lower elevations, one individual was captured above 3,048 meters (10,000 feet). In Colorado, spotted bats occur in the western semidesert canyonlands (Armstrong et al. 1994). It was also captured in southern Utah (Easterla 1965), and a few individuals were captured in Bighorn Canyon National Recreation Area and on Little Mountain Plateau near Lovell, Wyoming (Bogan and Cryan 2000). Two females were captured in Carbon County, Montana (Worthington 1991).
Subspecies Distribution: Monotypic species.

Ecology and Behavior. This species is a desert specialist most often occupying rough, rocky, semiarid terrain. It is often captured in open ponderosa pine woodlands. It roosts by day in rock crevices located on high cliffs (Watkins 1977). Foraging begins about one hour after dark and ends just before sunrise, and this species tends to forage 10–15 meters (33–50 feet) above the ground at or above treetops. Its echolocatory cries are high pitched but audible to the human

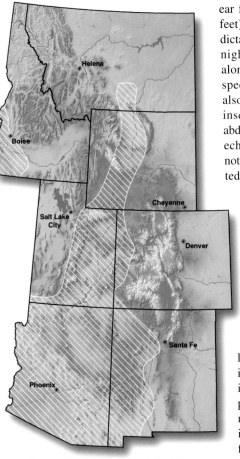

ear from distances of 251 meters (825 feet). The spotted bat is a highly predictable forager, using the same areas nightly and even arriving at points along the way at routine times. This species consumes mostly moths but also probably eats a variety of other insects. Curiously, moths that have abdominal ears adapted for hearing the echolocation of ultrasonic bats cannot hear the audible calls of the spotted bat. This may be the reason that the low-frequency call of spotted bats is adaptive. Their diet in Canada is almost exclusively noctuid moths and June beetles (Woodsworth et al. 1981; Leonard and Fenton 1984).

One specimen was captured in a ravine on the Colorado River, and two specimens were captured in a riparian zone occupied by cottonwoods, willows, seepwillows, and arrowweed in Arizona (Hoffmeister 1986). Other individuals have been taken in riparian areas with creosote bush, mesquite, tamarix, and desert willow in Utah (Ruffner et al. 1979). The first mammalogist to capture this species in the Rocky Mountain West did so in Rio Arriba County, New Mexico (Constantine 1961; Findley et al. 1975). The specimen was captured in piñon-juniper woodlands in proximity to sandstone cliffs. Spotted bats were added to the New Mexico Department of Game and Fish threatened species list in 1988 (Jones and Schmitt 1997).

Based on audible echolocation calls, spotted bats were found to occur at four canyons in Dinosaur National Monument, Colorado, foraging approximately ten meters above piñon-juniper woodlands as well as in riparian situations, such as over the Yampa and Green rivers (Navo et al. 1992). Spotted bats emerge to feed later than sympatric species, generally after midnight (Storz 1995), and occur in sagebrush, semidesert shrub, and piñon-juniper woodland habitats (Armstrong et al. 1994). This species was captured in southern Utah in areas containing sagebrush, rabbitbrush, creosote bush, snakeweed, blackbrush, bursage, and yucca (Easterla 1965; Poché and Bailie 1974; Poché and Ruffner

1975; Poché 1981; Jackson and Herder 1997). Montane and forest grasslands are also used (Foster et al. 1997); however, Jackson and Herder (1997) reported that 77 percent of *E. maculatum* captures were in riparian zones and only 23 percent were in ponderosa pine forests. Four individuals were found overwintering in a cave in Utah (Hardy 1941). Other researchers have captured active individuals in January and February in extreme southern Utah (Ruffner et al. 1979; Poché 1981). In Wyoming, there are eleven records of this species' occurrence in semidesert habitat (Priday and Luce 1999). Montana records are scant, although one individual was captured after entering a house in Billings, Yellowstone County (Nicholson 1950). Two others were captured in the Pryor Mountains, Carbon County, and vocalizations were heard throughout the Bighorn Canyon National Recreation Area along steep canyon cliffs (Worthington 1991).

Reproduction and Development. Very little is known of reproductive patterns in this bat. Judging from lactation records, young are born from mid-June until early July in Arizona (Hoffmeister 1986). In New Mexico, lactating females occur in late June and early July (Findley et al. 1975). Parturition occurs in June and results in the birth of a single offspring per pregnant female. In Montana, a lactating female and young were captured in the Pryor Mountains, Carbon County (Worthington 1991). As with other vespertilionid bats, newborn young lack adult coloration, weigh about four grams, and are altricial (Watkins 1977).

Conservation Status. **Threat High** in Wyoming, southern Idaho, and most of Utah. **Threat Medium** in Montana, northern Idaho, Colorado, northeastern Utah, New Mexico, and Arizona.

ALLEN'S BIG-EARED BAT
Idionycteris phyllotis Allen (1916)

Description. This bat weighs 8–16 grams (0.3–0.6 ounce) and has a wingspan of 31–35 centimeters (12–14 inches). A lappet projects from the base of each ear over the muzzle. The large ears of this species are nearly two-thirds the length of its body. Coloration is variable, ranging from yellowish gray to blackish brown. Dorsal fur is long and soft, and there is also a patch of white fur behind each ear.

Standard Measurements [sex (*n*) mean (range)]: **Arizona** (Hoffmeister 1986), **M** Union Pass, Mt. Elden, and Wilbanks; **F** Union Pass and Mount Elden: TL = **M**

(8) 112.9 (106–117), **F** (9) 112.0 (104–116); TAL = **M** 50.75 (49–54), **F** 47.9 (43–54); HFL = **M** 10.5 (10–11), **F** 10.6 (10–11); EL = **M** 40.25 (34–44), **F** 37.9 (36–39); FA = **M** 46.94 (45.8–48.85), **F** 44.56 (42.8–47.3).

Dental Formula: I 2/3, C 1/1, PM 2/3, M 3/3 = 36 teeth.

Echolocation. The calls of Allen's big-eared bat are broken, steep, modulated calls of low frequency that begin at about 25 kHz and end at about 10–12 kHz, and they are used to glean moths from vegetation in forested areas. Most of the call is audible to humans. The depicted spectrograph is from a real-time recording of an individual flying near a water tank on 7/13/98 at Weimer Springs, Coconino County, Arizona.

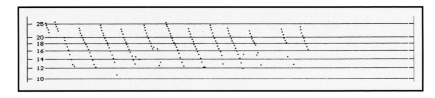

Distribution. This species occurs in southwestern United States to central Mexico. In the Rocky Mountain region, it occurs in southern Utah throughout most of Arizona and into southwestern New Mexico. In Arizona, this species is found most often at lower elevations; however, it has been trapped on occasion at higher locations (Hoffmeister 1986). Published reports of this species in Utah are from San Juan, Washington, and Garfield counties (Black 1970; Armstrong 1974; Poché 1975; Foster et al. 1997; Mollhagen and Bogan 1997). Agency reports cite captures from Grand, Wayne, and Kane counties (Oliver 2000).

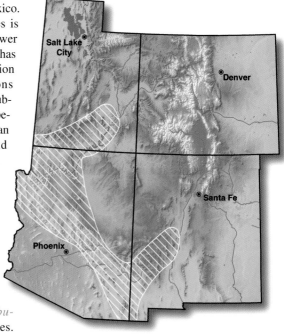

Subspecies Distribution: Monotypic species.

Ecology and Behavior. The biology of this species is poorly known. Allen's big-eared bat inhabits mountainous areas and is commonly found in pine-oak forested canyons and in coniferous forests. It has also been found, but to a lesser degree, in treeless, arid habitats. This species forms day roosts in rock crevices, caves, and mines and therefore typically prefers areas associated with cliffs, outcrops, boulder piles, or lava flows. Emergence from the day roost begins well after dark, and serial foraging takes place approximately 10 meters (33 feet) above the ground. Allen's big-eared bat uses both aerial foraging and gleaning to hunt primarily on small moths; however, soldier beetles, dung beetles, leaf beetles, roaches, and flying ants also compose the diet. Flight speeds tend toward the higher side of North American bats, but this bat can also be highly maneuverable and may even hover, or fly vertically (Czaplewski 1983).

In Arizona, this species is found most often in lower-elevation ponderosa pine forests, piñon-juniper woodlands, and Mexican woodlands, but it has been trapped on occasion in higher-elevation white fir forests. It also inhabits Mohave desertscrub, with opuntia, catclaw, yucca, and Joshua trees (Commissaris 1961; Findley and Jones 1961; Hayward and Johnson 1961). Cockrum and Musgrove (1964) observed 155 *I. phyllotis* over two years in Mohave County. This species is considered rare in Utah, but those few individuals captured were present in piñon-juniper woodlands (Black 1970). Armstrong (1974) captured individuals at Squaw Creek, southeastern Utah, whose habitat was composed of horsetail, cattail, bulrushes, rabbitfoot grass, little bluestem, sweet clover, and willows, with well-developed woodlands within one mile of the site. In southwestern Utah, *I. phyllotis* was captured among *Tamarix* and *Salix* in a wash with blackbrush and infrequent piñon pine and juniper on the adjacent uplands (Poché 1975). It has also been captured in areas of narrowleaf cottonwood, ponderosa pine, piñon-juniper, oakbrush (Toone 1994), and also submontane shrublands (Foster et al. 1997). Recent surveys showed that *I. phyllotis* was eighth in abundance of the thirteen species captured (Day and Peterson 1999a). Winter ecology of this species is little known, but single individuals have been observed hibernating in northern Arizona in a cave within piñon-juniper woodlands habitat (Hoffmeister 1986).

Reproduction and Development. Little is known about the reproductive biology of this species. Maternity roosts can occur in pine snags, on boulders beneath rock shelters, and in mine entrances. A single young is born in June or July. In Arizona, near Kingman, seventy-one females were found with thirteen male young of the year. Lactating females were observed on 31 July at Union Pass, along with a single young that was volant (Cockrum and Musgrove 1964). Apparently, young are born from mid- to late June and can fly by late July (Hoffmeister 1986). In New Mexico, a pregnant female with one embryo was collected on 23 June, and of females captured from 22 June through 2 August, most were lactating (Findley et al. 1975).

Conservation Status. **Threat High** throughout Rocky Mountain range.

SILVER-HAIRED BAT
Lasionycteris noctivagans Le Conte (1831)

Description. The silver-haired bat weighs 8–11 grams (0.3–0.4 ounce) and has a wingspan of 27–32 centimeters (11–13 inches). It has dark brown to black fur, with silvery-white tips imparting a frosted or silvery appearance. The tail membrane is furred dorsally to the tip. The ears are short and rounded, and flight membranes are black. This species is not likely to be confused with others.

Standard Measurements [sex (*n*) mean (range)]: **Arizona** (Hoffmeister 1986), White Mountains: TL = **M** (7), **F** (1) 99.3 (94–106); TAL = 42.5 (39–45); HFL = 9.3 (7–12); EL = 16.0 (14–19), FA = 41.00 (39.9–43.2). **Colorado** (Armstrong 1972), Estabrook, Park County: TL = **M** (15) 101.1; TAL = **M** 38.1 (36–40); HFL = **M** 8.8 (8–9); EL = **M** 15.1 (14–16); FA = **M** 40.53 (39.0–42.4). **Utah** (Durrant 1952) Moab: TL = **F** (1) 91; TAL = **F** 37; HFL = **F** 10; EL = **F** 17; FA = **F** 41.4. **Wyoming** (Long 1965),

Split Rock, Fremont County: TL = **M** (1) 92; TAL = 38; HFL = 9. Clark and Stromberg (1987), no localities, ranges only: TL = 92–115; TAL = 35–45; HFL = 7–10; EL = 12–17; FA = 38–43. **Idaho** (Davis 1939), means only: TL = 99; TAL = 38; HFL = 9. **Montana** (Foresman 2001): TL = **M** (5) 88.6, **F** (6) 98.8; TAL = **M** 34.8, **F** 40.3; HFL = **M** (2) 9.8, **F** (4) 9.8; EL = **M** (4) 12.5, **F** (4) 16.3.

Dental Formula: I 2/2, C 1/1, PM 3/3, M 3/3 = 36 teeth.

Echolocation. Silver-haired bats emit vocalizations in which the sweeps begin as broken, steeply modulated calls at about 45–55 kHz but become a more constant frequency toward the terminal and longer portion of the call that drops from 30 to 26 kHz. It uses this type of call for aerial pursuit of mostly moths in or near coniferous forests and usually near water. The depicted spectrograph is from a tape recording of an individual on 6/17/95 at Shingle Spring, Lincoln County, Nevada.

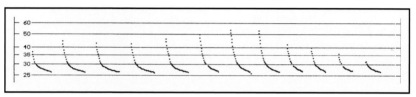

Distribution. This species occurs in suitable habitat throughout most of North America, ranging from southeastern Alaska, across the southern half of Canada, southward in the United States to Georgia, westward to New Mexico and Arizona, and southward to the Republic of Mexico. It has been captured in all of the Rocky Mountain states. Silver-haired bats are probably most abundant in the Northern Rockies, including Wyoming, Idaho, and Montana. In Arizona, it occurs throughout Mohave County during the migratory season (Cockrum et al. 1996). It also occurs in the Tunicha and the White Mountains, and on the North Rim of the Grand Canyon. In Colorado, on 9 September 1994, a male *L. noctivagans* was captured near Penrose, Fremont County, with the nearest previous record occurring fifty-two kilometers to the north-northwest in El Paso County (Valdez 1998).

Subspecies Distribution: Monotypic species.

Ecology and Behavior. Perhaps because silver-haired bats are so mobile and can fly such long distances, little is known about their abundance, population dynamics, mortality, and survivorship. This is a solitary, tree-roosting bat whose typical day roost is under loose bark. It has been found roosting in woodpecker holes and bird nests, and it will also use human-made structures such as open sheds, garages, and outbuildings. Silver-haired bats hibernate in trees, buildings, rock crevices, and similar protected shelters (Kunz 1982b).

This species emerges from the day roost earlier than most species and is one of the slowest-flying bats in North America. Foraging occurs over woodland ponds and streams, where they consume moths, true bugs, flies, leaf hoppers, midges, flying ants, mosquitoes, termites, and beetles. Silver-haired bats become active shortly after sunset and forage around the tops of trees and over bodies of water. Two foraging bouts, one before midnight and the other at dawn, seem to be typical behavior. This species is thought to be migratory, based on seasonal changes in abundance, and its winter range is unknown (Kunz 1982b). In the Tunicha and the White Mountains, Arizona, and on the North Rim of the Grand Canyon, this species forages in openings among fir and spruce trees. It is also known to forage along the Verde River among cottonwoods. They are active in wintertime in southern Arizona, and most individuals captured in the state are males (82%; Hoffmeister 1986).

In New Mexico, 94 percent of captures are male, and it is thought that most individuals leave the state in midsummer for cooler northern climes (Findley et al. 1975). In Colorado there are no overwintering records of silver-haired bats, and Armstrong et al. (1994) suggested that the practice of clear-cutting aspen stands may have serious consequences for this species by reducing the number of roost sites available to them. This species is captured in all habitat types in Colorado, with the exceptions of subhumid grasslands, plains wetlands, sagebrush, semidesert shrub, and highland stream banks (Armstrong et al. 1994). At two sites along Piceance Creek, west of Rio Blanco, *L. noctivagans* were captured in association with little brown myotis (*M. lucifugus*) at the first and hoary bats (*L. cinereus*) at the second (Finley et al. 1983). The diet of individuals captured in Elk Springs, Moffat County, consisted predominately of moths (Lepidoptera, 42.8%) and lacewings (Trichoptera, 14.3%; Freeman 1984). The silver-haired bat occurs statewide in Utah and is thought to be a summer resident of the Henry Mountains at elevations between 1,859 and 2,621 meters (6,100 and 8,600 feet; Mollhagen and Bogan 1997). This species occurs statewide in Idaho and Montana, and its ecology there is likely similar to that of other areas throughout its range.

Reproduction and Development. Most reproduction occurs in the northern tier states and in Canada. Females form small maternity colonies in hollow trees. Gestation is 50–60 days. Twinning is most common, and parturition occurs in June or early July. Newborn young grow rapidly and are weaned between three and four weeks of age (Kunz 1982b). Of twenty-five Coloradoan specimens examined, none were pregnant. Scrotal males are captured in Colorado in June, August, September, and October (Adams 1988).

Conservation Status. **Threat Medium** throughout Rocky Mountain range.

WESTERN RED BAT
Lasiurus blossevillii

Description. The western red bat weights 10–15 grams (0.4–0.5 ounce), and has a wingspan of 28–32 centimeters (11–13 inches). The pelage is brick red to rusty red with white patches on the shoulders. Individual hairs are white tipped, and the ventrum appears paler. It can be distinguished from the eastern red bat (*L. borealis*) by having more rusty, rather than brownish, coloration; fewer frosted hairs; and a scarcity of fur on the margins of the tail membrane (Bogan 1999).

Standard Measurements [sex (*n*) mean (range)]: **Arizona** (Hoffmeister 1986, as *L. borealis*), various localities: TL = **M** (3) 105.7 (100–109), **F** (4) 107.0 (98–114); TAL = **M** 49.3 (49–50), **F** 50.75 (45–54); HFL = **M** 9 (9–9), **F** 8.7 (7–10); EL = **M** 11.3 (10–12), **F** 12.0 (11–13).

Dental Formula: I 1/3, C 1/1, PM 2/2, M 3/3 = 32 teeth.

Echolocation. Calls of the western red bat are relatively high frequency and begin as a moderately sloped, modulated call, but take on a constant frequency

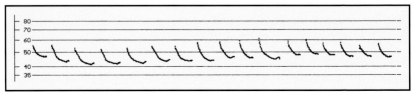

component after about the first third of each vocalization. Curiously, some of the calls end with an increased frequency relative to the middle third of the call. The FM calls begin at about 55–60 kHz and end at about 40–45 kHz and are used in aerial pursuit of moths and other insects over ponds and waterways. The spectrograph depicted is from a tape recording of an individual on 11/21/95 at Truttman House, Point Reyes National Seashore, California.

Distribution. Its distribution is western Canada, western United States, western Mexico, and Central America. In the Rocky Mountain region, it has been captured throughout Arizona and south-central and southwestern Utah. In Arizona's Mohave County, none have been observed since three were captured in 1902 (Cockrum et al. 1996). In Utah, a few records from Washington, Utah, and Carbon counties account for this species' occurrence in the state (Mollhagen and Bogan 1997).

Subspecies Distribution: Monotypic species.

Ecology and Behavior. This species is solitary and roosts in the foliage of large shrubs and trees in habitats bordering forests, rivers, cultivated fields, and urban areas. In the southwestern United States, western red bats roost in streamside habitats dominated by cottonwoods, oaks, sycamores, and walnuts; they are rarely found in desert habitat. This species is believed to be migratory throughout much of the Southwest and apparently is only a summer resident. The diet consists of moths and other insects (Harvey et al. 1999). In Arizona, *L. blossevillii* forages over ponds or along waterways surrounded by oaks, sycamores, and walnuts in the Huachuca and Graham Mountains, and among cottonwoods at Bright Angel Creek near the Colorado River. In the Sierra Ancha, western red bats forage in pine-fir forests (Hoffmeister 1986). They use riparian areas vegetated with sycamores and cottonwoods in New Mexico (Findley et al. 1975).

Reproduction and Development. Few reproductive data are available for this species. In mid-May to late June, as many as three offspring per female may be born (Harvey et al. 1999).

Conservation Status. **Threat High** throughout Rocky Mountain range.

EASTERN RED BAT
Lasiurus borealis Müller (1776)

Description. The eastern red bat has a distinctive dorsal coloration that is brick red to rusty red washed with white, whereas the ventrum is slightly paler, and anterior shoulders have buffy white patches. Red bats have long tails with a fully furred tail membrane, making them distinct from the western red bat (*L. blossevillii*). It is of moderate size, weighing 9–15 grams (0.3–0.5 ounce), with a wingspan of 28–33 centimeters (11–13 inches).

Standard Measurements: [sex (*n*) mean (range)]: **Utah** (Durrant 1952), Salt Lake City: TL = **M** (1) 130; TAL = 50; HFL = 13; EL = 19; FA = 52.5. **Wyoming** (Clark and Stromberg 1987), no localities, ranges only: TL = 90–120; TAL = 36–65; HFL

= 6–9; EL = 9–11, FA = 38–41. **Montana** (Shump and Shump 1980; Foresman 2001):
TL = **M** (12) 102.7, **F** (1) 107; TAL = 43.2 (9), 49 (1); HFL = **M** (12) 7.9, **F** (1) 7.0; EL
= **M** (6) 10.6, **F** (1) 9.

   Dental Formula: I 1/3, C 1/1, PM 2/2, M 3/3 = 32 teeth.

Echolocation. Eastern red bats have echolocation calls similar to western red
bats, except that in some parts of the sequence, the ending frequency increases
so abruptly, compared to that of the middle portion of the call, that a cuplike
appearance is evident in spectrographs. The vocalization begins as a steeply
swept, frequency-modulated call between 40 and 60 kHz, drops to as low as 27–40
kHz, and in some instances rebounds as much as 3–4 kHz above the lowest frequency when terminating. Eastern red bats use this call pattern during slow, fluttering, erratic flight that they begin at high altitude but then drop to treetop level in
aerial pursuit of mostly moths. The spectrograph depicted is from a taped recording of an individual on 10/31/98 near a pond at Carlton Campground, Arkansas.

Distribution. Eastern red bats occur mostly in the midwestern and eastern United
States and northeastern Mexico. In the Rocky Mountain states, only a few specimens have been captured, as this species appears restricted to northeastern
Montana, northeastern Wyoming, eastern Colorado, and east-central and southeastern New Mexico. This bat is rare in Colorado, found only occasionally as
accidental records east and southeast of the eastern foothills scattered through
nine counties (Armstrong et al. 1994). In Montana, this species is restricted mostly
to the eastern portion of the state. However, in 1880 an individual was collected
"on the Yellowstone" (no additional information), and in 1998 another individual
was captured near Big Sandy, Chouteau County. In 1997 an individual was captured in southeastern Montana near Ismay, Custer County (Foresman 2001).

   Subspecies Distribution: Monotypic species.

Ecology and Behavior. Eastern red bats generally spend the daytime hanging on the foliage of trees, usually by only a single foot, where they seem to mimic
dried leaves. Comparisons of thermal environments of diurnal roost sites with
other locations in the habitat showed that red bats prefer to hang in areas having
lower overall temperature and lower variance of temperature (Hutchinson and
Lacki 2001). They also appear to have a preference for the south side of trees.
This species apparently does not use caves as roosts but has been observed to

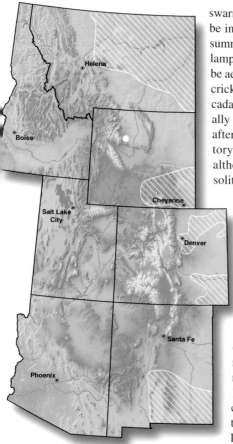

swarm at cave entrances in autumn and to be in flight on warm winter afternoons. In summer, it commonly feeds among street lamps in urban areas, and it is known to be aerially territorial as it consumes moths, crickets, flies, mosquitoes, true bugs, cicadas, and other insects. Red bats generally beginning to forage one to two hours after sunset. Eastern red bats are migratory and apparently migrate in groups, although most other times are spent as solitary individuals (Shump and Shump 1982a). In the eastern part of its range, female-dominated sex ratios were associated with warmer mean high temperatures, whereas male-dominated ratios occurred where monthly mean temperatures were lower (Ford et al. 2002). Little is known of this bat's ecology and behavior in the Rocky Mountain states. In Colorado, the rare occurrence of this species is limited to riparian corridors and urban ornamental woodlands (Armstrong et al. 1994). In Wyoming, an individual was captured roosting in a cottonwood tree near an isolated pond south of Laramie (Clark and Stromberg 1987).

Reproduction and Development. Generally, eastern red bats mate while in flight during August and September, and females give birth to one to five babies during late spring or early summer. Newborn young are hairless, their eyes are closed, and they weigh about 0.5 grams each. Mothers sometimes carry their young in flight and move them to new roosts daily, but not while foraging. Growth is fast, however, and within four weeks the pup's body is covered with short, dense fur, and it has grown to half the body weight of an adult. Pups are weaned between four and six weeks (Shump and Shump 1982a). Almost nothing is known of this species' reproductive patterns in the Rocky Mountain states. In Colorado, a lactating female was captured in Picture Canyon, Baca County, in early June (Ellinwood 1978), and in Wyoming, a female captured in Rawlins was pregnant with four 15-millimeter embryos (Clark and Stromberg 1987).

Conservation Status. **Threat Medium** throughout Rocky Mountain range.

HOARY BAT
Lasiurus cinereus Palisot de Beauvois (1796)

Description. The hoary bat is quite distinctive from any other bat in the Rocky Mountain states because of its large size and coloration. Body weight is 25–30 grams (0.9–1.1 ounces), and wingspan is 34–41 centimeters (13–16 inches). Hoary bats have mixed dark brownish and grayish fur, tinged with white to produce a frosty or hoary effect. It has white wrist and shoulder patches and a distinctively yellow throat patch. Hoary bats have very short, furred pinnae, which are apparently adapted to colder climates.

Standard Measurements [sex (*n*) mean (range)]: **Arizona** (Hoffmeister 1986), Chiricahua Mountains, Cochise County: TL = **M** (9) 136.1 (130–142); TAL = **M** 56.6 (51–60); HFL = **M** 11.7 (10–13); EL = **M** 17.2 (15–18); FA = **M** 52.17 (50.1–54.5). **Colorado** (Armstrong 1972), Estabrook, Park County: TL = **M** (28) 133.1 (123–142); TAL = **M** 53.4 (51–60); HFL = **M** 11.1 (9–12); EL = **M** 16.5 (13–18); FA = **M** 52.33 (50.0–55.6). **Utah** (Durrant 1952), Salt Lake City: TL = **F** (1) 130; TAL = **F** 50; HFL = **F** 13; EL = **F** 19; FA = **F** 52.5. **Wyoming** (Long 1965), Campbell County: TL = **F** (2) 143, 140; TAL = 54, 46; HFL = 11, 11; EL = 15, 16; FA = 55.2, 51.3. Clark and Stromberg (1987), no localities, ranges only: TL = 130–145; TAL = 55–58; HFL = 9–11; EL = 17–19; FA = 48–52. **Idaho** (Davis 1939), means only: TL = 140; TAL = 55; HFL = 13; EL = 17. **Montana** (Foresman 2001): TL = **M** (1) 130.1, **F** (1) 134.0; TAL = **M** 65.0, **F** 50.0; HFL = **M** 11.0, **F** 10.0; EL = **M** 15.0, **F** 11.0.
    Dental Formula: I 1/3, C 1/1, PM 2/2, M 3/3 = 32 teeth.

Echolocation. The calls of the hoary bat are of long duration and frequency modulated (FM) but also interspersed with some constant frequency (CF) calls that are useful in long-distance aerial pursuit of mostly moths in open habitats. In some cases, a single vocalization will incorporate both FM and CF components. The call varies in its initial frequency, sometimes beginning in the 25 kHz range and ending at about 18 kHz, and at other times beginning as high as 41 kHz and ending at 20–24 kHz. The spectrograph depicted was recorded from an individual flying near a small earthen tank on 6/30/95 at Oak Grove Tank, Kaibab National Forest, Coconino County, Arizona.

Distribution. The hoary bat is the most widespread of all American bats. It ranges from near the limit of trees in Canada, southward to at least Guatemala, and in South America from Brazil to Argentina and Chile. It also occurs on Hawaii. This species has been captured in all Rocky Mountain states. In Arizona, it likely occurs throughout the state during migration (Hoffmeister 1986). In Colorado, individuals have been captured at elevations exceeding 2,743 meters (9,000 feet; Armstrong et al. 1994). In Utah, two individuals were captured in Garfield County, one at Horn Spring (2,621 meters [8,600 feet]) on 3 June 1995, and another at Starr Spring (1,859 meters [6,100 feet]) on 26 May 1993 (Mollhagen and Bogan 1997). In Wyoming, only nine individuals have been captured over the last 120 years; however, because these captures occurred throughout the state, this species is considered widely distributed.
    Subspecies Distribution: L. c. cinereus: Rocky Mountain region.

Ecology and Behavior. The
hoary bat is solitary and roosts
primarily among the foliage in
trees. Individuals also have been
found to use unusual roost sites
such as woodpecker holes, caves,
the nests of gray squirrels, under driftwood planks, and the
sides of buildings. By day, this
bat prefers to roost 3–5 meters
(10–16 feet) above the
ground in trees at the edge of
a clearing. Individuals generally emerge late in the evening to
feed (Shump and Shump 1982b).
Little is known of its food habits,
and although the skull morphology is robust and reminiscent of a
beetle predator, this bat apparently prefers to consume moths
rather than harder-bodied insects. Other components of the
diet include beetles, flies, grasshoppers, dragonflies, and wasps
(Ross 1967; Black 1972). The hoary
bat also is known to be carnivorous, and in one case was reported to have attacked, killed,
and consumed a pipistrelle bat.
In captivity, they will eat the muscle
and liver of freshly killed mice (Shump
and Shump 1982b).

    In Arizona, this species shows a strong association with trees. Although
some females have been captured in Arizona in April, May, July, August, September, and October, males tend to dominate the area. For example, 78 percent of
eighty-eight captured individuals were males (Hoffmeister 1986). In New Mexico,
hoary bats were found to be active at about 1.5 hours after sunset and mostly
foraged in juniper scrub, riparian forests, and desert habitats after midnight (Jones
1965). In Colorado, males oversummer, but females are rare (Armstrong et al.
1994). Near Elk Creek in Moffat County, *L. cinereus* foraged predominately in
open areas, where its diet was composed mostly of moths (Lepidoptera, 50%) but
also contained large numbers of lacewings (Trichoptera, 30%; Freeman 1984).
Hoary bats made up 9.7 percent of captures at Rocky Mountain Arsenal, a high-
plains urban wildlife refuge near Denver, Colorado (Everette et al. 2001). This

species was the most abundant among cottonwoods and Douglas-fir between 2,000 and 2,300 meters (6,560 and 7,550 feet) at Piceance Creek, Rio Blanco County (Finley et al. 1983). In Utah, a hoary bat was found hanging from a cottonwood tree along the Virgin River (Stock 1965), but this species is also found roosting among buildings in urban settings (Hardy 1941; Crane 1948; Durrant 1952; Shuster 1957; Stock 1965; Hasenyager 1980). Records from the Wyoming State Veterinary Laboratory show equal ratios of males and females, with the former specimens recovered between July and October, and the latter specimens collected from May through October (Bogan and Cryan 2000). The diet of hoary bats in Montana consists of scarab beetles, a variety of moths, true bugs, and other insects (Jones et al. 1973).

Reproduction and Development. Sexes are segregated throughout the summer. Apparently females fly farther north and east during the summer than do males. This species gives birth to two offspring on average (ranges from one to four) in mid-May, June, or early July. Young cling to their mothers during the day but are left in the roost when the female leaves to feed at night. Newborns are covered with fine, silvery gray hair except on the belly, and the eyes and ears are closed. Their ears open by the third day and their eyes by the twelfth day. Juveniles are capable of flight at about one month (Shump and Shump 1982b). In Colorado, pregnant females were present in June and July (7/20), whereas none were pregnant in August, September, and October (0/12). Most scrotal males are present in August (14/14; Adams 1988). Two lactating females and one juvenile were captured at the Rocky Mountain Arsenal National Wildlife Refuge on 18 June and 3 August 1998 respectively (Everette et al. 2001).

Conservation Status. **Threat Medium** throughout Rocky Mountain range.

WESTERN YELLOW BAT
Lasiurus xanthinus Thomas (1897)

Description. This medium-sized bat species weighs 10–15 grams (0.4–0.5 ounce) and has a wingspan of 33–37 centimeters (13–15 inches). As its name implies, it is yellow in coloration. Unlike other lasiurines, the tail membrane is not heavily furred.

Standard Measurements [sex (*n*) mean (range)]: **Arizona** (Hoffmeister 1986, as *Lasiurus ega*), Phoenix, Tempe, Tucson, and Chiricahua Mountains: TL = **F** (6) 118.5 (105–126); TAL = **F** 52.5 (44–58); HFL = **F** 8.75 (8–9.5); EL = **F** 14.42 (11–16); FA = **F** 47.25 (46.5–48.0).

Dental Formula: I 1/3, C 1/1, PM 1/?, M 3/3 = 30 teeth.

Echolocation. The western yellow bat has a call pattern similar to other species of *Lasiurus,* but it is generally more steeply swept than that of the hoary bat. The sequence is somewhat more predictable as well, beginning usually at 60 kHz and ending at 32 kHz. As in *L. borealis,* the spectrograph depicts a slight cuplike appearance in some of the vocalizations where there is a gain in frequency at termination. The western yellow bat uses such calls in aerial pursuit of insects, primarily beetles. The spectrograph depicted was recorded from an individual flying through a pine grove on 7/9/96 at Borrego Palm Canyon, San Diego County, California.

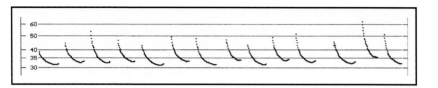

Distribution. This species occurs in the southwestern United States, including California, and across the Mexican Plateau to southern Mexico. In the Rocky Mountain region, it occurs in the very southwestern corner of New Mexico and westward through the southern third of Arizona. It is common in south-central Arizona but is not common elsewhere in the United States. Hoffmeister (1986) reports yellow bats north of Phoenix, and this species appears to be extending its range northward in Arizona, as it has been taken at several new sites in recent years. Cockrum et al. (1996) did not capture yellow bats in Mohave County, but because of the association of this species with palm trees, which are being planted commonly along the Colorado River, they speculated that yellow bats will soon become summer residents in that county. Spencer et al. (1988) noted the high probability of human-aided range extensions for populations of a closely related species, the southern yellow bat (*L. ega*), in Texas. In New Mexico, this bat occur mostly in the Animas Mountains (Cook 1986) and Guadalupe Canyon (Mumford and Zimmerman 1963; Baltosser 1980), Hidalgo County.

Subspecies Distribution: Monotypic species.

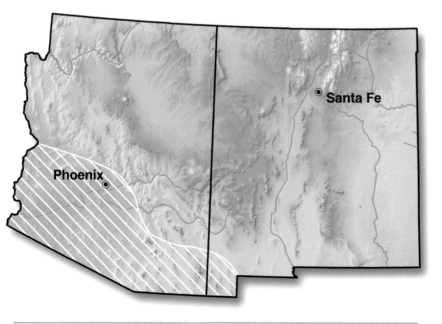

Ecology and Behavior. Western yellow bats prefer the dry, thorny vegetation of the Mexican Plateau; coastal western Mexico, including parts of Baja California; and southwestern deserts of the United States. Diet consists of medium-sized night-flying insects, especially beetles. This species is fast-flying and leaves its roosts just after sunset, staying active until midnight or beyond. The western yellow bat does not hibernate, although it does employ daily torpor on occasion (Barbour and Davis 1969).

In Arizona, some individuals have been found torpid in the dead fronds of palm trees in Tucson in January and February (Hoffmeister 1986; Cockrum et al. 1996). In New Mexico, they roost in hackberry and sycamore trees, and it is probable that their summer arrival coincides with the blooming of century plants (agaves) and perhaps yuccas as well (Findley et al. 1975). The western yellow bat is listed as threatened by the New Mexico Department of Fish and Game (Jones and Schmitt 1997).

Reproduction and Development. Mating probably occurs in autumn, as sperm storage has been noted in females of the closely related species *L. ega* (Meyers 1977). Parturition occurs as early as 1 May in the tropics but as late as 14 July in the United States. Twinning is common in this species, but the presence of up to four embryos, and the fact that females have four nipples rather than two, as in other vespertilionid bats, implies that litter size varies between one and four (Wilson and Ruff 1999). Newborn young are fed mother's milk for about two months as they learn to fly. It is believed that young bats probably breed in their first year (Barbour and Davis 1969).

Conservation Status. **Threat High** throughout Rocky Mountain range.

SOUTHWESTERN MYOTIS
Myotis auriculus Hoffmeister and Krutzsch (1955)

Description. The southwestern myotis is a medium-sized member of the genus. It weighs 5–8 grams (0.2–0.3 ounce) and has a wingspan of 26–30 centimeters (10–12 inches). Its long brown ears (> 17 millimeters) make it distinctive from most Rocky Mountain bats, with the exception of the fringed myotis *(Myotis thysanodes)*, northern long-eared myotis (*M. septentrionalis*), and western long-eared myotis (*M. evotis*). It can be distinguished from these other species by either ear color or ear size. This bat is dull brown on the dorsum, with hairs that possess a dark basal band. The ventral pelage is buffy, and the ears are long and brown.

Standard Measurements [(*n*) mean (range)]: **Arizona** (Hoffmeister 1986, not designated by sex), Sierra Ancha, Graham Mountains, and Huachuca Mountains: TL = (8) 91.4 (87–95); TAL = 42.0 (39–49); HFL = 9.5 (9–11); EL = 20.0 (19–21); FA = 37.6 (35.7–38.7).

Dental Formula: I 2/3, C 1/1, PM 3/3, M 3/3 = 38 teeth.

Echolocation. The southwestern myotis has a broken, staccato call that sometimes begins greater than 100 kHz, sweeping downward to as low as 40 kHz. This bat uses this style of echolocation in mostly gleaning insects from vegetation in ponderosa pine forests. The spectrograph depicted was recorded from an individual on 6/2/96 at Pitchfork Tank, Coconino County, Arizona.

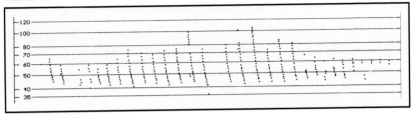

Distribution. Southwestern myotis occur from south-central Arizona eastward to western south-central New Mexico and southward into Mexico. Elevational range is from 366 to 2,226 meters (1,200–7,300 feet; Barbour and Davis 1969). In Arizona, this species ranges from the vicinity east of Phoenix, southeast to Santa Cruz and Cochise counties where it appears common between 1,524 and 1,828 meters (5,000 and 6,000 feet). Winter records are from Chiricahua Mountains only (Hoffmeister 1986). In New Mexico, the southwestern myotis is most common in the west-central and southwestern mountains, where it can be found night-roosting in caves (Findley et al. 1975). However, recently a pregnant female was captured in Harding County, extending the distributional range of this species 200 kilometers (125 miles) northeast from the nearest published record in Santa Fe County (Geluso 2002).

*Subspecies Distribution: **M. a. apache:** Arizona, New Mexico.*

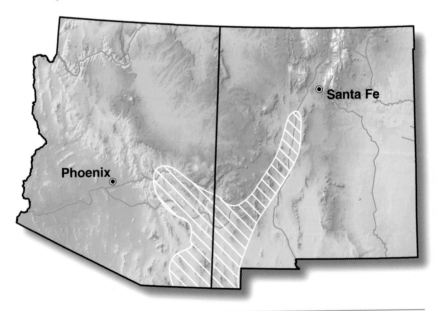

Ecology and Behavior. This species occurs often in ponderosa pine habitat but has a wide ecological range that includes mesquite and chaparral through oak forests into piñon-juniper woodland habitats, with greatest abundances coincident with rocky cliffs and the presence of water. Southwestern myotis are primarily active 1.5 to 2 hours after sunset, although this may vary with season and area. No day roosts have been located, but these bats have been found occupying night roosts in buildings, mines, and caves. Moths are the preferred diet, and the southwestern myotis gleans them from buildings and tree trunks, where it will sometimes land to grab its prey. Average flight speed for this species is 13 km per hour (8 mph). No hibernacula are currently known (Warner 1982).

In Arizona, foraging habitats include ponderosa pine, Douglas-fir, and white fir forests in the Graham Mountains (Hoffmeister 1986). An individual was captured near Flagstaff over water among ponderosa pine, Gambel's oak, and willow (Warner and Czaplewski 1981), and another was captured in deciduous-riparian habitat of willow, sycamore, box elder, some ponderosa pine and Douglas-fir (Hoffmeister 1986). In the Huachuca Mountains, it was captured among oaks (Hoffmeister 1986). Although found to occur mostly in the yellow pine zone of New Mexico, southwestern myotis have been captured in riparian zones containing cottonwoods and in the upper pine zone where Douglas-fir and white fir occur (Findley et al. 1975).

Reproduction and Development. Parturition takes place in June or early July and results in one offspring per female. Timing of birth is geographically variable and life span is estimated to be three years (Warner 1982). In Arizona, pregnant females are captured in June, and lactating females are captured in July and August (Findley et al. 1975).

Conservation Status. **Threat Medium** throughout Rocky Mountain range.

CALIFORNIA MYOTIS
Myotis californicus Audubon and Bachman (1842)

Description. The California myotis weighs 3–5 grams (0.1–0.2 ounce) and has a wingspan of 22–26 centimeters (9–10 inches). It is one of the smallest bats in the United States. This species is difficult to distinguish from the western small-footed myotis (*M. ciliolabrum*). Distinctive characters for *M. californicus* include tricolor hairs, a steeply sloping forehead, a rostrum that is short and delicate, an overall delicate body form (Simpson 1993), and a tail that does not extend beyond the border of the tail membrane (Constantine 1998).

Standard Measurements [sex (*n*) mean (range)]: **Arizona** (Hoffmeister 1986, sex not designated) , Sierra Ancha, Graham and Chiricahua mountains: TL = 80.0 (74–86); TAL = 37.8 (32–44); HFL = 8.2 (5–12); EL = 13.0 (9–13); FA = 32.56 (30.6–34.4). Grand Canyon: TL = 84.7 (78–90); TAL = 41.3 (36–44); HFL = 7.0 (6–8); EL = 12.7 (8–15), FA = 32.11 (30.2–33.9). **Colorado** (Armstrong 1972), Mesa Verde National Park: TL = **M** (2) 85, 78, **F** (1) 82; TAL = **M** 29, 34, **F** 38; HFL = **M** 5, 6, **F** 7; EL = **M** 13, 13, **F** 14; FA = **M** 31.4, 32.3, **F** 32.7. **Utah** (Durrant 1952), Kanab: TL = **M** (1) 85; TAL = **M** 42; HFL = **M** 6.7; EL = **M** 11.0. **Wyoming** (Clark and Stromberg 1987), no localities, ranges only: TL = 73–90; TAL = 29–45; HFL = 5–8; EL = 11–15; FA = 30–35. **Idaho** (Davis 1939), means only: TL = 82; TAL = 36; HFL = 7.5; EL = 11.5. **Montana** (Foresman 2001): TL = **M** (2) 81.5, **F** (1) 79.0; TAL = **M** 34.5, **F** 34.0; HFL = **M** 6.5, **F** 6.5; EL = **M** 14.3, **F** 14.0.

Dental Formula: I 2/3, C 1/1, PM 3/3, M 3/3 = 38 teeth.

Echolocation. The California myotis uses high-frequency calls that are modulated and sweep steeply from as high as 100 kHz down to about 50 kHz. The call is strictly frequency modulated and rapid. The California myotis uses this call pattern in aerial pursuit of moths and flies, usually along forest edge. The spectrograph depicted is from an individual recorded on 10/17/97 at Lime Kiln Canyon, Mohave County, Arizona.

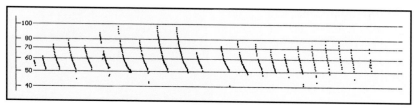

Distribution. This species occurs from southern Alaska and western Canada southward throughout most of Mexico. In the Rocky Mountain region, it occurs throughout Arizona to northeastern Utah, the western deserts of the Colorado Plateau in Colorado, and southward throughout the western half of New Mexico. In Wyoming, the California myotis is known only from Sweetwater County (Bogan and Cryan 2000), and these authors argue for lack of evidence of its occurrence in northern Wyoming. However, *M. californicus* does occur in western Montana (Foresman 2001). Thus, there appears to be a regionally disjunct northern distribution that includes northern Utah and extends throughout most of Idaho and into the westernmost regions of Montana.

Subspecies Distribution: M. c. californicus: Northwest corner of Utah into Idaho and Montana, central to southeastern Arizona, central to southwestern New Mexico. *M. c. stephensi:* Western and northern Arizona, northwest corner of New Mexico into Utah and Colorado.

Ecology and Behavior. A bat of arid regions, the California myotis inhabits areas close to water. Individuals leave the roost soon after sunset, and their flight is slow and erratic as they forage along the margins of vegetation clumps, tree canopies, and high above the ground in open areas. Roost sites are established in rock crevices, hollow trees, under loose bark, and in buildings. The sexes are segregated during the summer but are found roosting together in September and March. Caves and mines are used as hibernacula. The California myotis feeds on small flying insects, primarily flies, moths, and beetles that it captures using slow, maneuverable flight, seeking out concentrations that allow it to capture several insects simultaneously (Simpson 1993).

In Arizona, this species feeds over desertscrub up to the oak woodlands and along the edge of conifers. Individuals tend to leave their rock-crevice roosts early in the evening (Hoffmeister 1986). In New Mexico, this species is locally common from grasslands and desert through the ponderosa pine zone, and there is evidence of hibernation in the Little Hatchet Mountains in January (Findley et al. 1975). Gannon et al. (2001) found significant intraspecific differences in pinnae shape and echolocatory call morphology between *M. californicus* and *M. ciliolabrum*, with the latter having longer ears that correlated with a lower frequency call. In Colorado, the status of this species is poorly known, but it tends to occupy suitable low-elevation semidesert habitat throughout the Western Slope (Armstrong et al. 1994). Using stomach-content analysis, Freeman (1984) found that California myotis near Elk Springs, Moffat County fed mostly on moths (Lepidoptera), beetles (Coleoptera), and lacewings (Trichoptera).

This species occurs in Utah in a variety of settings, including cities, towns, and ranches. When in natural habitats, it is associated with lowland riparian, desert shrub, juniper-sagebrush, juniper, piñon-juniper, sagebrush-rabbitbrush, sagebrush-greasewood, montane meadows, and mixed forests. Mollhagen and Bogan (1997) found them to be seventh in abundance of fifteen species in the Henry Mountains of southern Utah. Hibernating sites have been located in southwestern Utah (Stock 1965), and despite their small body-size, individuals have been observed flying in winter (Ruffner et al. 1979). In Montana, Woodsworth et al. (1981) described the diet of this species as consisting of moths, true bugs, beetles, flies, and mosquitoes and observed most feeding to occur over water.

Reproduction and Development. Males and females breed in autumn, resulting in the birth of a single young in July. Females may form small maternity colonies during pregnancy, birth, and lactation. In Colorado, no pregnant females were collected in June or July, although embryos were taken from six of ten females collected in July (Adams 1988). Nonscrotal males were captured from Peacock and Burnwell Mines in La Plata County in early August (Freeman and Adams 1992; Armstrong et al. 1994).

Conservation Status. **Threat Medium** in south-central Wyoming, west-central Utah, and western Colorado. **Threat Low** in remainder of Rocky Mountain range.

WESTERN SMALL-FOOTED MYOTIS
Myotis ciliolabrum Merriam (1890)

Description. This species weighs 4–6 grams (0.1–0.2 ounce) and has a wing-span of 21–25 centimeters (8–10 inches). Its dorsal fur is light brown to yellowish brown, and the ventrum is a slightly lighter shade than the dorsum fur color. Its ears are black or dark brown, and it has a dark brown facial mask. It is easily confused with the California myotis (*Myotis californicus*) where the two species overlap in distribution. Distinguishing characteristics of the western small-footed myotis are: bicolored fur with a glossy sheen, small hind feet (less than half the length of the tibia), flat and broader cranium, and overall robust appearance. The tail extends 4 millimeters beyond the border of the tail membrane (Constantine 1998).

Myotis ciliolabrum has been known in recent times by several names, such as *M. subulatus* and *M. leibii*. *M. ciliolabrum* was once known as *M. l. ciliolabrum* and considered a western subspecies of *M. leibii*, which also had an eastern subspecies, *M. l. melanorhinus*. Van Zyll de Jong (1984) has shown convincing evidence that the western *M. ciliolabrum* is a distinct species from the eastern *M. leibii*.

Standard Measurements [sex (*n*) mean (range)]: **Arizona** (Hoffmeister 1986, sex not designated) , as *Myotis leibii*, South Rim of Grand Canyon: TL = (6) 89.7 (85–96); TAL = 41.8 (40–46); HFL = 7.5 (6–9); EL = 14.5 (13–16); FA = 33.65 (31.5–35.7); Vicinity of Kingman, Mohave County: TL = (14) 85.1 (76–93); TAL = 39.6 (33–45); HFL = 7.9 (7–9); EL = 14.7(13–16); FA = 33.34 (31.0–34.9). **Colorado** (Armstrong 1972), as *M. leibii*, Larimer County: TL = **M** (1) 85, **F** (1) 86; TAL = **M** 38, **F** 35; HFL = **M** 8, **F** 7; EL = **M** 14, **F** 15; FA = **M** 32.1, **F** 33.9. **Utah** (Durrant 1952), as *M. subulatus*, Colorado River and Parish Ranch: TL = **M** (2) 80, 71; TAL = **M** 30, 35; HFL = **M** 9, 5; EL = **M** 15, 11; FA = **M** 31, 31. **New Mexico** (Bogan 1974): TL = (34) 89.1; TAL = 41.5; HFL = 7.7; EL = 14.7; FA = 33.5. **Wyoming** (Long 1965), Campbell County: TL = (5) 77.4 (68–86); TAL = 31.2 (25–37); HFL = 6.8 (5–8), EL = 13 (11–14). Clark and Stromberg (1987), no localities, ranges only: TL = 68–86; TAL = 25–37; HFL = 5–8; EL = 11–14. **Montana** (Foresman 2001): TL = **M** (2) 77.0, **F** (1) 81.0; TAL = **M** 36.5, **F** 36.0; HFL = **M** (4) 6.25, **F** (1) 6.5; EL = **M** (4) 12.1, **F** (1) 14.0.

Dental Formula: I 2/3, C1/1, PM 3/3, M 3/3 = 38 teeth.

Echolocation. The small-footed myotis uses high-frequency, modulated vocalizations similar to those of *M. californicus*, but the call appears more staccato, or broken. Calls begin as high as 80–100 kHz and sweep abruptly down to 40 kHz. They are used in combination with slow, maneuverable flight in aerial pursuit of moths and flies along forest-edge habitats. The spectrograph depicted is that of an individual captured and hand-released on 6/12/95 at Tank 3, Buffalo Ranch, Coconino County, Arizona.

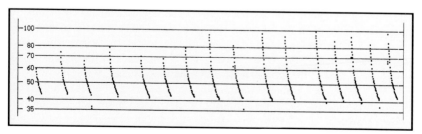

Distribution. The western small-footed myotis occurs from southern British Columbia, Alberta, and Saskatchewan into the southwestern United States. It occurs throughout the Rocky Mountain states, except for extreme northeastern Montana. In Colorado, it occurs at low to moderate elevation on either side of the Continental Divide and as high as 2,743 meters (9,000 feet) in the La Plata Mountains. In Washington County, Utah, *M. ciliolabrum* is most common above 1,066 meters (3,500 feet). It has not been captured in Teton County nor in Yellowstone National Park (Bogan and Cryan 2000).

Subspecies Distribution:
M. c. ciliolabrum: Montana into eastern Idaho, northeastern corner of Utah into Wyoming, eastern Colorado, and a small northeastern portion of New Mexico. *M. c. melanorhinus:* Northern Idaho through west-central Utah and western Colorado into Arizona and New Mexico.

Ecology and Behavior. The body size of this species increases in the southern portion of its range (Van Zyll de Jong 1985). Western small-footed myotis prefer arid habitats, where they are associated with cliffs, scree fields, and prairies located in the vicinity of clay buttes and steep riverbanks. It is common in deserts, badlands, and semiarid habitats but may also be found at higher elevations, in more mesic habitats in the southern part of its range. The western small-footed myotis begins to forage shortly before dark (Fenton et al. 1980), using slow, maneuverable flight (Norberg and Rayner 1987), and tends to forage within 1–3 meters (3–10 feet) of the ground along cliffs and rocky slopes. When co-occurring with *M. californicus*, resource partitioning has been noted (Woodsworth et al. 1981). *M. ciliolabrum* is known to roost in rock crevices in the Rocky Mountain region (Armstrong et al. 1994), but it is quite eclectic in its choices of roost sites.

In Arizona, little is known of this species' roosting ecology (Hoffmeister 1986). Merriam (1886) found small-footed myotis using abandoned swallow nests. Cockrum et al. (1996) found no day roosts for this species in Mohave County, although they were captured foraging in the area. In other parts of its range, the western small-footed myotis roosts under loose bark on trees and in buildings (Jones 1964) and even uses horizontal fractures in stream banks and water erosion crevices in the ground (Tuttle and Heaney 1974). In Arizona, small-footed myotis use many different habitats, such as hottest desert, oak woodlands, chaparral, and riparian habitat associated with junipers and oaks (Hoffmeister 1986). In the Hulalapai Mountains, Mohave County, most individuals were captured in July (thirty-four individuals), and the ratio of females to males was higher at lower elevations (Cockrum et al. 1996).

In New Mexico, this species forages mostly in the yellow pine zone (64%) but is also found along grassland/riparian habitats (24%) and woodland and encinal habitats (12%; Findley et al. 1975). Small-footed myotis form summer roosts beneath and between boulders in talus fields in Colorado as well as in rock crevices (Adams, unpubl. data; Armstrong et al. 1994). It roosts singly or in small groups (up to four individuals), even at maternity roosts (Adams, unpubl. data). Individuals were found hibernating in Colorado at 2,900 meters (9,500 feet) in the La Plata Mountains (Armstrong et al. 1994), in an irrigation tunnel in Larimer County (Armstrong 1972; Cramer 1994), and in Marchioness Tunnel, Boulder Canyon (Warren 1942). Small-footed myotis will hibernate with Townsend's big-eared bats (*Corynorhinus townsendii*). It has been observed in the eastern foothills of Colorado foraging along the edges of Douglas-fir forests and in ponderosa pine stands. This species was commonly captured in Colorado National Monument over small pools of water it visited to drink (Adams, unpubl. data). Freeman (1984), using stomach contents, found the diet of *M. ciliolabrum* near Elk Springs, Moffat County, to consist of 34 percent beetles (Coleoptera), 15 percent moths (Lepidoptera), and 13.2 percent lacewings (Trichoptera). In addition, he found that small-footed myotis foraged along rock cliffs 44.5 percent of the time.

In Utah, Hardy (1941) observed two individuals hibernating singly in a cave in Kane County, and Twente (1960) reported two individuals hibernating in a cave outside of Logan. In Montana, small-footed myotis are found roosting in caves, mines, trees, and rock outcrops. Maternity colonies form in buildings, caves, and mines, and evidence of hibernacula was found in a mine in Sydney County (Swenson and Shanks 1979). In Washington County, *M. ciliolabrum* is commonly captured near streams and lakes (Stock 1965). It is captured in southern Utah foraging in sagebrush and rabbitbrush habitats several miles from montane ponderosa pine forests (Easterla 1965), and it is even present in riparian habitats 23 percent of the time (Jackson and Herder 1997). It also occurs in montane grasslands, montane forests, and Douglas-fir/aspen forests (Foster et al. 1997) up to 2,713 meters (8,900 feet; Mollhagen and Bogan 1997) and may commonly be found in piñon-juniper forests (Chung-MacCoubrey 1996).

In Wyoming, maternity colonies of this species have not been definitively located, but hibernacula containing 1–31 individuals are found in the north-central and southwestern areas of the state and include the use of mines, caves, and a tunnel (Bogan and Cryan 2000). Colony sizes averaged 3.8 individuals (Priday and Luce 1996). In southeastern Montana, this species forages over water in short-grass prairie near ponderosa pine habitat (Jones et al. 1973; Lampe et al. 1974) and is known to inhabit caves of the Pryor Mountains, Carbon County, associated with Douglas-fir forests (Foreman 2001).

Reproduction and Development. In general, a single young is born, but twinning has been reported. Newborn young are hairless and weigh about 1.6 grams. In New Mexico, Findley et al. (1975) reported pregnant females in June, whereas lactating females occurred in late June and throughout July. Based on samples obtained from the Wyoming State Veterinary Laboratory, females were recovered more commonly in May through July, whereas males were higher in the sample in August and September (Bogan and Cryan 2000). A study based on specimens procured from the Colorado Department of Health showed embryos present in August (6/6) and September (4/5; Adams 1988). Lactating females are captured in mid-June in Colorado National Monument, whereas two pregnant females occurred in mid-June at the Peacock Mine, La Plata County (Armstrong et al. 1994). A pregnant female that appeared to be carrying twins was captured at Fort Laramie National Historical Site, Wyoming (Adams 1992). In Montana, pregnant females are captured in early July (Jones et al. 1973).

Conservation Status. **Threat Medium** in Wyoming, west-central and eastern Utah, western Colorado, Arizona, and New Mexico. **Threat Low** in remainder of Rocky Mountain range.

WESTERN LONG-EARED MYOTIS
Myotis evotis Miller (1897)

Description. This bat has the longest ears (> 21 millimeters [0.84 inches]) of any North American myotis. It weighs 5–8 grams (0.2–0.3 ounces) and has a wing-span of 25–30 centimeters (10–12 inches). The ears are long and blackish, and there is no conspicuous fringe of hairs on the trailing border of the tail membrane, such as in the fringed myotis (*M. thysanodes*). Its pelage is dull or palish brown to straw-colored, with individual hairs black at the base.

Standard Measurements [sex (*n*) mean (range)]: **Arizona** (Hoffmeister 1986, sex not designated), North Rim of Grand Canyon, White Mountains: TL = (12) 88.6 (82–94); TAL = 41.8 (36–45); HFL = 9.2 (8–10); EL = 22.1 (20–24), FA = 38.5 (36.9–39.8). **Colorado** (Armstrong 1972), Moffat County: TL = **M** (2) 94, 89; TAL = **M** 46, 44; HFL = **M** 10, 8; EL = **M** 23, 22; FA = **M** 39.2, 37.8. **Utah** (Durrant 1952, sex not designated), Zion National Park: TL = 85; TAL = 40; HFL = 9; EL = 19; FA = 38. **Wyoming** (Long 1965), Park, Sublette, and Weston counties: TL = **M** (1) **F** (2) 91.3 (87–96); TAL = 41.3 (39–43); HFL = 9.7 (9–11); EL = 20.3 (17–23). Clark and Stromberg (1987), no locality, range only: FA = 36–41. **Idaho** (Davis 1939), means only: TL = 87; TAL = 40; HFL = 9; EL = 22; FA = not given. **Montana** (Foresman

2001): TL = **M** (4) 82.3, **F** (6) 89.2; TAL = **M** 46.4, **F** 42.0; HFL = **M** (9) 8.3, **F** (10) 9.4; EL = **M** (8) 18.3, **F** (6) 18.8.
Dental Formula: I 2/3, C 1/1, PM 3/3, M 3/3 = 38 teeth.

Echolocation. The western long-eared myotis uses one of the lowest-frequency calls of the *Myotis* species. The vocalizations are highly broken and staccato throughout. They begin at around 80 kHz and sweep abruptly down to about 40 khz. Such a call sequence is adaptive for gleaning insects from leaves and other substrates while employing slow, maneuverable, and at times, hovering, flights through thick vegetation. The spectrograph depicted is of an individual recorded on 9/27/98 at Guzzler 19, Sage Creek, Sweetwater County, Wyoming.

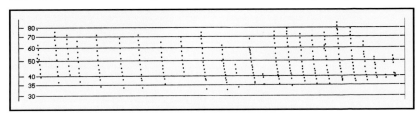

Distribution. The long-eared myotis inhabits the temperate west of North America. It ranges from central British Columbia, southern Saskatchewan, and Alberta southward along the Pacific Coast to Baja California and eastward through Nevada, the Rocky Mountain states of Montana, Idaho, Utah, Wyoming, and Colorado to New Mexico, as well as the western Dakotas. It occurs mostly along the Kaibab Plateau, Mogollon Plateau, and Chiricahua Mountains in the central and northern parts of Arizona (Hoffmeister 1986). In New Mexico, most records are in the western portion of the state (Findley et al. 1975). In Colorado, this species ranges on both sides of the Continental Divide up to about 2,591 meters (8,500 feet; Armstrong et al. 1994), and individuals have been captured in the foothills west of Boulder down to about 1,829 meters (6,000 feet; Adams, unpubl. data). In Utah, long-eared myotis occur throughout the state (Hasenyager 1980) and range from 1,430 to 2,895 meters (4,700 to 9,500 feet; Shuster 1957; Mollhagen and Bogan 1997). In Idaho, it occurs on the 2,286 meter (7,500 foot) summit of Smith Mountain, Adams County (Davis 1939). This species is thought to range widely throughout Wyoming, Idaho, and Montana in suitable habitats.
Subspecies Distribution: M. e. evotis: Throughout Rocky Mountain region.

Ecology and Behavior. This species is adapted for foraging in vegetatively dense habitats. It gleans insects from leaves and bark and locates them by listening for the sound of their fluttering wings. It uses echolocation to verify prey position just before attacking. Diet includes moths, beetles, flies, lace-winged insects, and true bugs. Males tend to consume more moths than do females. Long-eared myotis emerge from their roost site at dusk. Roost sites are located typically in rocky areas in a variety of habitats such as subalpine, semiarid

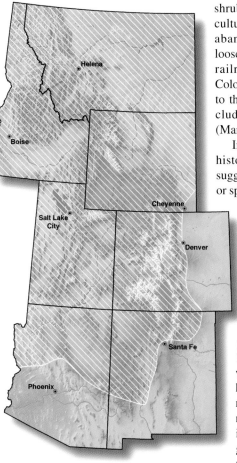

shrublands, sage, chaparral, and agricultural areas. This bat also roosts in abandoned buildings, hollow trees, loose slabs of bark, timbers of unused railroad trestles, caves, and mines. Colony size usually ranges from twelve to thirty individuals. Predators may include snakes, raccoons, and raptors (Manning and Jones 1989).

In Arizona, little is known of the life history of this species. Limited data suggest that it inhabits ponderosa pine or spruce-fir forests (Hoffmeister 1986). Day roosts include buildings and mine tunnels in New Mexico, and its distribution appears limited to higher elevations in the yellow pine zone and above (Findley et al. 1975). This species is common in coniferous woodlands and forests such as piñon-juniper and ponderosa pine (Armstrong et al. 1994) and is commonly captured at water holes located in Douglas-fir habitat outside of Boulder, Colorado (Adams et al. 1993). No hibernacula are known in the state, and it is thought that this species migrates to more suitable climes in winter (Armstrong et al. 1994). The diet of individuals captured near Elk Springs, Moffat County, Colorado, consisted of 32 percent moths (Lepidoptera), 24 percent beetles (Coleoptera), and 13.5 percent lacewings (Trichoptera), and individuals were captured 51 percent of the time in forested habitat (Freeman 1984). This species was captured in the highest numbers at pools adjacent to big sage, greasewood, and piñon-juniper woodland habitats in Rio Blanco County, Colorado (Finley et al. 1983). The long-eared myotis is known from a sage-grass community north of Blacktail Butte, Teton County, Wyoming (Negus and Findley 1959), and nine colonies have been located in the state, one a possible hibernaculum (Priday and Luce 1996). Nearly equal sex ratios were found in analysis of Wyoming State Veterinary Laboratory specimens (Bogan and Cryan 2000). In Utah, this species occurs in many habitat types, including narrowleaf cottonwood, sagebrush and rabbitbrush, subalpine tall shrublands, montane grasslands, subalpine low shrublands, and montane forests and woodlands (Foster et al. 1997). Use of various habitats in southern Utah was reported by Jackson and Herder (1997) in these percentages: riparian (9%), juniper-sagebrush (15%), juniper (6%), piñon-juniper (48%), and wet meadows in mixed forests (3%). Western long-eared myotis forage among firs and spruces at the summit of Smith Mountain in Idaho, and a dozen were found on 9 and 10 July roosting in Great Owl Cabin in Craters of the Moon National Monument (Davis 1939). In southeastern Montana, this species is found foraging over reservoirs in short-grass prairie adjacent to ponderosa pine–covered hills (Jones et al. 1973; Lampe et al. 1974). It is also found in caves of the Prior Mountains (Carbon County) located in Douglas-fir habitat at higher elevations and in association with drier Utah juniper–blacksage habitat of lower elevations (Worthington 1991). Some hibernation sites are present in Montana (Swenson and Shanks 1979).

Reproduction and Development. Female western long-eared myotis form small maternity colonies in summer, whereas males and nonpregnant females live singly or in small groups. A single pup is born in late June or early July, and individuals may live for twenty-two years or more (Manning and Jones 1989). Very little is known of its reproduction in the Rocky Mountain states. No pregnant females have been reported from New Mexico, although lactating individuals were captured on 27 and 28 July and young of the year were captured in late July (Findley et al. 1975). In Colorado, pregnant females occurred at Peacock Mine, La Plata County, in mid-June and early July (Freeman and Adams 1992; Armstrong et al. 1994). A mixed group of males with scrotal testes together with females captured in late July on Sugarloaf Mountain, Boulder County, Colorado, suggests that breeding may occur in the vicinity (Armstrong et al. 1994).

Conservation Status. **Threat Low** in Montana, northern Idaho, northeastern Utah, the central mountains and Eastern Slope of Colorado, and east-central New Mexico. **Threat Medium** in remainder of Rocky Mountain range.

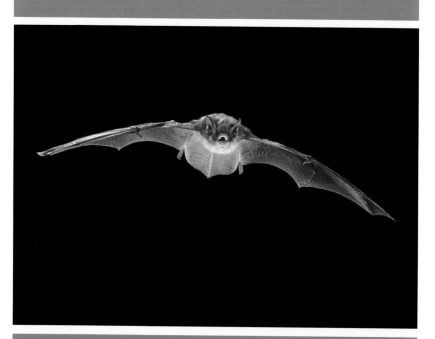

LITTLE BROWN MYOTIS
Myotis lucifugus Hollister (1909)

Description. The little brown myotis weighs 7–14 grams (0.3–0.5 ounce) and has a wingspan of 22–27 centimeters (9–11 inches). The lack of a keel on the calcar and the presence of hairs that extend beyond the toes of the hind foot are distinctive characters. This species can easily be confused with other myotis species and typically is distinctive in that it possesses none of the identifying characters of similar species. The fur exhibits a glossy appearance and ranges in dorsal coloration from a sooty brown, through paler golden brown and pallid, to yellowish or olive brown.

Standard Measurements [sex (*n*) mean (range)]: **Arizona** (Hoffmeister 1986, as *Myotis occultus*, sex not designated), Coconino and Yavapai counties: TL = (15) 89.0 (80–97); TAL = 38.1 (37–42); HFL = 8.9 (8–11); EL = 13.1 (11–16); FA = 38.72 (36.9–40.5). **Colorado** (Armstrong 1972), Lake County: TL = **F** (14) 94.9 (89–102); TAL = **F** 40.5 (37–44); HFL = **F** 10.6 (10–11); EL = **F** 14.7 (14–16); FA = **F** 38.13 (36.9–40.3). **Utah** (Durrant 1952), mouth of Bear River, Boxelder County: TL = **F** (7) 83 (79–90); TAL = **F** 36 (31–40); HFL = **F** 8.3 (8.0–9.0); EL = **F** 13.5 (12.0–14.5); FA = **F** 38.5 (37.5–39.0). **Wyoming** (Long 1965), 2.25 miles northeast of Pinedale, Sublette County: TL = (18) 90.5 (83–103); TAL = 38.1 (31–44); HFL = 11.0 (10–11); EL = 14.2

(13–15). Clark and Stromberg (1987), no localities, ranges only: HFL = 8–10; EL = 12.5–15.5; FA = 33–41. **Idaho** (Davis 1939), ranges only: TL = 80–87; TAL = 33–34; HFL = 8–10; EL = 10–13. **Montana** (Foresman 2001): TL = **M** (10) 81.7, **F** (10) 80.4; TAL = **M** 59.5, **F** 32.2; HFL = **M** 10.1, **F** 9.1; EL = **M**(5) 12.1, **F** (10) 12.1.

Dental Formula: I 2/3, C 1/1, PM 3/3, M 3/3 = 38 teeth.

Myotis occultus

Echolocation. The little brown myotis uses modulated calls of medium frequency and duration, beginning at about 70 kHz and sweeping down to 35–40 kHz. This bat uses a generalized call sequence for foraging on a diverse diet of flies, lacewings, small moths, and small beetles throughout many habitat types. The spectrograph depicted is of an individual captured and hand-released on 10/4/98 at Ray's Cave, Greene County, Nevada.

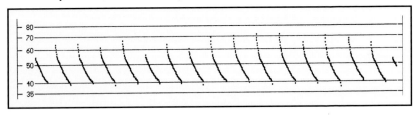

Distribution. This species is widely distributed from Alaska to central Mexico, occurring throughout much of the United States. In the Rocky Mountain region, it occurs in all states at almost all elevations but has never been captured in far eastern Colorado, eastern New Mexico, and far southern Arizona. The subspecies in Arizona (*M. l. occultus*) has species status (*M. occultus;* see photo on facing page) in some literature (see Hoffmeister 1986 for explanation); however, the evidence for this is contradictory. Analysis of 20 gene loci from 142 specimens collected from New Mexico, Colorado, and Wyoming suggests a single species, *Myotis lucifugus*, throughout the Rocky Mountains (Valdez, Choate, et al. 1999). Yet a recent study by Piaggio et al. (2002) using cytochrome-*b* and cytochrome oxidase II genes supported the assertion that *M. occultus* is a distinct species.

Subspecies Distribution: *M. l. occultus:* All of Arizona except the northern border region into New Mexico. *M. l. carissima:* The northern border area of Arizona and northwest corner of New Mexico through Utah, Colorado, and Wyoming to central Idaho through central and eastern Montana. *M. l. alascensis:* Northern Idaho into northwestern corner of Montana.

Ecology and Behavior. Little brown myotis are highly versatile in both their ecology and behavior. Day roosts include buildings (even ones occupied by humans), trees, under rocks, rock crevices, in piles of wood, caves, and under sheets of metal. Maternity colonies may reach thousands of individuals. This species usually hibernates in caves and mines, and there is no evidence that they use buildings as hibernacula. Little brown myotis prefer to forage over water but will also forage among trees or in open clearings. Though their diet is made up mostly of midges, it may also include craneflies, beetles, wasps, water boatmen, mosquitoes, and true bugs. The ability of this species to exploit a wide range of foods and roost sites likely contributes to the sustaining of large populations throughout its range. Females may move as far as several hundred kilometers between summer and winter roosts, and there is high fidelity of individuals to particular roosting sites. It is believed that populations of *M. lucifugus* (and perhaps most insectivorous bat populations) are limited mostly by roost availability rather than by food (Fenton and Barclay 1980).

In Arizona, this species in known from ponderosa pine or oak-pine woodlands, but a maternity colony was found in a riparian area containing cottonwoods, willows, and sycamores along the Middle Verde River (Hoffmeister 1986). Findley et al. (1975) suggested that little brown myotis are dependent upon permanent water sources and that the presence of such sources overrides the importance of vegetation zones in this species' distribution. The only known summer roosts for this species in New Mexico are in buildings, and there are no known hibernation sites (Findley et al. 1975). In Colorado, numbers of little brown myotis appear to have declined over recent decades (Armstrong et al. 1994). In 1997 a maternity colony containing approximately 120 females and young was located in a rock crevice west of Boulder (Adams, unpubl. data). Although commonly referred to as a "water bat," due to its propensity to forage over permanent water sources, this species was captured by Freeman (1984) only 33 percent of the time foraging over water in Moffat County. He determined the diet to consist of 28 percent moths (Lepidoptera), 28 percent flies (Diptera), 20 percent lacewings (Trichoptera), and 16 percent bees (Hymenoptera). Adams (1993) analyzed the diet of little brown myotis in Wyoming and found similar ratios of insects in the diet, but also noted that water boatmen (Hemiptera: Corixidae) made up a significant component in some years. In addition, diet differed among different age groups of juveniles, as well as between juveniles and adults. Habitat usage also differed among age/size groups, suggesting resource partitioning (Adams and Pedersen 1994; Adams 1996, 1997, 2000).

The extent of distribution of *M. lucifugus* in Utah is thought by some to include the entire state (Durrant 1952; Fenton and Barclay 1980; Hasenyager 1980), but their occurrence in the Henry Mountains is suspect (Mollhagen and Bogan 1997). Hibernation in the state is unknown (Twente 1960). This species has been captured over ponds in aspen groves and among spruces and aspens along a stream in a narrow canyon (Musser 1961). It has been captured in open areas in Rich County (Jensen 1965). Lengas (1994) captured little brown myotis at nine sites, with 53 percent of captures occurring in willows and aspens adjacent to lodgepole pine forests. Davis (1939) reported watching little brown myotis leave rock-crevice roosts in Idaho and foraging above open water at Salmon Creek Reservoir; he also observed them near Elba, foraging among willows bordering Cassia Creek. Little brown myotis are very common in parts of Montana, where more than four hundred were banded from a single cave (Worthington 1991), and large colonies have been located in human-made structures (Foresman 2001).

Reproduction and Development. Males and females mate in autumn, but individuals have also been observed copulating during hibernation. In addition, males copulate with several females, and females copulate with several males. A single young is born in May, June, or July, and newborns weigh about 25 percent of their mother's body mass. For the first eighteen days, pups dine only on milk. Curiously though, both insects and milk are found in the diet when young become volant at about three weeks (Anthony and Kunz 1977). There is apparent dietary and habitat partitioning between juveniles and adults during the flight-learning period (Adams 1996, 1997, 2000). Maximum longevity for an individual is more than thirty years in the wild (Fenton and Barclay 1980). In Idaho, a female collected at Elba on 16 June was pregnant, as was another captured at Granite Mountain on 14 July (Davis 1939). Six of thirteen, zero of two, and zero of fourteen females were lactating in June, July, and August respectively in Colorado. Scrotal males were found in June and July (seven of seven; Adams 1988). In Jackson Hole, Wyoming, one-third of females had given birth before the first week in July (Findley 1954), and in northeastern Wyoming, seven females and a newly born juvenile were captured on 4 July (Turner 1974).

Conservation Status. **Threat Medium** in west-central to eastern Utah, western Colorado, eastern New Mexico, and Arizona. **Threat Low** in remainder of Rocky Mountain range.

NORTHERN LONG-EARED MYOTIS
Myotis septentrionalis

Description. The northern long-eared myotis weighs 6–9 grams (0.2–0.3 ounce) and has a wingspan of 23–27 centimeters (9–11 inches). This species has a long, sharply pointed tragus. Until 1979, the northern long-eared myotis was considered a subspecies of Keen's myotis (*M. keenii*).

Standard Measurements [sex (*n*) mean (range)]: **Wyoming** (Long 1965, sex not designated), 2.5 miles east of Buckhorn, Weston County, as *Myotis keenii septentrionalis:* TL = (3) 87.3 (84–92); TAL = 39.7 (38–41); HFL = 9.0 (9.0–9.0); EL = 15.3 (15.0–16.0). **Montana** (Foresman 2001, from Smith 1993): TL = **M** (40) 92.9, **F** (10) 94.3; TAL = **M** 40.9, **F** 43.0; HFL = **M** 10.4, **F** 10.6; EL = **M** 17.8, **F** 18.2.

Dental Formula: I 2/3, C 1/1, PM 3/3, M 3/3 = 38 teeth.

Echolocation. The northern long-eared myotis has a call somewhat similar to other long-eared *Myotis* such as *M. evotis*. It uses relatively low-frequency, modulated, staccato calls to both pursue insects aerially and to glean them from vegetation in forested areas, usually hunting along forest-edge habitats. The majority of calls begin at about 80 kHz and sweep almost vertically downward to about 40 kHz. The spectrograph depicted is from an individual captured and hand-released on 5/27/96 at Tratchett's, Michigan.

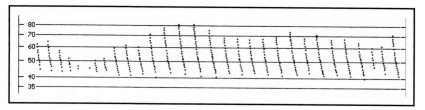

Distribution. This species ranges from southern Canada and the central and eastern United States southward into northern Florida. Its range barely extends into the Rocky Mountain states, with populations found only in extreme eastern Montana and extreme northeastern Wyoming.

This species is known from the Black Hills of Wyoming and may also occur in the Bear Lodge Mountains (Clark and Stromberg 1987, as *Myotis keenii septentrionalis*). Long (1965) referred to three individuals collected from 0.5 miles east of Buckhorn, Weston County, and although Clark and Stromberg (1987) noted specimens from Crook County, the whereabouts of these specimens is unknown (Bogan and Cryan 2000).

Subspecies Distribution: Monotypic species.

Ecology and Behavior. Northern long-eared myotis are apparently more solitary than other species of *Myotis*. They are commonly found roosting singly, but they also do form groups of up to one hundred individuals. Like many bats, they prefer tight crevices but will at times hang in the open. Moist caves and mines are used as hibernacula, and hibernation may begin as early as August and may last eight to nine months in northern areas. Forested hillsides and ridges are the preferred foraging areas for this species, which consumes a variety of insect prey.

Predation consists of homing in on the sounds of insects fluttering or making other wing movements and then gleaning the prey from the substrate. They take insects from the ground as well as from branches or foliage, and carry their prey to perches to ingest them (Caceres and Barclay 2000).

Priday and Luce (1996) discovered two night roosts of *M. septentrionalis* in Wyoming, one in a mine, the other in a building. In Montana, only a single specimen is known (Foresman 2001), an adult male that was hibernating in Culbertson Mine, Richland County, in mid-January (Swenson and Shanks 1979).

Reproduction and Development. As in other species of *Myotis*, mating occurs in autumn before hibernation. The formation of small maternity colonies apparently occurs in the spring, and females give birth to a single young. Life span may be more than eighteen years. Perhaps pertinent to the Wyoming population, females were lactating from late July to August in the nearby Black Hills of South Dakota (Clark and Stromberg 1987).

Conservation Status. **Threat Low** throughout Rocky Mountain range.

FRINGED MYOTIS
Myotis thysanodes Miller (1897)

Description. This species is a member of the large-eared group of North American myotis. It weighs 5–7 grams (0.2–0.3 ounces) and has a wingspan of 27–32 centimeters (11–13 inches). The most distinctive character of this species, as suggested by its common name, is a conspicuous fringe of stiff hairs that protrude along the trailing edge of the tail membrane (uropatagium). Because of this characteristic, this species is easily distinguished from other long-eared bats.

Standard Measurements [sex (*n*) mean (range)]: **Arizona** (Hoffmeister 1986, sex not designated): South Rim of Grand Canyon, Coconino County: TL = (13) 90.0 (80–99); TAL = 39.8 (36–45); HFL = 9.7 (8–12); EL = 17.6 (15–19); FA = 42.91 (40.9–45.3); Cochise County: TL = (12) 88.7 (82–97); TAL = 38.3 (35–44); HFL = 10.7 (10–11); EL = 18.6 (12–22); FA = 42.62 (40.3–44.7). **Colorado** (Armstrong 1972), Montezuma and Montrose counties: TL = **F** (2) 86, 81; TAL = **F** 37, 37; HFL = **F** 9, 11; EL = **F** 18, 21; FA = **F** 43.7, 39.4. **Wyoming** (Clark and Stromberg 1987), no localities, ranges only: TL = 77–104; TAL = 34–54; HFL = 7–9; EL = 16–20; FA = 40–47. **Montana** (O'Farrell and Studier 1980; Foresman 2001, no sex indicated except for HFL): TL = 43–53; TAL = 34–35; HFL = **M** 10.0, **F** none; EL = 16–20.

Dental Formula: I 2/3, C 1/1, PM 3/3, M 3/3 = 38 teeth.

Echolocation. The fringed myotis uses relatively low-frequency, modulated calls to hunt insects in forested areas. Like other long-eared myotis species, fringed myotis vary the beginning frequency of the call, sometimes initiating vocalizations at about 75 kHz and at other times beginning as low as 35 kHz. Calls consistently terminate at about 25–27 kHz, regardless of starting frequency. The spectrograph depicted is from an individual recorded on 6/12/96 at Jewell Cave National Monument, Custer County, South Dakota.

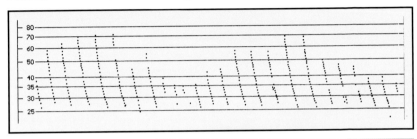

Distribution. This species ranges throughout western North America, from British Columbia southward into Mexico. Records are scattered throughout the mountainous regions of the Rocky Mountain states. There appears to be a large distributional gap between southwestern Utah and populations in north-central Idaho and western Montana. However, the range is contiguous extending through Nevada. No captures have occurred in the south-western corner of Arizona, but this spe-cies is abundant between 1,524 and 1,830 meters (5,000 and 6,000 feet) in the Chiricahua Mountains. In New Mexico, two females and two juveniles were captured recently in Harding County, extending this species' range eastward onto the plains (Geluso 2002). There appears to be a disjunct population in the Black Hills of Wyo-ming and South Dakota that is con-sidered a separate subspecies (*M. t. pahasapensis*). Colorado records are scattered at moderate eleva-

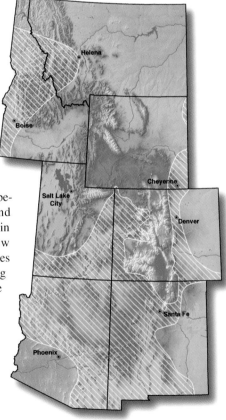

tions of 1,524–2,438 meters (5,000–8,000 feet) in mountainous parts of the state (Armstrong et al. 1994). Its elevational distribution in Utah covers 731 to 2,713 meters (2,400 to 8,900 feet; Jackson and Herder 1997).

Subspecies Distribution: M. t. thysanodes: Rocky Mountain states. Based on morphology, Bogan and Cryan (2000) believe that populations east of the Continental Divide in Wyoming are *M. t. pahasapensis.*

Ecology and Behavior. Although oak and piñon woodlands appear to be used commonly by this species, it also may be found abundant in fir-pine forests. Caves, mines, and buildings form suitable roost sites within which it typically hangs in the open. When in buildings, fringed myotis tend to roost tightly clustered in the open. This species is known to migrate, but to what extent is unclear. Diet includes beetles and moths that are taken in close proximity to the canopy. This bat's flight is slow and maneuverable. Most foraging activity occurs between one and two hours after sunset, but some activity may continue until 4.5 hours after sunset. This species is particularly susceptible to human disturbance, especially near maternity colonies (O'Farrell and Studier 1980).

In southern Arizona, the fringed myotis occurs mostly in oak woodlands but also uses most habitats from lowland chaparral to ponderosa pine (Cockrum and Ordway 1959; Jones 1965; Hoffmeister 1986). This is one of the most abundant species in oak-woodland habitat between 1,524 and 1,829 meters (5,000 and 1,000 feet) in the Chiricahua Mountains (Barbour and Davis 1969). In Mohave County, males, which form more numerous but smaller colonies, are found at higher elevations than are females during spring and summer (Cockrum et al. 1996). Sex differences in roost distribution have been documented throughout Arizona (Hoffmeister 1970). In New Mexico, Jones (1966) and Jones and Suttkus (1972) reported population fluctuations over an eleven-year period in the Mogollon Mountains and western New Mexico, with a small gain overall in relative numbers. Fringed myotis were captured in the middle Rio Grande Valley at an isolated water hole in desert grassland habitat containing scattered junipers and also along the Rio Grande in riparian forest habitat (Valdez, Stuart, et al. 1999).

In Colorado, the fringed myotis ranges across saxicoline brush and Douglas-fir forests on the Eastern Slope near Boulder (Adams et al. 1993) and in piñon-juniper and ponderosa pine woodlands in other parts of the state (Armstrong et al. 1994). The diet of this species near Elk Springs, Moffat County, was split fairly evenly across moths (Lepidoptera, 17.4%), beetles (Coleoptera, 21.7%), bees (Hymenoptera, 21.7%), and lacewings (Trichoptera, 21.7%; Freeman 1984). Roost sites occur in rock crevices (Adams, unpubl. data). In the Henry Mountains of Utah, fringed myotis composed 6 percent of the 572 bats captured, making it the seventh most common species of those captured (Mollhagen and Bogan 1997). It has been captured foraging in "treeless and rolling" terrain containing sagebrush and rabbitbrush (Easterla 1965) and also in montane forests in southern Utah containing Douglas-fir and aspen (Foster et al. 1997). Other habitats of capture in southern Utah are: riparian (20% of all captures), desert shrub (56%), piñon-juniper (8%), and juniper-sagebrush (8%; Jackson and Herder 1997).

Little is known of the fringed myotis throughout Wyoming; however, fourteen night roosts were found, eleven of these in Goshen County (Priday and Luce 1996; Luce 1998). In addition, two hibernacula were located in caves. No maternity colonies are known (Luce 1998). Adams (1996, 1997) captured no individuals of this species over three years of trapping in riparian and grassland habitats at Fort Laramie National Historical Site, Goshen County. In Montana, the fringed myotis has been captured in a variety of habitats, including grasslands, woodlands, shrublands, and spruce-fir forests, where it roosts in caves, mines, and buildings (Foresman 2001).

Reproduction and Development. Mating occurs in autumn, and females become highly secretive just before parturition. Birth of a single offspring occurs in late June or early July, after a gestation of fifty to sixty days. Upon birth, newborn young are placed in a cluster separate from the adults. Females visit the neonatal cluster, feed their young, and then return to the adult cluster. Neonates remain pink for about one week and weigh about 54 percent of adult weight at birth. The eyes are open and pinnae erect shortly after birth. Young are capable of limited flight at about sixteen days of age and are indistinguishable in flight ability from adults by twenty-one days (O'Farrell and Studier 1980).

In New Mexico, parturition occurred between 25 June and 5 July (O'Farrell and Studier 1973). In Colorado, females collected near Colorado Springs on 18 June were pregnant with single embryos (Barbour and Davis 1969), and Adams (unpubl. data) captured scrotal males in Colorado National Monument in June. Pregnant females were captured in Boulder County in July, and young were volant in August (Adams, unpubl. data). Maternity colonies tend to be about 30–35 individuals. However, in the Bradshaw Mountains of Arizona, a colony located in an old, vacant shack consisted of 100–150 adult females (Hoffmeister 1986).

Conservation Status. **Threat High** in southern Idaho, central and southern Wyoming, west-central to eastern Utah, and western Colorado. **Threat Medium** in Montana, northern Idaho, northwestern Wyoming, northeastern Utah, central Colorado, New Mexico, and Arizona.

CAVE MYOTIS
Myotis velifer Allen (1890)

Description. The cave myotis weighs 12–15 grams (0.4–0.5 ounce) and has a wingspan of 28–33 centimeters (11–13 inches). This is a medium-sized bat but is large for the genus *Myotis*. It has darkish dorsal fur, large feet, medium-sized ears, a long forearm, a long body, and no keel on the calcar. It has a stubby-nosed appearance. Ears reach only to the tip of the nose when bent forward.

Standard Measurements [sex (*n*) mean (range)]: **Arizona** (Hoffmeister 1986, sex not designated), Huachuca Mountains, Cochise County: TL = (12) 94.5 (87–100); TAL = 43.9 (41–47); HFL = 11.1 (10–12); EL = 15.7 (11–18); FA = 41.8 (40.05–43.1); Harquahala Mountains, Yuma County: TL = (12) 97.5 (93–100); TAL = 41.5 (37–47); HFL = 9.9 (9–11); EL = 15.6 (15–17); FA = 41.55 (40.1–42.6).

Dental Formula: I 2/3, C 1/1, PM 3/3, M 3/3 = 38 teeth.

Distribution. This species is distributed from southern Kansas and western Oklahoma through the southwestern United States and into northern Mexico. In the Rocky Mountain states, it occurs throughout much of Arizona except for the northern part of the state, and it is present in south-central and the southwestern corner of New Mexico.

Subspecies Distribution: M. v. velifer: Arizona and southwestern corner of New Mexico. *M. v. incautus:* South-central region of New Mexico.

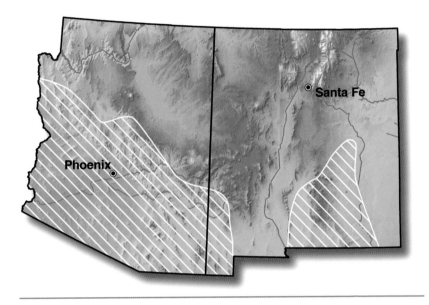

Ecology and Behavior. The cave myotis is highly gregarious, occurring in colonies of 2,000–5,000 individuals. Habitat associations vary from desert floodplains and rocky canyonlands, to the cave country of central Texas, to south-central Kansas. Summer roosts include caves and mines and, to a lesser extent, buildings (Fitch et al. 1981).

Most populations in Arizona appear to be seasonally migratory. This species uses mine shafts, caves, and bridges for roosts and forages in desert areas of creosote bush, palo verde, brittlebush, and cacti (Hoffmeister 1986). A study conducted in Arizona on the effects of cave tours on breeding behavior in this species showed negative effects and raised concerns about the conservation of this species (Mann 2002). It appears to be an opportunistic feeder (Hayward 1970) and to fly low over vegetation when foraging (Vaughan 1959). Moths are a large part of its diet (Ross 1967; Hayward 1970), but it has also been observed feeding on concentrations of flying ants (Vaughan 1980). When roosting in caves, this bat hangs clustered (Hayward 1970) and leaves the roost on average about thirty-seven minutes after sunset (Vaughan 1959). Cockrum et al. (1996) captured *M. velifer* in high numbers in Mohave County, Arizona. In New Mexico, the cave bat is found most commonly in the drainage basins of the lower Pecos River, near the San Francisco or Gila rivers, or in southern Hidalgo County (Findley 1987).

Reproduction and Development. Mating occurs in fall, but sperm are stored in the uterus until spring, when fertilization occurs. Gestation in this species lasts sixty to seventy days and results in a single young born in late June or early July. Neonates weigh about 3 grams and reach adult weight by week nine or ten. Females leave young behind while foraging. Juveniles begin to forage within one month after birth, with weaning occurring by thirteen weeks. Life span is ten to twelve years (Fitch et al. 1981).

Conservation Status. Not ranked by Western Working Group.

LONG-LEGGED MYOTIS
Myotis volans Miller (1914)

Description. The long-legged myotis is a 6–9 gram (0.2–0.3 ounce) bat with a wingspan of 25–30 centimeters (10–12 inches). It is very similar in appearance to the little brown myotis (*Myotis lucifugus*) but can be distinguished by its slightly larger size, fur extending from the ventrum to the elbow on the wing undersurface, and a keeled calcar.

Standard Measurements [sex (*n*) mean (range)]: **Arizona** (Hoffmeister 1986, sex not designated), South Rim of Grand Canyon, Coconino County: TL = (12) 99.7 (86–108); TAL = 46.4 (43–51); HFL = 8.9 (8–10); EL = 13.4 (12–14); FA = 39.69 (37.8–42.1); Graham and Chiricahua Mountains: TL = (11) 99.5 (92–112); TAL = 45.4 (39–51); HFL = 9.3 (8–11); EL = 13.8 (11–20); FA = 38.91 (37.5–40.5). **Colorado** (Armstrong 1972), 2.5 miles south of Estabrook, Park County: TL = **M** (6) 97.3 (96–99), **F** (9) 102.0 (99–106); TAL = **M** 41.2 (40–43), **F** 41.6 (38–46); HFL = **M** 9.0 (9–9), **F** 8.9 (8–9); EL = **M** 12.7 (12–13), **F** 12.3 (11–14); FA = **M** 37.75 (36.9–39.1), **F** 38.19 (37.2–38.8). **Utah** (Durrant 1952): TL = **M** (1) 91; TAL = **M** 38.2; HFL = **M** 8.0; FA = **M** 38.0. **Wyoming** (Long 1965), within eight miles of Moran, Teton County: TL = (3) 97, 95, 102; TAL = 48, 43, 47; HFL = 8, 10.5, 10; EL = 13, 13, 14. Clark and

Stromberg (1987), no localities, ranges only, sex not designated: TL = 95–103; TAL = 43–48; HFL = 8.5–11; EL = 11–14; FA = 34–41.2. **Idaho** (Davis 1939), means only: TL = 87; TAL = 34; HFL = 8; EL = 13. **Montana** (Foresman 2001): TL = **M** (3) 95.3, **F** (4) 95.0; TAL = **M** 42.3, **F** 42.0; HFL = **M** 8.1, **F** 8.4; EL = **M** 10.3, **F** (3) 12.3. *Dental Formula:* I 2/3, C 1/1, PM 3/3, M 3/3 = 38 teeth.

Distribution. This species is distributed from southern Alaska and western Canada southward into northern Mexico. It occurs in all of the Rocky Mountain states but is apparently absent from eastern Colorado (Armstrong et al. 1994) and eastern New Mexico (Findley et al. 1975). Fifty individuals were netted over a small water hole near Grandview Point on the Grand Canyon's South Rim, where better than a dozen females were either near full term or carrying newborn young on 23 June 1954 (Hoffmeister 1986). The long-legged myotis has been captured in high elevations of Black Rock Mountain, Mount Trumbull, and Hualapia Mountain, Arizona (Cockrum et al. 1996). It occurs on both sides of the Continental Divide in Colorado, and data suggest that it moves to higher elevation as the summer months get warmer. Records of occurrence are from elevations as high as 3,500 meters (11,500 feet; Armstrong et al. 1994). In New Mexico, a capture of three females in Harding County extends the range of this species onto the plains, somewhat east of the Sangre de Cristo Mountains (Geluso 2002).

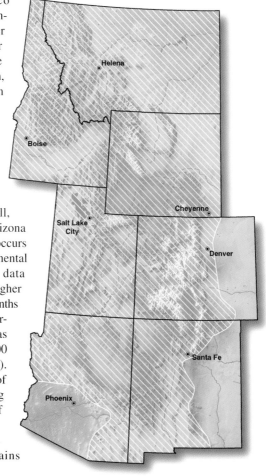

Subspecies Distribution: M. v. *interior:* Throughout Rocky Mountain states except northernmost Idaho into the northwestern corner of Montana. M. v. *longicrus:* Northernmost Idaho into the northwestern corner of Montana.

Ecology and Behavior. The long-legged myotis inhabits mostly forested areas, roosting in trees, rock crevices, crevices in stream banks, and buildings. This bat tends to be a direct flier that pursues prey over relatively long distances through and around forest canopies. Long-legged myotis tend to be active over long periods of the night, but their peak activity is within the first three to four hours after sunset. Hibernation occurs in caves and mines, and typically more males inhabit a hibernaculum than females. Diet consists primarily of moths, but long-legged myotis also consume other soft-bodied insects (Warner and Czaplewski 1984).

In Arizona, this species is common in ponderosa pine and coniferous forests, although it does occur in piñon-juniper and oak woodlands. In New Mexico, it is common at least from 10 May until 28 September in the ponderosa pine zone and above, although some individuals, including a pregnant female, were captured in grassland habitat (Findley et al. 1975). This species is one of saxicoline brush, piñon-juniper woodlands, ponderosa pine woodlands, mountain meadows, highland streams, and aspen woodlands in Colorado (Armstrong et al. 1994). It is associated with sagebrush, greasewood, and piñon-juniper woodlands habitats in Rio Blanco and Garfield counties (Finley et al. 1983). The diet of this species near Elk Creek, Moffat County (Freeman 1984), consisted of 42 percent moths (Lepidoptera), 20 percent lacewings (Trichoptera), and 12 percent beetles (Coleoptera).

Knowledge of *M. volans* in Utah has come a long way since the publication of four known records by Durrant (1952). The long-legged myotis apparently moves from lower to higher elevations between May and June in the Henry Mountains of Utah, where it is widespread and abundant (Hasenyager 1980; Mollhagen and Bogan 1997). This species hibernates in Utah at Logan Cave, where colonies of mixed-sex groups have been observed. Day and Peterson (1999a) reported capturing fifty-seven *M. volans* at the Grand Staircase in Escalante National Monument in south-central Utah, making it the fifth most common species captured during the census. It ranked seventh in a similar survey of bat species in southwestern Utah (Day and Peterson 1999b). This species occurs in steep canyons in proximity to spruce and aspen woodlands (Musser 1961) and was captured in highest number in piñon-juniper woodlands (38% of captures), followed by riparian (25%), juniper-sagebrush (19%), juniper (16%), and desert shrub (3%; Jackson and Herder 1997). This species is abundant in appropriate habitats in Wyoming, such as oak, ponderosa pine, and mixed deciduous forests above 1,310 meters (4,300 feet), where it roosts in tree crevices, snags, buildings, and rock crevices (Clark and Stromberg 1987). Little is known about this species in Idaho, but it likely occurs extensively throughout the state and "seems to frequent open forests," according to Miller and Allen (1928). In Montana, this is a bat of montane coniferous forests that occasionally occurs in riparian cottonwood woodlands (Swenson and Shanks 1979; Foresman 2001). It is known to use buildings, the underside of tree bark, and caves for roost sites (Worthington 1991). Some individuals are known to overwinter in mines in Richland County (Swenson and Shanks 1979).

Reproduction and Development. Rock crevices, trees, stream banks, or buildings serve as maternity roost sites. Females give birth to a single young per year. Life span may be up to twenty-one years (Warner and Czaplewski 1984). The highest proportion of lactating females in Colorado was in August (16/35), followed by July (11/34), and June (3/29). Pregnant females were captured in June (1/10), July (7/16), and August (6/25), and a pregnant female was present at Peacock Mine, La Plata County, in mid-June (Adams 1988; Freeman and Adams 1992). On 8 July, forty-five females were captured from the courthouse in Conejos in the San Luis Valley, Colorado (Barbour and Davis 1970). In Montana, pregnant and lactating females were captured on 9 and 17 July (Jones et al. 1973; Lampe et al. 1974).

Conservation Status. **Threat Medium** in southern Idaho, south-central Wyoming, Arizona, and western New Mexico. **Threat Low** in remainder of Rocky Mountain range.

YUMA MYOTIS
Myotis yumanensis H. Allen (1864)

Description. This bat weighs 4–6 grams (0.1–0.2 ounce) and has a wingspan of 22–26 centimeters (9–10 inches). This species may be confused with the little brown myotis (*M. lucifugus*) throughout its range, although in much of the Rocky Mountain region it is distinctive due to its pale brown ears and wings. Populations in Sonora and southeastern Arizona, however, are dark in color. Other distinctive traits include smaller size, lack of burnished tips on the fur, and a relatively steeply inclined forehead.

Standard Measurements [sex (*n*) mean (range)]: **Arizona** (Hoffmeister 1986, sex not designated), Victor, Kingman and Davis Dam, Mohave County: TL = (9) 79.1 (76–81); TAL = 34.8 (29–38); HFL = 9.3 (8–10); EL = 13.8 (13–14); FA = 33.93 (31.7–35.8); Grand Canyon, Coconino County: TL = 84.2 (77–89); TAL = 37.9 (36–40); HFL = 9.7 (8–10); EL = 14.4 (13–15); FA = 34.36 (32.7–35.9); Victor, Camp Verde, and Rimrock, Yavapai County: TL = (10) 82.4 (75–88); TAL = 35.2 (32–37); HFL = 8.9 (8–10); EL = 13.3 (12–14); FA = 33.45 (32.5–34.5). **Colorado** (Armstrong 1972), respectively Moffat, Conejos, and La Plata counties: TL = **M** (1) 85, **F** (3) 86, 86, 88; TAL = **M** 37, **F** 38, 39, 47; HFL = **M** 11, **F** 10, 10, 11; EL = **M** 16, **F** 15, 16, 15; FA = **M** 37.9, **F** 36.2, 37.9, 34.3. **Wyoming** (Clark and Stromberg 1987), no localities, ranges only: TL = 85–88; TAL = 37–39; HFL = 10–11; EL = 14–15.

Montana (Foresman 2001): TL = **M** (1) 85.0, **F** (8) 78.8; TAL = **M** 35.0, **F** 35.8; HFL = **M** 10.0, **F** (2) 8.8; EL = **M** none, **F** 12.8 (8).
Dental Formula: I 2/3, C 1/1, PM 3/3, M 3/3 = 38 teeth.

Echolocation. The Yuma myotis uses moderate-length, steeply swept frequency-modulated calls to hunt insects almost exclusively over water. The starting frequency varies widely, between 59 and 72 kHz, and sweeps abruptly down to 45–50 kHz. The spectrograph depicted is of an individual flying around a small earthen tank on 6/30/95 at Oak Grove Tank, Coconino County, Arizona.

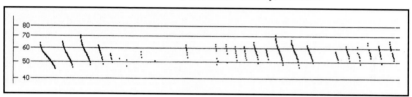

Distribution. This species occurs from southwestern British Columbia through the western United States and into central Mexico. In the Rocky Mountain region, it lives throughout Arizona and New Mexico, in south-central Colorado, in a southwest-northeast band across Utah, as well as in parts of western and central Montana and across much of Idaho. Until 1998, there was only a questionable record for Wyoming, but more recent surveys have verified night-roost sites for this species in the state (Luce 1998).

Subspecies Distribution: **M. y. yumanensis:** Rocky Mountain region.

Ecology and Behavior. Yuma bats, no matter the habitat, occur where there is open water. Often they occur in areas that are treeless. This species emerges from the day roost at darkness and forages over the surface

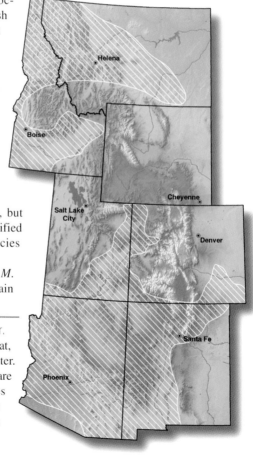

of streams and ponds. Night roosts occasionally are used. The diet includes beetles and soft-bodied insects such as flies, termites, moths, and mayflies. Peaks of foraging activity occur shortly after darkness (Barbour and Davis 1969).

In Arizona, this species is found active in proximity to standing water, over which individuals forage for food very close to the surface. They have been found roosting in narrow crevices in cliffs near the Verde River, where they had taken over abandoned cliff-swallow nests (Vaughan 1980). Cockrum et al. (1996) reported colonies numbering as high as 10,000 individuals in crevices at Davis Dam on the Colorado River on 17 September 1960, which they determined were used as transient roosting sites. They found no maternity or hibernating colonies in Mohave County. In New Mexico, abundance of this species is highest in desert, grasslands, and woodlands, and within riparian zones of these communities at elevations between 1,220 and 2,134 meters (4,000 and 7,000 feet; Findley et al. 1975). In Colorado, the Yuma myotis occurs in riparian woodlands, semidesert shrub, and piñon-juniper woodlands (Armstrong et al. 1994). It lives at lower elevations in Utah in such habitats as lowland riparian, desert shrub, sagebrush-grass, sagebrush-grass-piñon-juniper, piñon-juniper-sagebrush, piñon-juniper, mountain brush, sagebrush-juniper-maple canyon, aspen-willow canyon, sagebrush-grass-spruce-fir, mixed forests, and wet meadows in ponderosa pine forests (Hardy 1941; Ranck 1961; Stock 1965, 1970; Armstrong 1974; Oliver 2000). In southern Utah, it has been captured at 2,621 meters (8,600 feet; Mollhagen and Bogan 1997) and even as high as 3,048 meters (10,000 feet; Day and Peterson 1999b). This species appears strongly attracted to riparian areas (83% of captures) and less so to desert shrub (13%) and ponderosa pine forests (13%; Day and Peterson 1999a).

Reproduction and Development. Breeding occurs predominately in autumn with sperm storage by females. A single young is born in late May or early June, and females become reproductive the season after they are born. Nursery roosts are vacated in autumn. Maternity colonies are formed in buildings, caves, and mines, and under bridges, sometimes in abandoned cliff-swallow nests. Maternity roosts are abandoned quickly if disturbed. Males tend to lead a solitary life (Barbour and Davis 1969).

In Arizona, a maternity colony near Rimrock found on 5 July 1958 was located near standing water and contained volant young of the year, judged to have been born between 25 May and 5 June (Hoffmeister 1986). In Colorado, three females, one containing three embryos, were collected from a deserted house near Rio Blanco Lake on 6 and 7 July 1977 (Finley et al. 1983). Adams (1988) found 19 of 22 males captured in August in Colorado National Monument to be scrotal, and documented a foraging maternity colony of about 25 individuals that visited nightly a small pond near the west gate entrance of the monument. Juveniles were captured at the same site in early August. In Utah, a maternity colony of approximately 125 individuals was found in an attic in Kane County (Hasenyager 1980). Maternity colonies located in Hells Canyon, Idaho, ranged from 50–750 individuals, and cave temperatures were higher where colony size ranged between 500 and 750 bats (Betts 1997).

Conservation Status. **Threat Medium** in southern Idaho, northwestern corner of Utah, Arizona, and New Mexico. **Threat Low** in remainder of Rocky Mountain range.

WESTERN PIPISTRELLE
Pipistrellus hesperus Allen (1864)

Description. This is one of the smallest bats in the United States. Adults weigh 3–6 grams (0.1–0.2 ounce) and have a wingspan of 19–23 centimeters (7–9 inches). The tragus is blunt and slightly curved, and the hind foot is less than half as long as the tibia. Females are significantly larger than males.

Standard Measurements [sex (*n*) mean (range)]: **Arizona** (Hoffmeister 1986), Yuma County: TL = **M** (10) 70.6 (67–74), **F** (9) 74.8 (70–79); TAL = **M** 28.6 (26–30), **F** 30.6 (27–34); HFL = **M** 5.8 (4–7), **F** 5.95 (4–7); EL = **M** 10.9 (9–12), **F** 11.4 (10–12); FA = **M** 28.3 (26.2–29.5), **F** 29.6 (28.6–30.75). **Colorado** (Armstrong 1972), Four Corners, Montezuma County: TL = **M** (5) 70.5 (67–75), **F** (2) 68, 74; TAL = **M** 30.0 (27–33), **F** 29, 31; HFL = **M** 6.0 (5.6–6.8), **F** 6, 6; FA = **M** 30.4 (29.0–31.4), **F** 31.8, 31.5. **Utah** (Durrant 1952), five miles east of Moab Bridge: TL = **F** (6) 72 (70–75); TAL = **F** 30 (27–32); HFL = **F** 7 (6–7); EL = **F** 11 (10–11); FA = **F** 30.2 (29.6–31.3). **Idaho** (Davis 1939), means only: TL = 65; TAL = 23; HFL = 5; EL = 10.

Dental Formula: I 2/3, C 1/1, PM 2/2, M 3/3 = 34 teeth.

Distribution. Western pipistrelles occur from southern Washington across the southwestern United States to southern Mexico. In the Rocky Mountain states, this species occurs throughout Arizona, most of New Mexico and Utah, and at lower elevations of the western and southeastern parts of Colorado. Elevational distribution in Colorado is typically below 2,133 meters (7,000 feet); however, a hibernaculum was reported from 2,896 meters (9,500 feet; Armstrong et al. 1994). In Utah, records are lacking from the Uinta Mountains, Wasatch Mountains, and the mountains of the central part of the state. It appears to be restricted mostly to the southwestern part of Idaho.

Subspecies Distribution: P. h. hesperus: Rocky Mountain region.

Ecology and Behavior. This is primarily a desert species that inhabits rocky canyons, cliffs, and outcroppings to creosote bush flats. Western pipistrelles prefer rock crevices as day roosts but will also roost under rocks, in burrows made by other animals, in mines, and in buildings. Colony sizes are small, with the largest known colony housing only twelve individuals. Emergence from the day roost usually happens well before sunset, and activity may continue way past dawn. Western pipistrelles are weak and slow fliers as they forage between 2 and 25 meters (7 and 80 feet) above the ground. Diet consists of caddis flies, stoneflies, moths, small beetles, leafhoppers, flies, mosquitoes, ants, and wasps. This species is common throughout its range (Barbour and Davis 1965).

In Arizona, it forages along canyons, stream beds, and water holes through many habitats, including desertscrub and pine forests. It rarely ventures far from rocky outcrops, which are typically used for roosts. Other foraging habitats include mesquite–creosote bush deserts, cottonwoods and sycamores, palo verde and saguaro, piñon-juniper woodlands, and the spruce-fir forests of the higher mountains (Hoffmeister 1986). Western pipistrelles begin feeding earlier than any other bat in Arizona, well before sunset, sometimes two hours before dark. The diet of this species in Arizona consists of small-sized insects that occur in swarms (Hayward and Cross 1970). Of the hundreds of tunnels visited in Mohave County and summarized by Cockrum et al. (1996), only one contained a western pipistrelle, a single male. A single female was collected from a rock crevice in the Burro Creek area, Mohave County (Cockrum et al. 1996). In Colorado, western pipistrelles are known from the Western Slope from woodlands and semidesert shrublands (Armstrong et al. 1994). This species is abundant in Utah, particularly in lowland riparian and desert shrub habitats (Shuster 1957).

Reproduction and Development. Western pipistrelle females show proestrous morphological changes in late summer and autumn that continue into early spring. Permanent arousal from torpor and normal metabolism result in ovulation (Krutzsch 1975). Parturition occurs in June or July, and despite this species' small size, twinning is the rule. Newborn pups weigh less than one gram but grow quickly. Juveniles begin to fly by one month of age (Barbour and Davis 1969). Little has been published about reproduction in the Rocky Mountain states. In Colorado, an infant *P. hesperus* that fell to the floor was found in an abandoned house in Rio Blanco County (Scott et al. 1984), and a lactating female was captured in Colorado National Monument in 1989 (Adams, unpubl. data).

Conservation Status. **Threat Medium** in west-central and eastern Utah and western Colorado. **Threat Low** in remainder of Rocky Mountain range.

EASTERN PIPISTRELLE
Pipistrellus subflavus

Description. The eastern pipistrelle can be distinguished easily from the western pipistrelle and smaller-sized species of *Myotis*. It possesses distinctively tricolored hairs that are dark at the base, lighter and yellowish brown in the middle band, and dark at the tip. Eastern pipistrelles weigh 6–8 grams (0.2–0.3 ounce) and have a wingspan of 21–26 centimeters (8–10 inches).

Standard Measurements [range]: **Colorado** (Fitzgerald et al. 1994; sex not designated): TL = 70–90; TAL = 32–42; HFL = 8–11; EL = 12–14; FA = 30–35.

Dental Formula: I 2/3, C 1/1, PM 2/2, M 3/3 = 34 teeth.

Distribution. The distribution of this species is eastern Canada, most of eastern and central United States, and along the Caribbean coast of Mexico to Guatemala and Belize. In 1996, three individuals were found hibernating in a cave in southeastern Wyoming (Bogan and Cryan 2000), and a single record of an individual in Greeley, Colorado, in 1988 is available (Fitzgerald et al. 1994), documenting the species in the Rocky Mountain region. These localities are about 500 km (311 miles) from the previously known margins of its conterminous range in north-central Kansas, eastern Nebraska, and the Texas Panhandle.

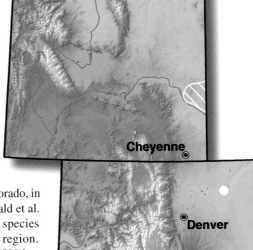

Subspecies Distribution: P. s. subflavus: Colorado and Wyoming.

Ecology and Behavior. This bat rarely occurs in buildings, and it appears that most roost in trees in summer. Caves, mines, and rock crevices are used as hibernacula and may be utilized as night roosts during the summer. Eastern pipistrelles are known to form small colonies of a few individuals using the same tree. They inhabit more caves in eastern North America than any other species. Eastern pipistrelles are very weak fliers that tend to be blown about on the wind, and they are so small they are occasionally mistaken for large moths. Foraging areas are small, with individuals utilizing forest edges and waterways. Two or three feeding bouts are interrupted by night roosting. The diet consists of moths, beetles, mosquitoes, true bugs, ants, and other insects that it pursues early in the evening, usually before other bats have emerged. Their flight is erratic and fluttery (Fujita and Kunz 1984).

In Colorado, the only individual captured in the state was collected from the side of a dwelling in Greeley in early September and appeared to be in good health (Fitzgerald et al. 1994). The species was first discovered to occur in Goshen County, Wyoming, in 1996, as reported in an annual report to the Wyoming Game and Fish Department (Priday and Luce 1996). A single male was found hibernating in the cave in February and was collected as a voucher specimen (Denver Museum of Nature and Science 8510). Two more individuals were observed in the cave the following March.

Reproduction and Development. Eastern pipistrelles give birth to twins in June or July and gestation is about forty days. Juveniles weigh only 1 gram at birth. Their bodies are pink, and their eyes are closed. They grow quickly and begin flying at about one month of age. Soon after birth they are capable of making loud, audible clicking sounds that may alert their mothers. Sexual maturity in females has occurred between three and eleven months of age. Whether or not this pattern is true throughout this species' range is unknown. Juveniles make practice flights for two or three nights before venturing out to forage. Females and juveniles begin to disperse from the maternity roost in late July and August (Fujita and Kunz 1984).

Conservation Status. Not ranked in Rocky Mountain region.

FAMILY MOLOSSIDAE

GREATER MASTIFF BAT
Eumops perotis Merriam (1890)

Description. This is the largest bat in North America north of Mexico, weighing 60–70 grams (2.1–2.5 ounces), with a wingspan of 53–58 centimeters (21–23 inches). It is distinguished from other molossids by its large size and lack of long rump hairs. As with all free-tailed bats, the tail extends far beyond the tail membrane (uropatagium). The dorsal fur is dark gray, and the ventrum barely contrasts with it. Males are larger than females.

Standard Measurements [sex (*n*) mean (range)]: **Arizona** (Hoffmeister 1986), Yuma and vicinity of Tucson, and Tempe and vicinity of Kingman: TL = **M** (2) 174 (none given), **F** (5) 176 (170–185); TAL = **M** 58 (none given), **F** 60.25 (55–65); HFL = **M** 17 (none given), **F** 16.0 (15–17); EL = **M** 41 (none given), **F** 44.3 (41–47); FA = **M** 76.3 (none given), **F** 76.3 (73.6–78.0).

Dental Formula: I 1/2, C 1/1, PM 2/2, M 3/3 = 30 teeth.

Echolocation. The greater mastiff bat uses very low frequency vocalizations that vary little and are referred to as constant frequency, or CF, calls. Such vocalizations are typical of a species that forages only in open areas using long-distance, high-speed pursuit with little maneuverability involved. The calls are audible to humans and begin at about 13–14 kHz, sweeping slightly and softly to about 9 or 10 kHz. The spectrograph depicted was recorded from an individual on 6/9/96 at the south end of Split Mountain, San Diego County, California.

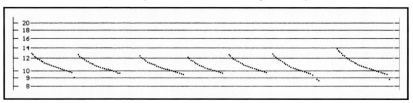

Distribution. The greater mastiff bat has an unusual distribution in that it occurs in two disjunct populations. One occurs from the western United States to southern Mexico, and the other is present from northern South America to north-central Argentina. In the southwestern United States, this species occurs from sea level in California up to 1,100 meters (3,600 feet) in Texas. In the Rocky Mountain states, it occurs throughout south-central and north-central Arizona in the lower Sonoran Desert and in the southwestern corner of New Mexico.

Subspecies Distribution: E. p. californicus: Arizona and New Mexico.

Ecology and Behavior. Roosts have large openings from below to allow for unobstructed approaches, but may become more narrow in the upper reaches. The wings of the greater mastiff bat are so adapted for fast, efficient flight that if an individual is grounded, it must climb to a height allowing for a substantial drop before takeoff. *Eumops perotis* is highly audible in its vocalizations, which can be heard more than 200 meters (656 feet) from the roost (Ohlendorf 1972), and when foraging as far away as 300 meters (984 feet) (Vaughan 1959). It emits high-pitched, piercing cries every two to three seconds as it flies (Vaughan 1959). Hibernation is unknown, but captive specimens are known to enter torpor. Unlike other molossids, it is not known to migrate (Best et al. 1996).

In Arizona, this species eats a diversity of insects, even diurnal ones such as cicadas, but primarily consumes the abdomens of large hawkmoths. Foraging periods are long, lasting more than 6.5 uninterrupted hours each night. The greater mastiff bat is present in Arizona every month except perhaps January. Its roosts in Arizona are known to occur in crevices and shallow cliffside caves (Cockrum 1960), where it may co-habit with white-throated swifts (Johnson and Johnson 1964; Cox 1965). It is also found to roost in human-made structures in the Tucson area (Krutzsch 1955). In Arizona, its diet consisted of 58 percent diurnal hymenopterous insects (wasps, ants, bees) in one study (Ross 1961) but primarily large moths (Lepidoptera) in another (Ross 1967). Foraging bouts in late July began at 8:00 P.M., with returns to the roost beginning at about 4:00 A.M. (Cox 1965).

Reproduction and Development. Ovulation in females is thought to occur shortly after copulation. Gestation period is unknown for this species, and births have occurred as early as April and as late as August. A single young per female is usual, and parturition typically occurs in late June to early July. Curiously, adult males are found roosting in maternity colonies. The young are born naked, with eyes open, and show a conspicuous gland on the throat that matures in the adults (Cockrum 1960).

Unlike most other bat species in the Rocky Mountain region, colonies are mixed sex throughout the year and move among several roosts seasonally (Howell 1920; Krutzsch 1955; Ohlendorf 1972). Little is known about reproduction in this species in the Rockies. In Arizona, males become reproductive in late March and have a well-developed throat gland that enlarges, producing a thick and odorous secretion during the mating season. A female was observed giving birth to a single young while hanging from a cactus clump on 10 August at 4:39 P.M. (Hoffmeister 1986).

Conservation Status. **Threat High** in west-central to eastern Utah and western Colorado. **Threat Medium** in Arizona and New Mexico.

UNDERWOOD'S MASTIFF BAT
Eumops underwoodi Bensen (1974)

Description. Underwood's mastiff bat weighs 50–60 grams (1.8–2.1 ounces) and has a wingspan of 50–55 centimeters (20–22 inches). This is a large-bodied bat, second in size in North America only to the greater mastiff bat. As in other free-tailed bats, the tail membrane does not extend to the tip of the tail. The lips are not wrinkled, and it has shorter ears than the greater mastiff bat (*E. perotis*), with which it can be confused. The dorsal pelage varies from cinnamon to mummy brown, and the ventral fur is hazel in color.

Standard Measurements [sex (*n*) mean (range)]: **Arizona** (Hoffmeister 1986), Baboquivari Mountains, Pima County: TL = **M** (4) 163.25 (160–167), **F** (4) 164.5 (158–172); TAL = **M** 54.5 (51–57), **F** 58.0 (52–64); HFL = **M** 18.7 (18–20), **F** 17.8 (16–19); EL = **M** 30.3 (29–32), **F** 28.3 (26–29); FA = **M** 69.85 (66.9–73.7), **F** 68.65 (67.85–69.5).

Dental Formula: I 1/2, C 1/1, PM 2/2, M 3/3 = 30 teeth.

Distribution. This species occurs in south-central Arizona, along the western coast of Mexico, and into Central America. In the Rocky Mountain region, it is known from only the Baboquivari Mountains of Arizona.

Subspecies Distribution: E. u. sonoriensis: Arizona.

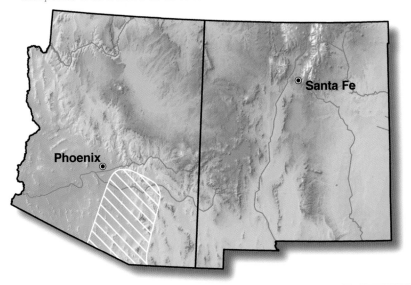

Ecology and Behavior. Underwood's mastiff bat is adapted for long-distance, high-speed flight in open habitats. Information on habitat associations in the United States is lacking, as it is known only from the mesquite desert. However, in Mexico and Central America, it occurs in arid lowlands, grasslands, and pine-oak and deciduous forests. Roost sites include large, hollow trees and probably rock crevices, from which individuals emerge well after dark. It uses loud, audible vocalizations when flying, similar to *Eumops perotis* (see previous species account). Diet includes grasshoppers, leafhoppers, moths, and a variety of beetles. Winter distribution is unknown (Barbour and Davis 1969; Kiser 1995).

Underwood's mastiff bat is known from Pima County, Arizona, where two males were captured flying over a reservoir (Hoffmeister 1986). Eight females and three males were captured over water tanks near Sasabe, Arizona, close to the Mexican border in mesquite desert at 1,220 meters (4,000 feet) between 8:45 P.M. and 5:00 A.M. on 16 July (Cockrum and Gardner 1960). The diet of this species in Pima County, Arizona, consisted of 47 percent scarab beetles (Coleoptera; Ross 1967).

Reproduction and Development. Almost nothing is known about reproduction in this species. A single young is born in late June or early July. In Pima County, Arizona, seven of eight females captured in July were lactating, and the other was near term (Cockrum and Gardner 1960).

Conservation Status. **Threat Medium** throughout Rocky Mountain range.

POCKETED FREE-TAILED BAT
Nyctinomops femorosaccus Merriam (1889)

Description. This species weighs 10–14 grams (0.4–0.5 ounce) and has a wing-span of 34–37 centimeters (13–15 inches). The pocketed free-tailed bat is a small-to medium-sized molossid with ears joined at the base and deep vertical grooves in the upper lip. Its fur is brown to grayish brown, and the hairs are whitish at their base. The ventral fur is lighter and slightly paler than the dorsal. Its most distinguishing characteristic, however, is a shallow fold of skin on the underside of the membrane between its legs (interfemoral membrane), near the knee, which forms a pocketlike structure.

Standard Measurements [sex (*n*) mean (range)]: **Arizona** (Hoffmeister 1986, cited as *Tadarida femorossacca*), Southern Arizona, one specimen of unknown sex: 7 **F**, 1 **M**: TL = 108.7 (99–118); TAL = 42.8 (41–45); HFL = 10.4 (8–14); EL = 19.8 (16–23); FA = 45.9 (44.3–47.4).

Dental Formula: I 1/2, C 1/1, PM 2/2, M 3/3 = 30 teeth.

Echolocation. The pocketed free-tailed bat has a call that is shallow sloped and frequency modulated. This component begins at about 24 kHz and ends at about 17–18 kHz. Another component of the call is steeply sloped and frequency modulated, much of which is staccato in nature. This component begins at about 59 kHz and ends at about 16 kHz. Parts of the call below 20 kHz are audible to humans. The spectrograph depicted was recorded from an individual on 6/9/96 at the south end of Split Mountain, San Diego County, California.

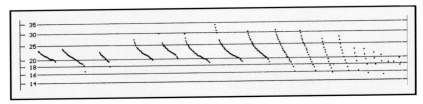

Distribution. This species occupies the southwestern United States to south-central Mexico. In the Rocky Mountain region, it occurs throughout south-central Arizona and in areas of the southwestern and southeastern corners of New Mexico. In Arizona, its distribution is restricted to riparian corridors below 1,250 meters (4,100 feet); elsewhere throughout its Rocky Mountain range it is found up to 2,250 meters (7,380 feet).

Subspecies Distribution: Monotypic species.

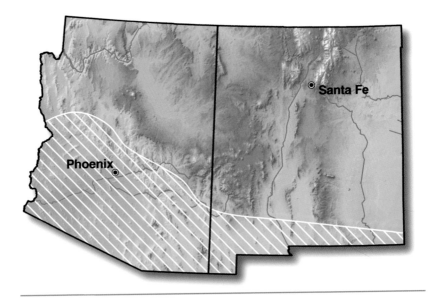

Ecology and Behavior. This bat prefers arid environments, roosting predominately in rock crevices of rugged cliffs, slopes, and tall, rocky outcrops, where it forms small colonies of fewer than one hundred individuals. Emergence from the day roost happens well after dark and coincides with a series of shrill, sharp, high-pitched calls. Flight is swift and direct, and the diet consists of mostly moths, but it will also ingest beetles, flying ants, flies, leafhoppers, crickets, stinkbugs, lacewings, and grasshoppers. Visiting open water holes, it hits the surface hard as it opens its mouth, drinking on the wing (Kumirai and Jones 1990). In Arizona, this species is associated with sycamore-and-mesquite-vegetated open floodplains bounded by large cliffs and mountains (Cockrum and Musgrove 1965). Its diet has not been documented in Arizona, but in nearby parts of its range, 36.9 percent of its diet by volume was large moths (Lepidoptera; Easterla and Whitaker 1972).

Reproduction and Development. A single young is born in late June, although more commonly in early July. Juveniles are flying by mid- to late August. In Arizona, a female near full-term was captured on 15 July (Hoffmeister 1986), and in New Mexico, a pregnant female was captured on 4 July (Easterla 1973).

Conservation Status. **Threat Medium** throughout Rocky Mountain range.

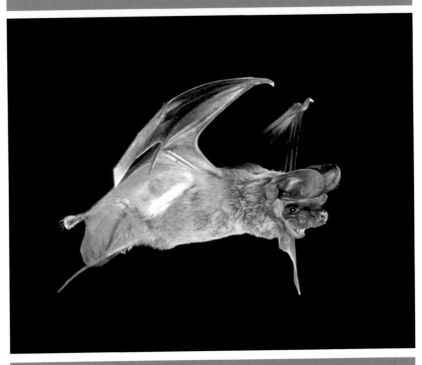

BIG FREE-TAILED BAT
Nyctinomops macrotis Gray (1839)

Description. This bat weighs 25–30 grams (0.9–1.1 ounce) and has a wingspan of 42–46 centimeters (17–18 inches). The pelage is glossy and each hair is bicolored, with a nearly white base, distinguishing it from the Brazilian free-tailed bat (*Tadarida brasiliensis*). Its large, broad ears are joined at their base, and its upper lip is deeply creased by vertical wrinkles. The muzzle is slender.

Standard Measurements [sex (*n*) mean (range)]: **Arizona** (Hoffmeister 1986, as *Tadarida macrotis*), Nixon Springs, Mohave County, and Canyon del Muerto, Apache County: TL = **F** (11) 131.8 (120–139); TAL = **F** 50.45 (40–57); HFL = **F** 9.3 (7–11); EL = **F** 27.2 (25–32); FA = **F** 60.01 (58.3–62.5). **Colorado** (Armstrong 1972, as *Tadarida macrotis*), El Paso County: TL = **M** (1) 130; TAL = **M** 52; HFL = **M** 16; EL = **M** 10; FA = **M** 60.0.

Dental Formula: I 1/2, C 1/1, PM 2/2, M 3/3 = 30 teeth.

Echolocation. The big free-tailed bat has calls similar to the greater mastiff bat because they are both singularly adapted for open aerial foraging using straight-line pursuit. However, the big free-tailed bat uses a slightly higher frequency, at times beginning at 18 kHz and sweeping slightly to about 12 kHz. These calls are audible to humans. The spectrograph depicted was recorded from an individual flying over a large pond on 6/21/95 at Parashant Field Station, Mohave County, Arizona.

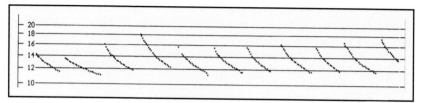

Distribution. The big free-tailed bat occurs from the southwestern United States to south-central Mexico. In the Rocky Mountain states, it occurs from central Utah and Colorado southward throughout Arizona and New Mexico. A single record has been reported from Jackson Hole, Wyoming. In New Mexico, this species occurs up to 2,438 meters (8,000 feet) in evergreen forests (Jones 1965) but is most common below 1,829 meters (6,000 feet). A new record from Harding County, New Mexico, represented by the capture of a postlactating female and the obvious calls of other individuals overhead, extends the range 200 kilometers (125 miles) eastward from a previous record in Sandoval County (Geluso 2002). Recent work by Navo and Gore (2001) reported the presence of individuals and roost sites in the western canyon country of Colorado, in particular along the Dolores River, Montrose County. In Wyoming, a male was captured at West Gros Ventre Butte, Teton County, at 1,880 meters (6,168 feet; Bogan and Cryan 2000).

Subspecies Distribution: **Monotypic** species.

Ecology and Behavior. This species prefers rocky landscape, roosting high on cliff faces. It also uses buildings for day roosts and occasionally roosts in tree cavities. Like most molossids, it leaves the roost long after dark, using fast, powerful flight and emitting a loud, piercing chatter as it hunts large moths. Big free-tailed bats also feed on crickets, flying ants, stinkbugs, and leafhoppers. In Arizona, it forages in a variety of habitats such as ponderosa pine forests, Douglas-fir forests, and Sonoran Desert scrub (Hoffmeister 1986). Cockrum and Ordway (1959) captured fifty individuals over a twenty-day census between 17 June and 7 July near the Southwestern Research Station, Cochise County, and all but seven were females. Their diet in Arizona consisted almost entirely of large moths (Ross 1967). In New Mexico, colonies are formed in crevices of large sandstone rock shelters (Findley et al. 1975). In Colorado, few specimens have been collected, but these individuals were taken mostly in open country at moderate elevations (Armstrong et al. 1994). In Utah, this species is rare (Durrant 1952; Hasenyager 1980) but has been captured in lowland riparian, desert shrub, and montane forests (Forester et al. 1997; Jackson and Herder 1997), and it occurs in the Henry Mountains (Mollhagen and Bogan 1997).

Reproduction and Development. Females form maternity colonies, and individuals give birth to a single offspring in June or July. Juveniles begin flying in late August. The only known maternity colony for this species in the United States is located in Big Bend National Park, Texas; however, reproductive females were captured near Natural Bridges National Monument, Utah (Mollhagen and Bogan 1997).

Conservation Status. **Threat High** in west-central to eastern Utah and western Colorado. **Threat Medium** in Arizona, southern Utah, southwestern Colorado, and western New Mexico. **Threat Low** in northeastern Utah, central and eastern Colorado, and eastern New Mexico.

BRAZILIAN FREE-TAILED BAT
Tadarida brasiliensis Saussure (1860)

Description. The Brazilian free-tailed bat weighs 11–15 grams (0.4–0.5 ounce) and has a wingspan of 30–35 centimeter (12–14 inches). This species has a uniform brown pelage and is readily distinguished from other molossids in the Rocky Mountain states by its smaller size and the fact that the ears are not joined at the midline.

Standard Measurements [sex (*n*) mean (range)]: **Arizona** (Hoffmeister 1986), Nogales and Baboquivari Mountains: TL = **M** (10) 98.3 (91–105), **F** (10) 95.0 (88–100); TAL = **M** 37.2 (30–42), **F** 34.3 (32–38); HFL = **M** 9.75 (9–10), **F** 9.8 (9–10); EL = **M** 18.6 (17–20), **F** 18.0 (17–19); FA = **M** 42.5 (40.2–44.6); **F** 42.8 (41.8–44.4). **Colorado** (Armstrong 1972), New Castle, Garfield County: TL = **M** (4) 100.5 (97–102); TAL = **M** 34.7 (33–38); HFL = **M** 10.2 (10–11); FA = **M** 43.3 (42.7–44.0). **Utah** (Durrant 1952, as *Tadarida mexicana*), Salt Lake City: TL = **M** (1) 90; TAL = **M** 32; HFL = **M** 9; EL = **M** 18; FA = **M** 43. **Wyoming** (Clark and Stromberg 1987), no localities, ranges only: TL = 90–105; TAL = 32–38; HFL = 9–11; EL = 42–44; FA = 36–46.

Dental Formula: I 1/3, C 1/1, PM 2/2, M 3/3 = 32 teeth.

Echolocation. The Brazilian free-tailed bat has a unique echolocation call that varies between an almost pure constant frequency to that of a steep, frequency-modulated call. The constant-frequency component begins at about 28 kHz and sweeps slightly to about 25 kHz, whereas the frequency-modulated segment begins at about 60 kHz and sweeps abruptly to about 25 kHz. This bat is an open aerial straight-line pursuer of moths and other insects. The spectrograph depicted is recorded from an individual in real-time on 7/13/98 at Weiner Springs, Coconino County, Arizona.

Distribution. This species occurs throughout the southern United States and into Mexico, Central America, and South America. It also occurs on some Caribbean islands. In the Rocky Mountains, it occurs in the Four Corners states of Utah, Colorado, Arizona, and New Mexico. Although ranging to elevations of 2,500 meters (8,200 feet) on occasion in New Mexico, this species usually occurs below 1,829 meters (6,000 feet; Findley et al. 1975). Adams and Thibault (1999) documented a northern range extension for this species along the Front Range of Colorado with the capture of a male at a water hole in ponderosa pine habitat near Boulder. There is a single record from Cheyenne, Wyoming, of a male individual (Stromberg 1982), and two females were recovered from Big Horn and Sublette counties (Bogan and Cryan 2000). Records of this species in Wyoming come solely from the Wyoming State Veterinary Laboratory collections.

Subspecies Distribution: Monotypic species.

Ecology and Behavior. Brazilian free-tailed bats forage in a variety of habitats, from tropical forests to the deserts of the Colorado Plateau. This species forms enormous maternity colonies. The largest known colony in the world, estimated at twenty million adults, occupies Bracken Cave outside San Antonio, Texas. Colony size nearly doubles when the young are born, and it is estimated that there are currently one hundred million Brazilian free-tailed bats inhabiting south-central Texas. Individuals migrate southward for the winter. In the southeastern United States, colonies resident in human-made structures are unknown. Throughout its range, high-temperature roosts in attics or caves are preferred. Diet consists mostly of moths and beetles. Long, narrow wings allow for high-speed, long-distance flights, and individuals routinely fly 50 kilometers (30 miles) or more from their roost and to altitudes of 2,987 meters (9,800 feet) when foraging. Because of their large colony aggregations and large home ranges, this species is a major predator on night-flying insects, and studies have shown that they consume vast quantities of agricultural pests (McCracken 1999; Lee and McCracken 2002). Diet among individuals of the same colony is strikingly similar (Whitaker et al. 1996). Migrations of up to 1,840 kilometers (1,142 miles) have been documented (Glass 1982; Wilkins 1989). Roadrunners (*Geococcyx californianus*) are known to visit Brazilian free-tailed bat roosts to prey on individuals (Herreid 1960; Lee and Kuo 1999).

In Arizona, Brazilian free-tailed bats inhabit caves, mines, and occasionally old buildings and bridges. Large colonies are found in the vicinity of Eagle Creek, Greenlee County, in areas of desertscrub, but they occasionally move to higher elevations (Hoffmeister 1986). Large numbers were observed roosting in crevices over spillways at Davis Dam, Mohave County, in 1962 (Cockrum et al. 1996). In New Mexico, females arrive pregnant in spring at Carlsbad Caverns (Findley et al. 1975).

A bachelor colony inhabiting an abandoned mine in the San Luis Valley of Colorado is estimated to be 230,000 individuals (Adams 1989). Females and juveniles captured in the same valley later in the season suggest a nearby maternity roost (Svoboda and Choate 1987). The male individual captured at a water hole by Adams and Thibault (1999) was foraging in open ponderosa pine woodlands at about 1,829 meters (6,000 feet). In Utah, this species is known to roost in buildings (Long 1940; Hardy 1941; Musser 1961) but may also use caves (Stock 1965). Jackson and Herder (1997) reported captures of *T. brasiliensis* in riparian habitat mostly (76% of captures) but also in desert shrub (18%) and ponderosa pine (3%). Individuals were captured in riparian habitat in a small canyon in the Grand Staircase-Escalante National Monument as well (Day and Peterson 1999a).

Reproduction and Development. A single offspring is born per female in early to mid-June. Passage of the pup through the birth canal requires as little as ninety seconds. During the six weeks of parental care, pups are gathered into large "crèches" in densities that may exceed five thousand pups per square meter. Mothers roost apart from the pups but visit the crèche to feed them two or three times daily (Jones 2000). They locate their own offspring using spatial memory as well as audible calls and odor from the pup. In Texas, body mass of pups increased linearly over the first three weeks, with pups reaching about 80 percent of adult mass during this time (Kunz and Robson 1995). Females typically suckle their young for six to seven weeks and are known to suckle only their own offspring (McCracken 1984; McCracken and Gustin 1991; Kunz et al. 1995). Pups will alternate between teats up to five times during a single feeding (McCracken and Gustin 1991). Unlike temperate, hibernating vespertilionid bats, this species does not store sperm (Krutzsch et al. 2002). Life span is about ten years (Wilkins 1989). In Colorado, few females have been captured. Lactating females were captured at the Orient Mine, San Luis Valley, in 1978, and postlactating individuals occurred in 1979 (Freeman and Wunder 1988). A female captured in Colorado National Monument was lactating (Adams 1988), and a maternity colony of approximately two hundred individuals was photographed on 16 September 1996 by Joe Hall in Grand Junction, Mesa County.

Conservation Status. **Threat Medium** in west-central to eastern Utah and western Colorado. **Threat Low** in remainder of Rocky Mountain range.

Selected References

GENERAL

Altringham, J. D. 1996. *Bat: Biology and behaviour.* United Kingdom: Oxford University Press.

Armstrong, D. M. 1982. *Mammals of the canyon country: A handbook of mammals of Canyonlands National Park and vicinity.* Moab, Utah: Canyonlands Natural History Association.

———— 1987. *Rocky Mountain mammals.* Boulder: Colorado Associated University Press.

Armstrong, D. M., R. A. Adams, K. Navo, J. Freeman, and S. J. Bissell. 1995. *Bats of Colorado: Shadows in the night.* Denver: Colorado Division of Wildlife.

Clark, T. W, and M. R. Stromberg. 1987. *Mammals in Wyoming.* Lawrence: University Press of Kansas.

Findley, J. S. 1987. *The natural history of New Mexican mammals.* Albuquerque: University of New Mexico Press.

————. 1993. *Bats: A community perspective.* Cambridge: Cambridge University Press.

Foresman, K. R. 2001. *The wild mammals of Montana.* Lawrence, Kans.: American Society of Mammalogists, Allen Press.

Harvey, M. J., J. S. Altenbach, and T. L. Best. 1999. *Bats of the United States.* Asheville: Arkansas Game and Fish Commission.

Kunz, T. H. 1982. *Ecology of bats.* New York: Plenum Press.

Nowak, R. M. 1994. *Walker's bats of the world.* Baltimore: John Hopkins University Press.

Tuttle, M. D. 1988. *America's neighborhood bats.* Austin: University of Texas Press.

Ulrich, T. J. 1986. *Mammals of the Northern Rockies.* Missoula, Mont.: Mountain Press Publishing.

Wassink, J. L. 1993. *Mammals of the Central Rockies.* Missoula, Mont.: Mountain Press Publishing.

Wilson, D. E. 1997. *Bats in question*. Washington, D.C., and London: Smithsonian Institution Press.

Wilson, D. E, and S. Ruff. 1999. *The Smithsonian book of North American mammals.* Washington, D.C.: Smithsonian Institution Press.

Some Dissertations and Theses on Western Bats

Adams, R. A. 1989. Growth and development of flight morphology in the little brown bat, *Myotis lucifugus*. Master's thesis, University of Colorado, Boulder.

Adams, R. A. 1992. Developmental ecomorphology of the little brown bat, *Myotis lucifugus*. Ph.D. diss., University of Colorado, Boulder.

Bosworth, W. R. 1994. Characteristics of winter activity in *Plecotus townsendii* in southeastern Idaho. Master's thesis, Idaho State University, Pocatello.

Cramer, H. K. 1994. Torpor patterns and metabolic rate characteristics of *Myotis lucifuga*: Metabolic rate variability and effect of two ambient temperatures. Master's thesis, University of Colorado, Boulder.

Doering, R. W. 1996. Thermal implications of roost site selection in hibernating *Plecotus townsendii*. Master's thesis, Idaho State University, Pocatello.

Ellinwood, S. R. 1978. A survey of bats in southeastern Colorado. Master's thesis, University of Northern Colorado, Greeley.

Freeman, J. 1984. Ecomorphological analysis of an assemblage of bats: Resource partitioning and competition. Ph.D. diss., University of Colorado, Boulder.

Gannon, W. L. 1997. Assessing ecological interactions between bat species using morphological and acoustic techniques. Ph.D. diss., University of New Mexico, Albuquerque.

Lutch, D. J. 1996. Maternity roost characteristics and habitat selection of three forest-dwelling bat species in Arizona. Master's thesis, Arizona State University, Tempe.

Miller, P. H. 1964. The ecological distribution of mammals in Colorado National Monument, Mesa County, Colorado. Master's thesis, Oklahoma State University, Stillwater.

Reidinger, R. F., Jr., 1972. Factors influencing Arizona bat population levels. Ph.D. diss., University of Arizona, Tucson.

Sidner, R. 1997. Studies of bats in southeastern Arizona with emphasis on aspects of life history of *Antrozous pallidus* and *Eptesicus fuscus*. Ph.D. diss., University of Arizona, Tucson.

Wackenhut, M. C. 1990. Bat species overwintering in lava-tube caves in Lincoln, Gooding, Blaine, Bingham, and Butte counties, Idaho, with special reference to annual return of banded *Plecotus townsendii*. Master's thesis, Idaho State University, Pocatello.

Worthington, D. J. 1991. Abundance and distribution of bats in the Pryor Mountains of south-central Montana and northwestern Wyoming. Master's thesis, University of Montana, Missoula.

Wright, D. T. 1966. Morphological variation in the fringed myotis, *Myotis thysanodes* Miller (Vespertilionidae). Master's thesis, University of Arizona, Tucson.

CHAPTER 1: INTRODUCTION

Armstrong, D. M. 1995. A bat by any other name. *The Chiropteran* 3: 1.

Fenton, M. B. 1999. Describing the echolocation calls and behaviour of bats. *Acta Chiropterologica* 1: 127–136.

Freeman, P. W. 1998. Form, function, and evolution in skulls and teeth of bats. In *Bat biology and conservation,* ed. T. H. Kunz and P. A. Racey, pp. 140–156. Washington and London: Smithsonian Institution Press.

Gould, E. 1955. The feeding efficiency of insectivorous bats. *Journal of Mammalogy* 36: 399–406.

Griffin, D. G., R. A. Webster, and C. R. Michael. 1960. The echolocation of flying insects by bats. *Animal Behavior* 8: 141–154.

Griffin, D. R. 1958. *Listening in the dark.* New Haven: Yale University Press.

Hartridge, H. 1920. The avoidance of objects by bats. *Journal of Physiology* 54: 54–57.

Hill, J. E., and J. D. Smith. 1984. *Bats: A natural history.* Austin: University of Texas Press, in association with the Natural History Museum, London.

Kunz, T. H., and P. A. Racey. 1998. *Bats: Biology and conservation.* Washington, D.C.: Smithsonian Institution Press.

McCracken, G. F., and M. K. Gustin. 1987. Batmom's daily nightmare. *Natural History* 96: 66–73.

Reddell, J. R. 1968. The hairy-legged vampire, *Diphylla ecaudata,* in Texas. *Journal of Mammalogy* 49: 769.

Schutt, W. A., Jr. 1993. Digital morphology in Chiroptera: The passive digital lock. *Acta Anatomica* 148: 219–227.

———. 1998. Chiropteran hindlimb morphology and the origin of blood feeding in bats. In *Bat biology and conservation,* ed. T. H. Kunz and P. A. Racey, pp. 157–168. Washington and London: Smithsonian Institution Press.

Simmons, N. B. 2001. Reassessing bat diversity: How many species of bats are there in the world? *Bat Research News* 42: 179.

CHAPTER 2: PHYSIOGRAPHY AND ZOOGEOGRAPHY OF THE ROCKY MOUNTAIN REGION

Armstrong, D. M. 1972. *Distribution of mammals in Colorado.* Monograph No. 3. Lawrence: Museum of Natural History, University of Kansas.

———. 1982. *Mammals of the canyon country: A handbook of mammals of Canyonlands National Park and Vicinity.* Moab, Utah: Canyonlands Natural History Association.

———. 1992. Biogeography of the foothills of the Colorado Front Range. In *Colorado Field Studies,* ed. A. D. Hill, pp. 97–106. Boulder: Interdependence in Geographical Education, Commission on Geographical Education, International Geographical Union, University of Colorado.

Chronic, H. 1980. *A roadside geology of Colorado.* Missoula, Mont.: Mountain Press Publishing.

Durrant, S. D. 1952. *Mammals of Utah: Taxonomy and distribution.* Lawrence: University of Kansas Press.

Elias, S. A. 2002. *Rocky Mountains.* Smithsonian Natural History Series. Washington, D.C., and London: Smithsonian Institution Press .

Findley, S. J., A. H. Harris, D. E. Wilson, and C. Jones. 1975. *Mammals of New Mexico.* Albuquerque: University of New Mexico Press.

Fitzgerald, J. P., C. A. Meaney, and D. M. Armstrong. 1994. *Mammals of Colorado.* Denver and Boulder: Denver Museum of Natural History and University Press of Colorado.

Gregg, R. E. 1965. *The ants of Colorado.* Boulder: University of Colorado Press.

Hall, E. R. 1981. *The mammals of North America.* New York: John Wiley and Sons.

Hoffmeister, D. F. 1986. *Mammals of Arizona.* Tucson: University of Arizona Press.

Merriam, C. H. 1890. Results of a biological survey of the San Francisco Mountain region and desert of the Little Colorado in Arizona. *North American Fauna* 3: 5–34.

Mutel, C. F., and J. C. Emerick. 1992. *Grassland to glacier.* Boulder: Johnson Books.

Tranquellini, W. 1979. *Physiological ecology of the alpine timberline.* Berlin: Springer-Verlag.

Zwinger, A. H., and B. E. Willard. 1972. *Land above the trees: A guide to American alpine tundra.* New York: Harper and Row.

CHAPTER 3: EVOLUTIONARY ORIGINS AND ADAPTATIONS OF ROCKY MOUNTAIN BATS

Buchler, E. R., and S. B. Childs. 1982. Use of post sunset glow as an orientation clue by the big brown bat (*Eptesicus fuscus*). *Journal of Mammalogy* 63: 243–247.

Griffin, D. R. 1070. Migration and homing of bats. In *Biology of bats,* Vol. 1, ed. W. A. Wimsatt, pp. 233–264. New York: Academic Press.

Jepson, G. L. 1966. Early Eocene bat from Wyoming. *Science* 154: 1333–1339.

———. 1970. Bat origins and evolution. In *Biology of bats,* Vol. 1, ed. W. A. Wimsatt, pp. 1–64. New York: Academic Press.

Novacek, M. J. 1985. Evidence for echolocation in the oldest known bat. *Nature* 315: 140–141.

Schall, C. T., and W. Ziegler, eds. 1992. *Messel: An insight into the history of life and of the earth.* Oxford: Clarendon Press.

Smith, J. D., and G. Storch. 1981. New middle Eocene bats from Grube Messel near Darmstadt, W. Germany. *Senkenbergiana Biologica* 61: 153–167.

CHAPTER 4: BATS IN ROCKY MOUNTAIN ECOSYSTEMS

Adams, R. A. 1988. Trends in the reproductive biology of some bats in Colorado. *Bat Research News* 29: 21–25.

———. 1990. Biogeography of bats in Colorado: Ecological implication of species tolerances. *Bat Research News* 31: 17–21.

Aldridge H.D.J.N., and R. M. Brigham. 1991. Factors influencing foraging time in two aerial insectivores: the bird *Chordeiles minor* and the bat *Eptesicus fuscus. Canadian Journal of Zoology* 69: 62–69.

Arlettaz, R., G. Jones, and P. A. Racey. 2001. Effect of acoustic clutter on prey detection by bats. *Nature* 414: 742–745.

Benedict, A. D. 1991. *A Sierra Club naturalist guide: The Southern Rockies.* San Francisco: Sierra Club Books.

Brigham, R. M. 1990. Prey selection by big brown bats (*Eptesicus fuscus*) and common nighthawks (*Chordeiles minor*). *American Midland Naturalist* 124: 73–80.

Faure, P. A., and R.M.R. Barclay. 1992. The sensory basis of prey detection by the long-eared bat, *Myotis evotis,* and the consequences for prey selection. *Animal Behavior* 44: 31–39.

Finley, R. B., Jr., and M. A. Bogan. 1995. New records of terrestrial mammals in northwestern Colorado. *Proceedings of the Denver Museum of Natural History,* Series 3, 10: 1–6.

Fisher, C., D. Pattie, T. Harston. 2000. *Mammals of the Rocky Mountains.* Renton, Wash.: Lone Pine Publishing.

Fleming, T. H. 1993. Plant-visiting bats. *American Scientist* 81: 460–467.

Fullard, J. H., J. A. Simmons, and P. A. Sallant. 1994. Jamming bat echolocation: The dogbane tiger moth *Cynia tenera* times its clicks to the terminal attack calls of the big brown bat *Eptesicus fuscus. Journal of Experimental Biology* 194: 285–298.

Griffin, D. R. 1970. Migration and homing in bats. In *Biology of bats,* Vol. 1, ed. W. A. Wimsatt, pp. 233–246. New York: Academic Press.

Hoffmann, R. S., and D. L. Pattie. 1968. *A guide to Montana mammals: Identification, habitat, distribution and abundance.* Missoula: University of Montana Foundation.

CHAPTER 5: ROCKY MOUNTAIN BAT CONSERVATION STRATEGIES

Adams, R. A. 1990. Biogeography of bats in Colorado: Ecological implication of species tolerances. *Bat Research News* 31: 17–21.

———. 2000. Location and distribution of diurnal roosts, roost site parameters, and the use of water resources by Boulder County bats. Unpublished report to the City of Boulder Open Space Department.

Adams, R. A., and S. C. Pedersen. 1994. Wings on their fingers: Despite 50 million years of evolution, bats don't become expert fliers overnight. *Natural History* 103: 48–55.

Adams, R. A., S. C. Pedersen, K. M. Thibault, J. Jadin, and B. Petru. 2003. Calcium as a limiting resource to insectivorous bats: can water holes provide a supplemental calcium source? *Journal of Zoology* 260: 189–194.

Adams, R. A., and J. A. Simmons. 2002. Directionality of drinking passes at water holes: Is there cooperation? *Acta Chiropterologica* 4: 195–198.

Altenbach, J. S. 1998. Abandoned mines as bat habitat. *Cultural Resource Magazine* 7: 5–10.

Altenbach, J. S., and H. E. Milford. 1995. Evaluation and management of bats in abandoned mines in New Mexico. In *Proceedings of the 1993 Cave Management Symposium,* ed. D. Pate, pp. 326–330. Carlsbad, N.Mex.: National Cave and Karst Management Symposium.

Altenbach, J. S., and E. D. Pierson. 1995. The importance of mines to bats: An overview. In *Inactive mines as bat habitat: Guidelines for research, survey, monitoring and mine management in Nevada,* ed. B. R. Riddle, pp. 7–18. Reno: Biological Research Center, University of Nevada.

Annett, E. B., and J. P. Hayes. 2000. Influence of availability of snags and roost trees on presence and habitat use of bats in the Oregon Cascades. *Bat Research News* 41: 107.

Anonymous. 1992. Report of the 1992 Colorado Bat Trend Survey. *The Chiropteran* 2: 3–4.

Barclay, R.M.R., and R. M. Brigham. 1996. *Bats and forest symposium.* Working Paper 23. Victoria, B. C.: Ministry and Forests Research Program, British Columbia.

Bureau of Land Management (BLM). 1995. Prevention of potential bird and bat mortalities caused by production equipment design. Information Bulletin, Colorado IB–95–1.

———. 1996. Modification of oil and gas facilities to minimize bird and bat mortality. Information Bulletin, NTL 96–01.

Clark, D. R., Jr. 1991. Bats, cyanide, and gold mining. *Bats* 9: 17–18.

Codd, J., B. Clark, and K. Sanderson. 1999. Drinking by the common bent-wing bat *Miniopterus schreibersii* and calcium in cave water. *Bat Research News* 40: 9–10.

Crawford, R. L., and W. W. Baker. 1981. Bats killed at a north Florida television tower: A 25-year record. *Journal of Mammalogy* 62: 651–652.

Dahl, T. E. 1990. Wetlands: Losses in the United States, 1780–mid-1980. U.S. Fish and Wildlife Service Report to Congress, Washington, D.C.

Eisener, R., D. R. Clark, Jr., S. N. Wiemeyer, and C. J. Henny. 1999. Sodium cyanide hazards to fish and other wildlife from gold mining operations. In *Environmental impacts of mining activities: Emphasis on mitigation and remedial measures,* ed. J. M. Azcue, pp. 55–67. Berlin: Springer-Verlag.

Hall, J. 1993. Results of the Third Annual Bat Trend Survey. *The Chiropteran* 5: 3.

Humes, M. L., J. P. Hayes, and M. W. Collopy. 1999. Bat activity in thinned, unthinned, and old-growth forests in western Oregon. *The Journal of Wildlife Management* 63: 553–558.

Huston, A. M., S. P. Mickleburgh, and P. A. Racey. 2001. *Microchiropteran bats; global status survey and conservation action plan.* Gland, Switzerland, and Cambridge, UK: IUCN/SSC Chiropteran Specialist Group, IUCN.

Keeley, B. W., and M. D. Tuttle. 1999. *Bats in American bridges.* Resource Publication No. 4. Austin: Bat Conservation International.

Mann, S. L. 2002. Effects of cave tours on breeding *Myotis velifer. Journal of Wildlife Management* 66: 618–624.

Navo, K. W. 2001. The survey of evaluation of abandoned mines for bat roosts in the west: Guidelines for natural resource managers. *Proceedings of the Denver Museum of Nature and Science* 4: 1–12.

Navo, K. W., T. E. Ingersoll, L. R. Bonewell, A. J. Piaggio, N. Lamantia-Olson, and C. E. Wilkey. 2001. A Colorado case study to secure underground mines for bat habitat. In *Proceedings of bat conservation and mining: A technical interactive forum,* ed. K. C. Vories and D. Throgmorton, 96–100. N.p.: U.S. Department of Interior, Office of Surface Mining; Bat Conservation International, Inc.; and Coal Research Center, Southern Illinois University, Carbondale.

Osborn, R. G., K. F. Higgins, C. D. Dieter, and R. E. Usgaard. 1996. Bat collisions with wind turbines in southwestern Minnesota. *Bat Research News* 37: 105–110.

O'Shea, T. J., D. R. Clark, Jr., and T. P. Boyle. 2001. Impacts of mine-related contaminants on bats. In *Proceedings of bat conservation and mining: A technical interactive forum,* ed. K. C. Vories and D. Throgmorton, pp. 205–215. U.S. Department of Interior, Office of Surface Mining; Bat Conservation International, Inc.; and Coal Research Center, Southern Illinois University at Carbondale.

O'Shea, T. J., A. L. Everette, and L. E. Ellison. 2000. Cyclodiene insecticide, DDE, DDT, arsenic and mercury contamination of big brown bats (*Eptesicus fuscus*) foraging at a Colorado Superfund site. *Archives of Environmental Contamination and Toxicology* 40: 112–120.

Patriquin, K. 2000. Habitat use by bats in logged forests in northern Alberta. *Bat Research News* 41: 132.

Pierson, E. D. 1998. Tall trees, deep holes, and scarred landscapes: Conservation biology of North American bats. In *Bat biology and conservation,* ed. T. H. Kunz and P. A. Racey, pp. 309–325. Washington, D.C., and London: Smithsonian Institution Press.

Ramirez, P., Jr. 1999. Fatal attraction: oil field waste pits. *Endangered Species Bulletin* 104: 10–11.

———. 2000. Wildlife mortality risk in oil field waste pits. U.S. Fish and Wildlife Service Region 6 Contamination Bulletin. Cheyenne, Wyo.: U.S. Fish and Wildlife Service.

Saunders, W. E. 1930. Bats in migration. *Journal of Mammalogy* 11: 225.

Theis, M. L., K. Theis, and K. McBee. 1996. Organochloride pesticide accumulation and genotoxicity in Mexican free-tailed bats from Oklahoma and New Mexico. *Archives of Environmental Contamination and Toxicology* 30: 178–187.

Thibault, K. M, and R. A. Adams. 1998. Roosting behavior of bats in the Front Range of Colorado. Twenty-eighth North American Symposium on Bat Research, Hot Springs, Arkansas. *Bat Research News* 39: 190.

Thomas, D. W. 1988. The distribution of bats in different ages of Douglas-fir forests. *Journal of Wildlife Management* 52: 619–626.

CHAPTER 6: ACCOUNTS OF SPECIES

Adams, R. A. 1988. Trends in the reproductive biology of some bats in Colorado. *Bat Research News* 29: 21–25.

———. 1989. Population status of Brazilian free-tailed bats at the Orient Mine. Processed report, Colorado Division of Wildlife, Denver.

————. 1990. Biogeography of bats in Colorado: Ecological implications of species tolerances. *Bat Research News* 31: 17–21.

————. 1992. Comparative growth and development of the forearm between the little brown bat (*Myotis lucifugus*) and the Norway rat (*Rattus norvegicus*). *Journal of Morphology* 214: 251–260.

————. 1993. Consumption of water boatmen (Hemiptera: Corixidae) by little brown bats, *Myotis lucifugus*. *Bat Research News* 34: 66–67.

————. 1996. Size-specific resource partitioning among juvenile little brown bats (*Myotis lucifugus*): Is there an ontogenetic shift? *Canadian Journal of Zoology* 74: 1204–1210.

————. 1997. Onset of juvenile volancy and foraging patterns of little brown bats, *Myotis lucifugus*. *Journal of Mammalogy* 78: 239–246.

————. 2000. Wing ontogeny, niche dimensions, and adaptive landscapes. In *Ontogeny, functional ecology, and evolution of bats*, ed. R. A. Adams and S. C. Pedersen, pp. 275–316. Cambridge: Cambridge University Press.

Adams, R. A., and S. C. Pedersen. 1994. Wings on their fingers. *Natural History* 103: 48–55.

Adams, R. A., and K. M. Thibault. 1999. Records of the Brazilian free-tailed bat, *Tadarida brasiliensis* (Chiroptera: Molossidae) in Colorado. *The Southwestern Naturalist* 44: 542–543.

Adams, R. A., S. C. Pedersen, K. M. Thibault, J. Jadin, and B. Petra. 2003. Calcium as a limiting resource to insectivorous bats: can water holes provide a supplemental calcium source. *Journal of Zoology*, London, 260: 189–194.

Agosta, S. J. 2002. Habitat use, diet and roost selection by the big brown bat (*Eptesicus fuscus*) in North America: A case for conserving an abundant species. *Mammal Review* 32: 179–198.

Anderson, S. 1969. Macrotus waterhousii. Mammalian Species, American Society of Mammalogists, 1: 1–4.

Anthony, E.L.P., and T. H. Kunz. 1977. Feeding strategies of the little brown bat, *Myotis lucifugus*, in southern New Hampshire. *Ecology* 58: 775–786.

Arita, H. T., and S. R. Humphrey 1988. Revisión taxonómica de los murciélagos magueyeros del género *Leptonycteris* (Chiroptera: Phyllostomidae). *Acta Zoológica Mexicana*, Nueva Serie, 29: 1–60.

Armstrong, D. M. 1972. *Distribution of mammals in Colorado*. Monograph No. 3. Lawrence: Museum of Natural History, University of Kansas.

————. 1974. Second record of the Mexican big-eared bat in Utah. *The Southwestern Naturalist* 19: 114–115.

Armstrong, D. M., R. A. Adams, and J. Freeman. 1994. Distribution and ecology of bats in Colorado. *University of Colorado Museum, Natural History Inventory* 15: 1–82.

Arroyo-Cabrales, J., R. R. Hollander, and J. Knox Jones, Jr. 1987. Choeronycteris mexicana. Mammalian Species, American Society of Mammalogists, 291: 1–5.

Baltosser, W. H. 1980. A biological inventory of endangered species occurring in Guadalupe Canyon, Hidalgo County, New Mexico. New Mexico Department of Game and Fish, Contract 519–68–06, Final Report: 1–73. Unpublished technical report.

Barbour, R. W., and W. H. Davis. 1969. *Bats of America*. Lexington: University Press of Kentucky.

Beatty, L. D. 1955. The leafchin bat in Arizona. *Journal of Mammalogy* 36: 290.

Bell, G. P. 1985. The sensory basis of prey location by the California leaf-nosed bat, *Macrotus californicus* (Chiroptera: Phyllostomatidae). *Behavioral Ecology and Sociobiology* 16: 343–347.

Bell, G. P., G. A. Bartholomew, and K. A. Nagy. 1986. The role of energetics, water economy, foraging behavior, and geothermal refugia in the distribution of the bat, *Macrotus californicus. Journal of Comparative Physiology* 156B: 441–450.

Bell, G. P., and M. B. Fenton. 1986. Visual acuity, sensitivity, and binocularity in a gleaning insectivorous bat, Macrotus californicus (Chiroptera: Phyllostomatidae). *Animal Behavior* 34: 409–414.

Best, T. L., W. M. Kiser, and P. W. Freeman. 1996. Eumops perotis. Mammalian Species, American Society of Mammalogists, 291: 1–5.

Betts, B. J. 1997. Microclimate in Hell's Canyon mines used by maternity colonies of *Myotis yumanensis. Journal of Mammalogy* 78: 1240–1250.

Black, H. L. 1970. Occurrence of the Mexican big-eared bat in Utah. *Journal of Mammalogy* 51: 190.

———. 1972. Differential exploitation of moths by the bats *Eptesicus fuscus* and *Lasiurus cinereus. Journal of Mammalogy* 53: 598–601.

———. 1974. A north temperate bat community: Structure and prey populations. *Journal of Mammalogy* 55: 138–157.

Bleier, W. 1975. Early embryology and implantation in the California leaf-nosed bat, *Macrotus californicus. Anatomical Record* 182: 237–253.

Bogan, M. A. 1974. Identification of *Myotis californicus* and *M. leibii* in southwestern North America. *Proceedings of the Biological Society of Washington* 87: 49–56.

———. 1975. Geographic variation in *Myotis californicus* in the southwestern United States and Mexico. Fish and Wildlife Service, Wildlife Research Report, 3: 1–31.

———. 1999. Family Vespertilionidae. In *Mamíferos del noroeste de México*, ed. S. T. Alvarez-Castañeda and J. L. Patton, pp. 139–181. La Paz: Centro de Investigaciones Biológicas del Noroeste, S.C.

Bogan, M. A., and P. M. Cryan. 2000. The bats of Wyoming. In *Reflections of a Naturalist: Papers Honoring Professor Eugene D. Fleharty*, ed. J. R. Choate. Fort Hays Studies, Special Issue 1: 71–94.

Bradshaw, G. 1962. Reproductive cycle of the California leaf-nosed bat, *Myotis californicus. Science* 136: 645–646.

Caceres, M. C., and R.M.R. Barclay. 2000. Myotis septentrionalis. Mammalian Species, American Society of Mammalogists, 634: 1–4.

Chung-MacCoubrey, A. L. 1996. Bat species composition and roost use in piñon-juniper woodlands of New Mexico. In *Bats and forest symposium*, ed. R. M. R. Barclay and R. M. Brigham, pp. 118–123. Working Paper 23. Victoria: British Columbia Ministry Forestry.

Clark, B. S., D. M. Leslie, Jr., and T. S. Clark. 1993. Foraging activity of adult female Ozark big-eared bats (*Plecotus townsendii ingens*) in summer. *Journal of Mammalogy* 74: 422–427.

Clark, T. W., and M. R. Stromberg. 1987. *Mammals in Wyoming*. Lawrence: University Press of Kansas.

Cockrum, E. L. 1960. Distribution, habitat and habits of the mastiff bat, *Eumops perotis*, in North America. *Journal of the Arizona Academy of Science* 1: 79–84.

Cockrum, E. L., and A. L. Gardner. 1960. Underwood's mastiff bat in Arizona. *Journal of Mammalogy* 41: 510–511.

Cockrum, E. L., and B. F. Musgrove. 1964. Additional records of the Mexican big-eared bat, *Plecotus phyllotis* (Allen), from Arizona. *Journal of Mammalogy* 45: 472–474.

———. 1965. Extension of known range of the pocketed free-tailed bat. *Journal of Mammalogy* 46: 509.

Cockrum, E. L., B. Musgrove, and Y. Petryszyn. 1996. Bats of Mohave County, Arizona: Populations and movements. Occasional Papers 157. Lubbock: The Museum, Texas Tech University.

Cockrum, E. L., and E. Ordway. 1959. Bats of the Chiricahua Mountains, Cochise County, Arizona. American Museum Novitiates, 1938: 1–35.

Commissaris, L. R. 1961. The Mexican big-eared bat in Arizona. *Journal of Mammalogy* 42: 61–65.

Constantine, D. G. 1961. Spotted bat and big free-tailed bat in northern New Mexico. *Southwestern Naturalist* 6: 92–97.

———. 1998. An overlooked character to differentiate *Myotis californicus* and *Myotis ciliolabrum* (Vespertilionidae). *Journal of Mammalogy* 79: 624–630.

Cook, J. A. 1986. The mammals of the Animal Mountains and adjacent areas, Hidalgo County, New Mexico. Occasional Papers 4: 1–45. Albuquerque, N.Mex.: Museum of Southwestern Biology.

Cox, T. J. 1965. Behavior of the mastiff bat. *Journal of Mammalogy* 46: 687–688.

Cramer, H. K. 1994. Torpor patterns and metabolic rate characteristics of *Myotis lucifuga*: Metabolic rate variability and effects of two ambient temperatures. Master's thesis, University of Colorado, Boulder.

Crane, H. S. 1948. The mammals of Salt Lake County. Master's thesis, University of Utah, Salt Lake City.

Cryan, P. M., and M. A. Bogan. 2000. Recurrence of the Mexican long-tongued bat (*Choeronycteris mexicana*) at historical sites in Arizona and New Mexico. Unpublished technical report, U.S. Biological Survey.

Czaplewski, N. J. 1983. Idionycteris phyllotis. Mammalian Species, American Society of Mammalogists, 208: 1–4.

Davis, R. 1968. Wing defects in a population of pallid bats. *American Midland Naturalist* 79: 388–395.

Davis, R., and E. L. Cockrum. 1962. Repeated homing exhibited by a female pallid bat. *Science* 137: 341–342.

Davis, R. B., C. F. Herried II, and H. L. Short. 1962. Mexican free-tailed bats in Texas. *Ecological Monographs* 32: 311–346.

Davis, W. B. 1939. *The recent mammals of Idaho.* Caldwell, Idaho: Caxton Printers.

Davis, W. B., and R. Russell, Jr. 1954. Mammals of the Mexican state of Morelos. *Journal of Mammalogy* 35: 63–80.

Davis, W. B., and J. D. Schmidly. 1994. The mammals of Texas. Austin: Texas Parks and Wildlife, Nongame and Urban Program, and University of Texas Press.

Day, K. S., and L. C. Peterson. 1999a. 1998 baseline inventory of bat species in Grand Staircase–Escalante National Monument, Utah. Unpublished report submitted to the Bureau of Land Management, Grand Staircase-Escalante National Monument, Kanab, Utah.

———. 1999b. A bat survey of selected locations on Cedar City and Pine Valley Ranger Districts of Dixie National Forest, Utah: 1999. Unpublished report, United States Forest Service, Dixie National Forest, Cedar City, Utah.

Durrant, S. D. 1952. *Mammals of Utah: Taxonomy and distribution.* Vol. 6. Lawrence: Museum of Natural History, University of Kansas.

Easterla, D. A. 1965. The spotted bat in Utah. *Journal of Mammalogy* 46: 665–668.

———. 1972. Additional records of the pocketed free-tailed bat for New Mexico. *The Texas Journal of Science* 24: 543.

———. 1973. Ecology of eighteen species of Chiroptera at Big Bend National Park, Texas. *Northwest Missouri State University Studies* 34: 1–165.

Easterla, D. A., and J. O Whitaker, Jr. 1972. Food habits of some bats from Big Bend National Park, Texas. *Journal of Mammalogy* 53: 887–890.

Eger, J. L. 1977. Systematics of the genus *Eumops* (Chiroptera: Molossidae). Life Sciences Contribution 110: 1–69. Toronto: Royal Ontario Museum.

Ellinwood, S. R. 1978. A survey of bats in southeastern Colorado. Master's thesis, University of Northern Colorado, Greeley.

Everette, L. A., T. J. O'Shea, L. E. Ellison, L. A. Stone, and J. L. McCance. 2001. Bat use of high-plains urban wildlife refuge. *Wildlife Society Bulletin* 29: 967–973.

Faure, P. A., and R. M. R. Barclay. 1994. Substrate-gleaning versus aerial-hawking: Plasticity in the foraging and echolocation behaviour of the long-eared bat, *Myotis evotis. Journal of Comparative Physiology* 174: 651–660.

Faure, P. A., J. H. Fullard, and J. W. Dawson. 1993. The gleaning attacks of the northern long-eared bat, *Myotis septentrionalis*, are relatively audible to moths. *Journal of Experimental Biology* 178: 173–189.

Fenton, M. B. 1983. *Just bats.* Toronto: University of Toronto Press.

Fenton, M. B., and R. M. R. Barclay. 1980. Myotis lucifugus. Mammalian Species, American Society of Mammalogists, 142: 1–8.

Fenton, M. B., C. G. van Zyll de Jong, G. P. Bell, D. B. Campbell, and M. Laplante. 1980. Distribution, parturition dates, and feeding of bats in south-central British Columbia. *Canadian Field Naturalist* 94: 416–420.

Findley, J. S. 1954. Reproduction in two species of *Myotis* in Jackson Hole, Wyoming. *Journal of Mammalogy* 35: 434.

———. 1987. *The natural history of New Mexican mammals.* Albuquerque: University of New Mexico Press.

Findley, J. S., and C. Jones. 1961. A new United States record of the Mexican big-eared bat. *Journal of Mammalogy* 42: 97.

Findley, J. S., and G. L. Traut. 1970. Geographical variation in *Pipistrellus hesperus. Journal of Mammalogy* 51: 741–765.

Findley, J. S., A. H. Harris, D. E. Wilson, and C. Jones. 1975. *Mammals of New Mexico.* Albuquerque: University of New Mexico Press.

Finley, R. B., Jr., W. Caire, and D. E. Wilhelm. 1983. Bats of the Colorado oil shale region. *Great Basin Naturalist* 43: 554–560.

Fitch, J. H., and K. A. Shump, Jr. 1979. Myotis keenii. Mammalian Species, American Society of Mammalogists, 121: 1–3.

Fitch, J. H., K. A. Shump, Jr., and A. U. Shump. 1981. Myotis velifer. Mammalian Species, American Society of Mammalogists, 149: 1–5.

Fitzgerald, J. P., C. A. Meaney, and D. M. Armstrong. 1994. *Mammals of Colorado.* Denver and Boulder: Denver Museum of Natural History and University Press of Colorado.

Fitzgerald, J. P., D. Taylor, and M. Prendergast. 1989. New records of bats from northeastern Colorado. *Journal of the Colorado-Wyoming Academy of Science* 21: 22.

Ford, W. M., M. A. Menzel, J. M. Menzel, and D. J. Welch. 2002. Influence of summer temperature on sex ratios in eastern red bats (*Lasiurus borealis*). *American Midland Naturalist* 147: 179–184.

Foresman, K. R. 2001. *The wild mammals of Montana.* Lawrence, Kans.: American Society of Mammalogists, Special Publication No. 12, Allen Press.

Foster, D. A., L. Grignon, E. Hammer, and B. Warren. 1997. Inventory of bats in high plateau forests of central and southern Utah. In *Proceedings of the Third Biennial Conference of Research on the Colorado Plateau*, C. van Riper III and E. T. Deshler, pp. 63–72. Transactions and Proceedings Series. Flagstaff, Ariz.: National Park Service.

Freeman, J. 1984. Ecomorphological analysis of an assemblage of bats: Resource partitioning and competition. Ph.D. diss., University of Colorado, Boulder.

Freeman, J., and R. A. Adams. 1992. Project report: Conservation of Colorado's bat fauna; the effects of gating inactive mines on bat activity. Processed report to the Colorado Division of Wildlife, Denver.

Freeman, J., and L. Wunder. 1988. Observations of a colony of the Brazilian free-tailed bat (*Tadarida brasiliensis*) in southern Colorado. *The Southwestern Naturalist* 33: 102–104.

Freeman, P. W. 1981. A multivariate study of the family Molossidae (Mammalia: Chiroptera): Morphology, ecology, evolution. *Fieldiana, Zoology,* New Series, 7: 1–173.

Fujita, M. S., and T. H. Kunz, 1984. Pipistrellus subflavus. Mammalian Species, American Society of Mammalogists, 228: 1–6.

Gannon, W. L., R. E. Sherwin, T. N. deCarvalho, and M. J. O'Farrell. 2001. Pinnae and echolocation call differences between *Myotis californicus* and *M. ciliolabrum* (Chiroptera: Vespertilionidae). *Acta Chiropterologica* 3: 77–91.

Gardner, A. L. 1977. Feeding habits. In *Biology of bats of the New World family Phyllostomatidae,* Part 2, ed. R. J. Baker, J. K. Jones, and D. C. Carter, 293–350. Special Publications 13. Lubbock: The Museum, Texas Tech University.

Geluso, K. 2002. Records of mammals from Harding County, New Mexico. *The Southwestern Naturalist* 47: 325–329.

Glass, B. P. 1982. Seasonal movements of Mexican free-tailed bats *Tadarida brasiliensis mexicana* banded in the Great Plains. *The Southwestern Naturalist* 27: 127–133.

Hall, E. R. 1981. *Mammals of North America.* Vol. 1. New York: John Wiley and Sons.

Handley, A. H. 1959. A revision of American bats of the genera *Euderma* and *Plecotus. Proceedings of the United States National Museum* 110: 95–246.

Hardy, R. 1941. Some notes on Utah bats. *Journal of Mammalogy* 22: 289–295.

Harvey, M. J., J. S. Altenbach, and T. L. Best. 1999. *Bats of the United States.* Asheville: Arkansas Game and Fish Commission.

Hasenyager, R. N. 1980. *Bats of Utah.* Publication No. 80–15:109. Salt Lake City: Utah Division of Wildlife Resources.

Hayward, B. J. 1970. The natural history of the cave bat, *Myotis velifer.* Western New Mexico University Research in Science, Occasional Paper 1: 1–74.

Hayward, B. J., and E. L. Cockrum. 1971. The natural history of the western long-nosed bat *Leptonycteris sanborni.* Western New Mexico University Research in Science, Occasional Paper 1: 75–123.

Hayward, B. J., and S. P. Cross. 1979. The natural history of *Pipistrellus hesperus* (Chiroptera: Vespertilionidae). Western New Mexico University Office of Research, No. 3: 1–36.

Hayward, B. J., and R. Johnson. 1961. Notes on *Plecotus phyllotis* from Arizona. *Journal of Mammalogy* 42: 402.

Herly, R. H. 1979. Dietary habits of two nectar-feeding bats in southern Arizona and northern Mexico. *Journal of Arizona-Nevada Academy of Science* 14: 13–18.

Hermanson, J. W., and T. J. O'Shea. 1983. Antrozous pallidus. Mammalian Species, American Society of Mammalogists, 213: 1–8.

Herreid, C. F. II. 1960. Roadrunner a predator of bats. *The Condor* 62: 67.

Hill, J. E., and J. D. Smith. 1984. *Bats: A natural history.* Austin: University of Texas Press, in association with the Natural History Museum, London.

Hoffmeister, D. F. 1970. The seasonal distribution of bats in Arizona: A case for improving mammalian range maps. *The Southwestern Naturalist* 15: 11–22.

———. 1986. *Mammals of Arizona.* Tucson: University of Arizona Press.

Holloway, G. L., and R.M.R. Barclay. 2001. Myotis ciliolabrum. Mammalian Species, American Society of Mammalogists, 670: 1–5.

Howell, A. B. 1920. Contribution to the life history of the California mastiff bat. *Journal of Mammalogy* 1: 111–117.

Howell, D. J. 1974. Acoustic behavior and feeding in glossophagine bats. *Journal of Mammalogy* 55: 293–308.

————. 1980. Adaptive variations in the diet of desert bats has implications for evolution of feeding strategies. *Journal of Mammalogy* 61: 730–733.

Hoying, K. M, and T. H. Kunz. 1998. Variations in size at birth and postnatal growth in the eastern pipistrelle bat, *Pipistrellus subflavus* (Chiroptera: Vespertilionidae). *Journal of Zoology* (London) 245: 15–27.

Hoyt, R. A., J. S. Altenbach, and D. J. Hafner. 1994. Observations on the long-nosed bats (*Leptonycteris*) in New Mexico. *The Southwestern Naturalist* 39: 175–179.

Huey, L. M. 1925. Food for the California leaf-nosed bat. *Journal of Mammalogy* 6: 196–197.

Hutchinson, J. T., and M. J. Lacki. 2001. Possible microclimate benefits of roost site selection in the red bat, *Lasiurus borealis*, in mixed mesophytic forests of Kentucky. *Canadian Field Naturalist* 115: 205–209.

Jackson, J. G., and M. J. Herder. 1997. Baseline bat inventory of southern Utah using mist nets and ultrasonic detectors. Internal Report No. 97: 1–20. Cedar City, Utah: Utah Division of Wildlife Resources.

Jensen, J. N. 1965. The mammals of Rick County, Utah. Master's thesis, University of Utah, Salt Lake City.

Johnson, R. R., and J. E. Johnson. 1964. Notes on the distribution of bats and other mammals in Arizona. *Journal of Mammalogy* 45: 322–324.

Jones, C. 1965. Ecological distribution and activity periods of bats on the Mogollon Mountains area of New Mexico and adjacent Arizona. *Tulane Studies in Zoology* 12: 93–100.

————. 1966. Changes in populations of some western bats. *American Midland Naturalist* 76: 522–528.

Jones, C., and C. G. Schmitt. 1997. Mammal species of concern in New Mexico. In *Life among the Muses: Papers in honor of James S. Findley*, ed. T. L. Yates, W. L. Gannon, and D. E. Wilson, pp. 179–205. Special Publication 3. Albuquerque, N.Mex.: Museum of Southwestern Biology.

Jones, C., and R. D. Suttkus. 1972. Notes on netting bats for eleven years in western New Mexico. *The Southwestern Naturalist* 16: 261–266.

Jones, G. 2000. The ontogeny of behavior: A functional perspective. In *Ontogeny, functional ecology, and evolution of bats,* ed. R. A. Adams and S. C. Pedersen, pp. 362–392. Cambridge: Cambridge University Press.

Jones, J. K., Jr. 1964. *Distribution and taxonomy of mammals of Nebraska.* University of Kansas Publications 16. Lawrence, Kans.: Museum of Natural History.

Jones, J. K., Jr., R. P. Lampe, C. A. Spenrath, and T. H. Kunz. 1973. Notes on the distribution and natural history of bats in southeastern Montana. Occasional Papers 15. Lubbock: The Museum, Texas Tech University.

Keller, B. L., and R. T. Saathoff. 1995. A survey of day roosting by *Plecotus townsendii* in lava-tube caves at Craters of the Moon National Monument, Butte County, Idaho. Unpublished report, National Park Service, Arco, Idaho.

Kiser, W. M. 1995. Eumops underwoodi. Mammalian Species, American Society of Mammalogists, 516: 1–4.

Koopman, K. F. 1993. Order Chiroptera. In *Mammal species of the world: A taxonomic and geographic reference,* ed. D. E. Wilson and D. M. Reeder, pp. 137–241. Washington, D.C.: Smithsonian Institution Press.

Krutzsch, P. H. 1955. Observations on the California mastiff bat. *Journal of Mammalogy* 36: 407–414.

———. 1975. Reproduction of the canyon bat, *Pipistrellus hesperus,* in southwestern United States. *Journal of Anatomy* 143: 163–200.

Krutzsch, P. H., T. H. Fleming, and E. G. Crichton. 2002. Reproductive biology of male Mexican free-tailed bats (*Tadarida brasiliensis mexicana*). *Journal of Mammalogy* 83: 489–500.

Krutzsch, P. H., R. H. Watson, and C. D. Lox. 1976. Reproductive biology of the male leaf-nosed bat, *Macrotus waterhousii,* in southwestern United States. *Anatomical Record* 184: 611–635.

Kumirai, A., and J. K. Jones, Jr. 1990. Nyctinomops femorosaccus. Mammalian Species, American Society of Mammalogists, 349: 1–5.

Kunz, T. H. 1973. Population studies of the cave bat (*Myotis velifer*) reproduction, growth, and development. Occasional Papers of the Museum of Natural History, no. 15. Lawrence: University of Kansas.

———. 1974. Reproduction, growth, and mortality of the vespertilionid bat, *Eptesicus fuscus,* in Kansas. *Journal of Mammalogy* 55: 1–12.

———. 1982a. *Ecology of bats.* New York: Plenum Press.

———. 1982b. Lasionycteris noctivagans. Mammalian Species, American Society of Mammalogists, 172: 1–5.

Kunz, T. H., and W. R. Hood. 2000. Parental care and postnatal growth in the Chiroptera. In *Reproductive biology of bats,* ed. E. G. Crichton and P. H. Krutzsch, pp. 415–468. New York: Academic Press.

Kunz, T. H., and R. A. Martin. 1982. Plecotus townsendii. Mammalian Species, American Society of Mammalogists, 175: 1–6.

Kunz, T. H., and S. K. Robson. 1995. Postnatal growth and development in the Mexican free-tailed bat (*Tadarida brasiliensis mexicana*): Birth size, growth rates, and age estimation. *Journal of Mammalogy* 76: 769–783.

Kunz, T. H., J. O. Whitaker, Jr., and M. D. Wadanoli. 1995. Dietary energetics of the insectivorous Mexican free-tailed bat (*Tadarida brasiliensis*) during pregnancy and lactation. *Oecologia* 101: 407–415.

Kurta, A., G. P. Bell, K. A. Nagy, and T. H. Kunz. 1989. Energetics of pregnancy and lactation in free-ranging little brown bats (*Myotis lucifugus*). *Physiological Zoology* 62: 804–818.

Kurta, A., T. H. Kunz, and K. A. Nagy. 1990. Energetics and water flux of free-ranging big brown bats (*Eptesicus fuscus*) during pregnancy and lactation. *Journal of Mammalogy* 71: 59–65.

Kurta, A., and G. C. Lehr. 1995. Lasiurus ega. Mammalian Species, American Society of Mammalogists, 515: 1–7.

Kurta, A. T., and R. H. Baker. 1990. Eptesicus fuscus. Mammalian Species, American Society of Mammalogists, 356: 1–10.

Lampe, R. P., J. K. Jones, Jr., R. S. Hoffman, and E. C. Birney. 1974. The mammals of Carter County, southeastern Montana. Occasional Papers of the Museum of Natural History, no. 25. Lawrence: University of Kansas.

Lausen, C., and R.M.R. Barclay. 2002. Roosting behavior and roost selection of female big brown bats (*Eptesicus fuscus*) roosting in rock crevices in southeastern Alberta. *Canadian Journal of Zoology* 80: 1069–1076.

Lee, Y., and Y. Kuo. 1999. Roadrunner preys on Mexican free-tailed bat. *Bat Research News* 40: 4–5.

Lee, Y., and G. F. McCracken. 2002. Foraging activity and food resource use of Brazilian free-tailed bats, *Tadarida brasiliensis* (Molossidae). *Ecoscience* 9: 306–313.

Lengas, B. J. 1994. Summer 1993 bat survey of the Ashley National Forest. Unpublished report, Ashley National Forest, Vernal, Utah.

Leonard, M. L., and M. B. Fenton. 1984. Echolocation calls of *Euderma maculatum* (Vespertilionidae): Use in orientation and communication. *Journal of Mammalogy* 65: 122–126.

Lewis, L. 1994. Assessment of bat inventory and monitoring data in the Shoshone District BLM. Unpublished report, Bureau of Land Management, Shoshone District, Shoshone, Idaho.

Lewis, S. E. 1987. Low roost-site fidelity in pallid bats: Associated factors and effect on group stability. *Behavioral Ecology and Sociobiology* 39: 335–344.

———. 1995. Roost site fidelity of bats. *Journal of Mammalogy* 76: 481–496.

Long, C. A. 1965. The mammals of Wyoming. Vol. 14: 493–758. Lawrence: Natural History Museum, University of Kansas.

Long, W. S. 1940. Notes on the life history of some Utah mammals. *Journal of Mammalogy* 21: 170–180.

López-Wilchis, R., G. López-Ortega, and R. D. Owen. 1994. Noteworthy record of the western small-footed myotis (Mammalia: Chiroptera: *Myotis ciliolabrum*). *The Southwestern Naturalist* 39: 211–212.

Luce, R. 1998. Wyoming's bats: Wings of the night. *Wyoming Wildlife* (August): 17–31.

Mann, S. L. 2002. Effects of cave tours on breeding *Myotis velifer*. *Journal of Wildlife Management* 66: 618–624.

Manning, R. W. 1993. Systematics and evolutionary relationships of the long-eared myotis, *Myotis evotis*. Special Publication 37. Lubbock: The Museum, Texas Tech University.

Manning, R. W., and J. K. Jones, Jr. 1989. Myotis evotis. Mammalian Species, American Society of Mammalogists, 329: 1–5.

Martin, C. O., and D. J. Schmidly. 1982. Taxonomic review of the pallid bat, *Antrozous pallidus* (LeConte). Special Publications 18. Lubbock: The Museum, Texas Tech University.

McCracken, G. F. 1984. Communal nursing in Mexican free-tailed bat maternity colonies. *Science* 223: 1090–1091.

———. 1999. Brazilian free-tailed bat. In *The Smithsonian book of North American mammals,* ed. D. E. Wilson and S. Ruff, pp. 127–128. Washington, D.C.: Smithsonian Institution Press.

McCracken, G. F., and M. K. Gustin. 1991. Nursing behavior in Mexican free-tailed bat maternity colonies. *Ethology* 89: 305–321.

Merriam, C. H. 1886. Description of a new species of bat from the western United States (*Vespertilio ciliolabrum* sp. nov.). *Proceedings of the Biological Society of Washington* 4: 1–4.

Meyers, P. 1977. Patterns of reproduction of four species of vespertilionid bats in Paraguay. *University of California Publications in Zoology* 107: 1–41.

Miller, G. S., Jr., and G. M. Allen. 1928. The American bats of the genera Myotis and Pizonyx. *Bulletin of the United States National Museum* 144: 1–218.

Milner, J., C. Jones, and J. K. Jones, Jr. 1990. Nyctinomops macrotis. Mammalian Species, American Society of Mammalogists, 351: 1–4.

Mollhagen, T. R., and M. A. Bogan. 1997. Bats of the Henry Mountains region of southeastern Utah. Occasional Paper 170. Lubbock: The Museum, Texas Tech University.

Morales, J. C., and J. W. Buckley. 1995. Molecular systematics of the genus *Lasiurus* (Chiroptera: Vespertilionidae) based on restriction-site maps of the mitochondrial ribosomal gene. *Journal of Mammalogy* 76: 730–749.

Mumford, R. E., L. L. Oakley, and D. A. Zimmerman. 1964. June bat records from Guadalupe Canyon, New Mexico. *The Southwestern Naturalist* 9: 43–45.

Mumford, R. E., and D. A. Zimmerman. 1963. The yellow bat in New Mexico. *Journal of Mammalogy* 44: 417–418.

Musser, G. G., 1961. Mammals of the Tushar Mountains and Pavant Range in southwestern Utah. Master's thesis, University of Utah, Salt Lake City.

Nagorsen, D. W., and R. M. Brigham. 1993. *Bats of British Columbia.* Vancouver: Royal British Columbia Museum, University of British Columbia.

Navo, K. W., and J. A. Gore. 2001. Distribution of the big free-tailed bat (*Nyctinomops macrotis*) in Colorado. *The Southwestern Naturalist* 46: 370–376.

Navo, K. W., J. A. Gore, and G. T. Skiba. 1992. Observations on the spotted bat, *Euderma maculatum*, in northwestern Colorado. *Journal of Mammalogy* 73: 547–551.

Negus, N. C, and J. S. Findley. 1959. Mammals of Jackson Hole, Wyoming. *Journal of Mammalogy* 40: 371–381.

Nicholson, A. J. 1950. A record of the spotted bat (*Euderma maculatum*) for Montana. *Journal of Mammalogy* 31: 197.

Norberg, U. M., and J.M.V. Rayner. 1987. Ecological morphology and flight in bats (Mammalia: Chiroptera): Wing adaptations, flight performance, foraging strategy, and echolocation. *Philosophical Transactions of the Royal Society of London B* 316: 335–427.

O'Farrell, M. J., and E. H. Studier. 1973. Reproduction, growth, and development in *Myotis thysanodes* and *M. lucifugus* (Chiroptera: Vespertilionidae). *Ecology* 54: 18–30.

———. 1980. Myotis thysanodes. Mammalian Species, American Society of Mammalogists, 137: 1–5.

Ohlendorf, H. M. 1972. Observations on a colony of *Eumops perotis* (Molossidae). *The Southwestern Naturalist* 17: 297–300.

Oliver, G. V. 2000. *The bats of Utah: A literature review.* Publication No. 00–14. Salt Lake City: Utah Division of Wildlife Resources.

Paradiso, J. L., and A. M. Greenhall. 1967. Longevity records for American bats. *American Midland Naturalist* 78: 251–252.

Piaggio, A. J., E. W. Valdez, M. A. Bogan, and G. S. Spicer. 2002. Systematics of *Myotis occultus* (Chiroptera: Vespertilionidae) inferred from sequences of two mitochondrial genes. *Journal of Mammalogy* 83: 386–395.

Poché, R. M. 1975. New record of the bat *Plecotus phyllotis* from Utah. *Great Basin Naturalist* 35: 452.

———. 1981. Ecology of the spotted bat (*Euderma maculatum*) in southwest Utah. Publication No. 81: 1–63. Salt Lake City: Utah Division of Wildlife Resources.

Poché, R. M., and G. L. Bailie. 1974. Notes on the spotted bat (*Euderma maculatum*) from southwest Utah. *Great Basin Naturalist* 35: 121–122.

Poché, R. M. , and G. A. Rufner. 1975. Roosting behavior of male *Euderma maculatum* from Utah. *Great Basin Naturalist* 35: 121–122.

Priday, J., and R. Luce. 1996. Inventory of bats and bat habitat associated with caves and mines in Wyoming: Completion report. In *Endangered and Nongame Bird and Mammal Investigations. Annual Completion Report,* pp. 67–116. Cheyenne: Nongame Program, Wyoming Game and Fish Department.

———. 1999. New distributional record for the spotted bat, *Euderma maculatum*, in Wyoming. *Great Basin Naturalist* 59: 97–101.

Ranck, G. L. 1961. Mammals of the east Tavaputs Plateau. Master's thesis, University of Utah, Salt Lake City.

Reducker, D. W., T. L. Yates, and I. F. Greenbaum. 1983. Evolutionary affinities among southwestern long-eared *Myotis* (Chiroptera: Vespertilionidae). *Journal of Mammalogy* 64: 666–677.

Ross, A. 1961. Notes on food habits of bats. *Journal of Mammalogy* 42: 66–71.

———. 1967. Ecological aspects of the food habits of insectivorous bats. *Proceedings of the Western Foundation of Vertebrate Zoology* 1: 205–264.

Ruffner, G. A., R. A. Poché, M. Meirkord, and J. A. Neal. 1979. Winter bat activity over a desert wash in southwestern Utah. *The Southwestern Naturalist* 24: 447–453.

Schmidly, J. D. 1991. *The bats of Texas.* College Station: Texas A&M University Press.

Scott, J., D. M. Armstrong, S. J. Bissell, and J. Freeman. 1984. The bats of Colorado: Shadows in the night. Colorado Division of Wildlife, Denver. Pamphlet.

Sherwin, R. E., W. L. Gannon, J. S. Altenbach, and D. Strickland. 2000. Roost fidelity of Townsend's big-eared bat in Utah and Nevada. *Transactions of the Western Section of the Wildlife Society* 36: 15–20.

Shryer, J., and L. Flath. 1980. First record of the pallid bat (*Antrozous pallidus*) from Montana. *The Great Basin Naturalist* 40: 115.

Shump, K. A., and A. U. Shump. 1982a. Lasiurus borealis. Mammalian Species, American Society of Mammalogists, 183: 1–6.

———. 1982b. Lasiurus cinereus. Mammalian Species, American Society of Mammalogists, 185: 1–5.

Shuster, E. D. 1957. The taxonomy and distribution of the bats of Utah. Master's thesis, University of Utah, Salt Lake City.

Simpson, M. R. 1993. Myotis californicus. Mammalian Species, American Society of Mammalogists, 428: 1–4.

Smith, J. D. 1972. *Systematics of the chiropteran family Mormoopidae.* Miscellaneous Publications, no. 56. Lawrence: Museum of Natural History, University of Kansas.

Spencer, S. G., P. C. Choucair, and B. R. Chapman. 1988. Northward expansion of the southern yellow bat, *Lasiurus ega*, in Texas. *The Southwestern Naturalist* 33: 493.

Stock, A. D. 1965. Systematics and distribution of mammals of Washington County, Utah. Master's thesis, University of Utah, Salt Lake City.

———. 1970. Notes on the mammals of southwestern Utah. *Journal of Mammalogy* 51: 429–433.

Storz, J. F. 1995. Local distribution and foraging behavior of the spotted bat *(Euderma maculatum)* in northwestern Colorado and adjacent Utah. *Great Basin Naturalist* 55: 78–83.

Stromberg, M. R. 1982. New records of Wyoming bats. *Bat Research News* 23: 42–44.

Svoboda, P. L., and J. R. Choate. 1987. Natural history of the Brazilian free-tailed bat in the San Luis Valley of Colorado. *Journal of Mammalogy* 68: 224–234.

Swenson, J. E. 1970. Notes on distribution of *Myotis leibii* in eastern Montana. *Blue Jay* 28: 173–174.

Swenson, J. E., and J. C. Bent. 1977. The bats of Yellowstone County, south-central Montana. *Proceedings Montana Academy of Science* 37: 82–84.

Swenson, J. E., and G. F. Shanks. 1979. Noteworthy records of bats from northeastern Montana. *Journal of Mammalogy* 60: 650–652.

Toone, R. A. 1994. General inventory for bats in the Abajo and La Sal mountains, Manti-La Sal National Forest, Utah, with emphasis on the spotted bat (*Euderma maculatum*) and Townsend's big-eared bat (*Plecotus townsendii*). Unpublished report, United States Forest Service, Cedar City, Utah.

Turner, R. W. 1974. *Mammals of the Black Hills of South Dakota and Wyoming*. Miscellaneous Publication, no. 60. Lawrence: Museum of Natural History, University of Kansas.

Tuttle, M. D., and L. R. Heaney. 1974. Maternity habits of *Myotis leibii* in South Dakota. *Bulletin of the Southern California Academy of Science* 73: 173–174.

Twente, J. W. 1960. Environmental problems involving hibernation in bats in Utah. *Proceedings of the Utah Academy of Science* 37: 67–71.

Valdez, E. L. 1998. Noteworthy records of bats from southern Colorado. *The Prairie Naturalist* 30: 181–182.

Valdez, E. W., J. R. Choate, M. A. Goban, and T. L. Yates. 1999. Taxonomic status of *Myotis occultus*. *Journal of Mammalogy* 80: 545–552.

Valdez, E. W., J. N. Stuart, and M. A. Bogan. 1999. Additional records of bats from the middle Rio Grande Valley, New Mexico. *The Southwestern Naturalist* 44: 398–400.

Van de Water, P. K., and W. D. Peachey. 1997. Dietary analysis of the Mexican long-tongued bat (*Choeronycteris mexicana*) using pollen analysis of guano collected at Cienega Creek Natural Preserve. *Bat Research News* 38: 181.

Van Zyll de Jong, C. G. 1984. Taxonomic relationship of Nearctic small-footed bats of the *Myotis leibii* group (Chiroptera: Vespertilionidae). *Canadian Journal of Zoology* 62: 2519–2526.

———. 1985. *Handbook of Canadian Mammals*. Part 2, *Bats*. Ottawa: National Museum of Natural Sciences.

Vaughan, T. A. 1959. *Functional morphology of three bats, Eumops, Myotis, Macrotus*. Publication No. 12. Lawrence: Museum of Natural History, University of Kansas.

———. 1980. Opportunistic feeding by two species of *Myotis*. *Journal of Mammalogy* 61: 118–119.

Vaughan, T. A., and T. J. O'Shea. 1976. Roosting ecology of the pallid bat, *Antrozous pallidus*. *Journal of Mammalogy* 57: 19–42.

Wackenhut, M. C. 1990. Bat species over-wintering in lava-tube caves in Lincoln, Gooding, Blaine, Bingham, and Butte counties, Idaho. Master's thesis, Idaho State University, Pocatello, Idaho.

Wai-Ping, V., and M. B. Fenton. 1989. Ecology of the spotted bat (*Euderma maculatum*) roosting and foraging behavior. *Journal of Mammalogy* 70: 617–622.

Warner, R. M. 1982. Myotis auriculus. Mammalian Species, American Society of Mammalogists, 191: 1–3.

Warner, R. M., and N. J. Czaplewski. 1981. Presence of *Myotis auriculus* (Vespertilionidae) in northern Arizona. *The Southwestern Naturalist* 26: 439–440.

———. 1984. Myotis volans. Mammalian Species, American Society of Mammalogists, 224: 1–4.

Warren, E. R. 1942. *The mammals of Colorado*. Second rev. ed. Norman: University of Oklahoma Press.

Watkins, L. C. 1977. Euderma maculatum. Mammalian Species, American Society of Mammalogists, 77: 1–4.

Whitaker, J. O., Jr. 1972. Food habits of bats from Indiana. *Canadian Journal of Zoology* 50: 877–883.

Whitaker, J. O, Jr., and S. L. Gummer. 1992. Hibernation of the big brown bat, *Eptesicus fuscus*, in buildings. *Journal of Mammalogy* 73: 312–316.

Whitaker, J. O., Jr., C. Neefus, and T. H. Kunz. 1996. Dietary variation in the Mexican free-tailed bat (*Tadarida brasiliensis mexicana*). *Journal of Mammalogy* 77: 716–724.

Wilkins, K. T. 1989. Tadarida brasiliensis. Mammalian Species, American Society of Mammalogists, 331: 1–10.

Wilson, D. E, and S. Ruff, eds. 1999. *The Smithsonian book of North American mammals.* Washington, D.C.: Smithsonian Institution Press.

Winchell, J. M., and T. H. Kunz. 1996. Time-activity budgets of day-roosting eastern pipistrelle bats (*Pipistrellus subflavus*). *Canadian Journal of Zoology* 74: 432–441.

Woodsworth, G. C., G. P. Bell, and M. B. Fenton. 1981. Observations of echolocation, feeding behavior, and habitat use of *Euderma maculatum* (Chiroptera: Vespertilionidae) in south central British Columbia. *Canadian Journal of Zoology* 59: 1099–1102.

Worthington, D. J. 1991. Abundance, distribution, and sexual segregation of bats in the Pryor Mountains of south-central Montana. Master's thesis, University of Montana, Missoula.

Appendix 1
Bat
Conservation Programs

This Appendix is intended to be a resource for those interested in bat conservation at any level, from international or national to regional, state, or local. It provides information to help guide interested individuals to various organizations' web pages. Short descriptions and attributes of agencies and organizations are provided to give the reader some idea of their scope before venturing to the Internet. Descriptions are derived directly from web-site postings or other documents obtained from those organizations. Nonprofit organizations dedicated to the conservation of bats and to public education about the plight of bats are also included. The list begins with the groups of broadest scope and ends with regional and local grassroots organizations within the Rocky Mountain states.

UNITED NATIONS ENVIRONMENTAL PROGRAMME—WORLD CONSERVATION MONITORING CENTRE

The World Conservation Monitoring Centre (WCMC) was established in 2000 as the world biodiversity information and assessment center for the United Nations Environment Programme (UNEP). The Centre's roots date to 1979, when the International Union for Conservation and Nature (IUCN) established an office in Cambridge, United Kingdom, to monitor endangered species. In 1988 the independent, nonprofit World Conservation Monitoring Centre was founded jointly by IUCN, the World Wildlife Fund (WWF), and the United Nations Environmental Programme (UNEP). The transition to UNEP in 2000 received the full

Table A1.1. Summary of IUCN Threatened Bat Species per Risk Category

EX	EW	Sub-total	CR	EN	VU	Sub-total	LR/CD	LR/NT	DD	Total
12	0	12	29	37	173	239	0	209	60	520

EX = extinct	EN = endangered	CD = conservation dependent
EW = extinct in the wild	VU = vulnerable	NT = near threatened
CR = critically endangered	LR = lower risk	DD = data deficient

support of IUCN and WWF, as well as the political and financial backing of the UK government. A high-level Scientific Advisory Council that is closely linked to the UNEP Programme on Environmental Information, Assessment and Early Warning guides the Centre's work. At the WCMC web site (http://ims.wcmc.org.uk), data can be found on current listings and rankings of bat species living in the United States.

THE 2000 IUCN RED LIST OF THREATENED SPECIES

The International Union for Conservation and Nature (IUCN), through its Species Survival Commission (SSC), has for almost four decades assessed the conservation status of species, subspecies, varieties, and even selected subpopulations on a global scale. The Commission's motivation is to highlight taxa threatened with extinction and promote their conservation. Although today's IUCN operates in a very different political, economic, social, and ecological arena than when the initial IUCN Red Data Book was published, the SSC remains firmly committed to providing the world with the most objective, scientifically based information on the current status of globally threatened biodiversity. The taxa assessed for the IUCN Red List denote genetic diversity and the building blocks of ecosystems, and information on their conservation status and distribution provides the foundation for making informed decisions about preserving biodiversity at local to global levels.

The 2000 IUCN Red List of Threatened Species (www.redlist.org) provides taxonomic data, conservation status, and population distribution information on taxa evaluated using the IUCN Red List categories. This system is designed to determine the relative risk of extinction, and the main purpose of the IUCN Red List is to catalogue and highlight those taxa that are facing a higher risk of global extinction. The IUCN Red List also includes information on taxa that are categorized as Extinct or Extinct in the Wild, on taxa that cannot be evaluated because of insufficient data, and on Lower Risk taxa that are either near the threatened thresholds or would be threatened were it not for ongoing taxon-specific conservation efforts. Currently, a total of 520 of the 950 known species of bats are listed on the IUCN threatened species list. See A. M. Huston, S. P. Mickleburgh, and P. A.

Table A1.2. Natural Heritage Program Rankings of Bat Species in Rocky Mountain States

Species	Montana	Idaho	Wyoming	Utah	Colorado	New Mexico	Arizona
Townsend's big-eared bat *Corynorhinus townsendii*	G4/S2S3	G4/S2	G4/S1	ND	G4/S2	G4/S2	G4/S3
Allen's big-eared bat *Idionycteris phyllotis*	NO	NO	NO	NO	NO	ND	G3G4/S2S3
Big brown bat *Eptesicus fuscus*	ND	ND	ND	ND	ND	G5/S5	G5/S4S5
Silver-haired bat *Lasionycteris noctivagans*	ND	ND	ND	ND	ND	G5/S5	G5/S3S4
Western red bat *Lasiurus blossevillii*	NO	NO	NO	NO	NO	G5/S2	G5/S2
Hoary bat *Lasiurus cinereus*	ND	G5/S2	ND	ND	ND	G5/S3	G5/S4
Western yellow bat *Lasiurus xanthinus*	NO	NO	NO	NO	NO	G5/S1	G5/S1
Lesser long-nosed bat *Leptonycteris curasoae*	NO	NO	NO	NO	NO	G3/S1	G3/S2
Mexican long-tongued bat *Choeronycteris mexicana*	NO	NO	NO	NO	NO	NA	/S1
Southwestern myotis *Myotis auriculus*	NO	NO	NO	NO	NO	G5/S4	G5/S3S4
California myotis *Myotis californicus*	ND	G5/S1	ND	ND	ND	G5/S5	G5/S3S4

continued on next page

Table A1.2—Continued

Species	Montana	Idaho	Wyoming	Utah	Colorado	New Mexico	Arizona
Western small-footed myotis *Myotis ciliolabrum*	ND	G5/S4	ND	ND	ND	G5/S5	G5/S3
Western long-eared myotis *Myotis evotis*	ND	ND	G5/S1	ND	ND	G5/S4	G5/S3S4
Little brown myotis *Myotis lucifugus*	ND	ND	ND	ND	ND	G5/S5	G5/S3
Occult myotis *Myotis occultus*	NO	NO	NO	NO	NO	G5/S3	G5T3T4/S3
Northern long-eared myotis *Myotis septentrionalis*	G4/S2	NO	NO	NO	NO	NO	NO
Fringed myotis *Myotis thysanodes*	ND	G4G5/S1	G5/S1	ND	G5/S3	G4G5/S5	G4G5/S3S4
Cave myotis *Myotis velifer*	NO	NO	NO	NO	NO	G5/S4	G5S3
Long-legged myotis *Myotis volans*	ND	G5/S3	ND	ND	ND	G5/S5	G5/S3S4
Yuma myotis *Myotis yumanensis*	ND	G5/S3	G5/S1	ND	ND	G5/S5	G5/S3S4
Western pipistrelle *Pipistrellus hesperus*	ND	G5/S1	ND	ND	ND	G5/S5	G5/S5
Pocketed free-tailed bat *Nyctinomops femorosaccus*	NO	NO	NO	ND	ND	G4/S1	G4/S2S3
Big free-tailed bat *Nyctinomops macrotis*	NO	NO	NO	ND	G5/S1	G5/S2	G5/S2S3

Species								
Greater mastiff bat *Eumops perotis* *E. p. californicus*	NO	NO	NO	NO	NO	NO	ND	G5/S2S3 G5/S1S2
Underwood's mastiff bat *Eumops underwoodi*	NO	NO	NO	NO	NO	NO	ND	G4/S1S2
Brazilian free-tailed bat *Tadarida brasiliensis*	ND	ND	ND	ND	G5/S1	G5/S2	G5/S2	G5/S3S4
Pallid bat *Antrozous pallidus*	G5/S1	G5/S1	G5/S1	G5/S1	ND	ND	G5/S5	ND
Spotted bat *Euderma maculatum*	G4/S1	G4/S2	G4/S1	ND	ND	G4/S2	G4/S3	G4/S2
California leaf-nosed bat *Macrotus californicus*	NO	NO	NO	NO	NO	NO	ND	G4/S3
Ghost-faced bat *Mormoops megalophylla*	NO	NO	NO	NO	NO	NO	ND	G4/S1

KEY: G = Global Status
S = State Status
National Heritage Program Numerical Ranking System:
1 = critically imperiled or extremely rare; generally 5 or fewer occurrences
2 = imperiled or very rare; usually 6–20 occurrences
3 = very rare or found in a restricted range; 21–100 occurrences
4 = apparently secure
5 = demonstrably secure
NO = no known occurrence of species in that state
ND = no data on species in state

Racey, *Microchiropteran bats: global status survey and conservation action plan* (Gland, Switzerland, and Cambridge: IUCN/SSC Chiropteran Specialist Group, IUCN, 2001), 258.

UNITED STATES FEDERALLY LISTED ENDANGERED BAT SPECIES

In 1973 the United States Congress enacted the Endangered Species Act (ESA). The ESA requires the Fish and Wildlife Service to identify species of wildlife and plants that are endangered or threatened worldwide, based on the best available scientific information. Since its inception, thirteen bat species have been listed. These are the gray bat, *Myotis grisescens* (USA, central and southeastern); Hawaiian hoary bat, *Lasiurus cinereus semotus* (USA, HI); Indiana bat, *Myotis sodalis* (USA, eastern and midwestern); lesser long-nosed bat, *Leptonycteris curasoae yerbabuenae* (USA, AZ, NM; Mexico, Central America); little Mariana fruit bat, *Pteropus tokudae* (USA, western Pacific Ocean; Guam); Mariana fruit bat, *Pteropus marianus marianus* (USA, western Pacific Ocean; Guam, Rota, Tinian, Saipan, Agiguan); Mexican long-nosed bat, *Leptonycteris nivalis* (USA, NM, TX; Mexico, Central America); Ozark big-eared bat, *Corynorhinus townsendii ingens* (USA, MO, OK, AR); Virginia big-eared bat, *Corynorhinus townsendii virginianus* (USA, KY, NC, WV, VA); Singapore roundleaf horseshoe bat, *Hipposideros ridleyi* (Malaysia); bumblebee bat, *Craseonycteris thonglongyai* (Thailand); Bumbler's fruit bat, *Aproteles bulmerae* (Papua New Guinea); and Rodrigues flying fox, *Pteropus rodricensis* (Indian Ocean, Rodrigues Island). Only two of the bat species listed occur in the Rocky Mountain states, the Mexican long-nosed bat, *Leptonycteris nivalis,* and the lesser long-nosed bat, *Leptonycteris curasoae yerbabuenae*, both of which are pollinators of keystone desert plants.

Formerly, the Department of Interior used a category called Species of Concern that listed the western small-footed myotis (*Myotis ciliolabrum*), long-eared myotis *(M. evotis)*, fringed myotis (*M. thysanodes*), cave myotis (*M. velifer*), long-legged myotis *(M. volans)*, occult myotis (*M. occultus*), Yuma myotis (*M. yumanensis*), Townsend's big-eared bat (*Corynorhinus townsendii*), hoary bat (*Lasiurus cinereus*), spotted bat (*Euderma maculatum*), Brazilian free-tailed bat (*Tadarida brasiliensis*), big free-tailed bat (*Nyctinomops macrotis*), western mastiff bat (*Eumops perotis*), Underwood's mastiff bat (*E. underwoodi*), lesser long-nosed bat (*Leptonycteris curasoae*), Mexican long-nosed bat (*L. nivalis*), Mexican long-tongued bat (*Choeronycteris mexicana*), and the California leaf-nosed bat (*Macrotus californicus*). All of these species live in the Rocky Mountain West, and though a formal list of Species of Concern no longer exists, almost all are currently categorized as Sensitive Species by the Bureau of Land Management (BLM). In some cases, species are listed similarly by the United States Forest Service and in state-designated sensitive species documents. Species listed on the Sensitive List have no legal protection but are considered imperiled and in need of conservation efforts. Typically, such species are highlighted during management planning.

STATE AGENCY CONSERVATION EFFORTS AND LISTINGS

As mentioned above, some of the states in the Rocky Mountain region have established Sensitive Species lists based on rankings by the federal government or independent listings provided by conservation organizations, such as The Nature Conservancy's Natural Heritage Program (discussed in the following section). In the Rocky Mountain region, several state government agencies provide data on the status of bat populations.

Arizona

Arizona's Heritage Data Management System can be found at http://www.cnhp.colostate.edu/Projects/NSF/PowerPoint/Schwartz/Schwartz.htm. The web site lists the status of most species in the state, including bats. The data are portrayed in various formats, and the reader can sort the lists by scientific names, common names, or distributions among watersheds and counties.

Colorado

The Colorado Wildlife Commission consists of a ten-member board appointed by the governor, eight voting members and two nonvoting members. The nonvoting, or "ex-officio," members are the Executive Director for the Colorado Department of Natural Resources and the State Agriculture Commissioner.

The Wildlife Commission sets Colorado Division of Wildlife (CDOW) regulations and policies for hunting, fishing, watchable wildlife, nongame, and threatened and endangered species programs. The Commission also makes decisions about buying or leasing property for habitat and public access and approves the Division's annual budget proposals and long-range plans.

The CDOW has a bat page on its web site (http://wildlife.state.co.us) with general information on bat biology as well as bat houses and a species list for the state. In 1995, the CDOW published a free-to-the-public booklet entitled *Bats of Colorado: Shadows in the Night* (Armstrong et al. 1995).

New Mexico

The New Mexico Department of Game and Fish has established a database called Biota Information System of New Mexico, or BISON. BISON was developed by interagency cooperation between the New Mexico Department of Game and Fish and the Fish and Wildlife Information Exchange (College of Natural Resources, Fisheries and Wildlife Department, Virginia Polytechnic Institute and State University, Blacksburg, VA). Other contributing agencies include the U.S. Bureau of Land Management, U.S. Forest Service, U.S. Fish and Wildlife Service, U.S. Bureau of Reclamation, U.S. Army Corps of Engineers, New Mexico State Land Office, and New Mexico Natural Heritage Program (University of New Mexico). BISON contains accounts and rankings for all vertebrate and many invertebrate species of wildlife occurring in New Mexico and Arizona (including all threatened, endangered, and sensitive species). Many accounts are incomplete, although new information is added and the site does warn that errors in data entry may occur. Users are cautioned to refer back to the original cited source to assess completeness and correctness before using the information. Web updates are intermittent, not continuous, therefore some dynamic information such as legal status may not be current. The database is completely searchable when installed on stand-alone personal computers, and limited searches are available at http://nmnhp.unm.edu/bisonm/BISONM.CFM. Accounts can be accessed directly at www.fw.vt.edu/.

Utah

The Utah Conservation Data Center (http://www.dwrcdc.nr.utah.gov/ucdc/) of the State of Utah Natural Resources Division of Wildlife Resources contains data on "sensitive" as well as federally listed species. The web site also contains a publication produced in partnership with the Utah Natural Heritage Program entitled, *The Bats of Utah: A Literature Review* (Oliver 2000) that can be downloaded with Adobe Acrobat Reader. The paper has an extensive bibliography that includes hard-to-find literature and technical reports produced by individuals gathering data on bats in the state. This report gives taxonomy, distribution, wintering habits, abundance, habitat, and conservation information on the eighteen bat species inhabiting Utah.

STATE NONGAME PROGRAMS

Arizona

The Arizona Game and Fish Nongame Programs (http://www.gf.state.az.us/) includes the western red bat (*Lasiurus blossevillii*) on the department's draft list of Arizona Wildlife of Special Concern. It currently is not listed or proposed for listing by the U.S. Fish and Wildlife Service as endangered or threatened. In Arizona, all bats are protected through Commission Order 14, and cannot be taken alive or dead under the auspices of a hunting license. Bats cannot be imported, exported, or otherwise possessed without a special permit issued pursuant to Article 4 (Live Wildlife Rules). Although detailed information is lacking, loss of riparian and other broad-leaved deciduous forests is suspected to have had a negative effect on western red bats. Protecting riparian areas is cited as the best means of ensuring this bat species' continued existence. In addition, studies determining its basic life history information, population status and trends, and roost requirements are sorely needed.

Colorado

The Colorado Division of Wildlife's nongame efforts are supported in part by a state income tax program that allows residents to contribute on their state income tax form any amount they check off either from their tax refund or as a donation added to their total state tax bill. The contribution is tax deductible the following year. Since the inception of the checkoff program in 1978, the Division of Wildlife has used these monies to help fund some recovery efforts, including research projects leading to the conservation of bat species. In particular, studies have been conducted at the Orient Mine, located in the San Luis Valley, which houses a colony of Brazilian free-tailed bats *(Tadarida brasiliensis)* numbering in the hundreds of thousands. Money has also funded the Bat/Inactive Mine Program, whose mission is to census abandoned mines throughout the state and to gate mine openings where substantial bat populations are found to occur, especially colonies of Townsend's big-eared bat *(Corynorhinus townsendii)*.

Idaho

Idaho's Fish and Game Department's Nongame Wildlife Program (www2.state.id.us/ fishgame/info/nongame/nongame.htm) states that more than 80 percent, or 419 species, of Idaho's wild animals are classified as "nongame" wildlife. These include songbirds, waterbirds, raptors, small mammals, reptiles and amphibians, and threatened and endangered wildlife. Educational publications about bats consist of "Idaho's Bats: Description, Habitats and Conservation" (12 pp.) and "Building a Bat House" (1 p.). Under monitoring and research projects, they state that fourteen species of bats are known to occur in Idaho and that although studies and surveys have been conducted in some areas of the state, relatively little is known regarding the distribution and status of most species. The Department, the Bureau of Land Management, and the U.S. Forest Service (USFS) have begun an intensive effort to determine status, distribution, and habitat associations for bat species in Idaho. The nongame program also assisted Eastern Oregon State College and the USFS with the location automatic temperature and humidity recorders to measure environmental conditions in mines used as bat maternity sites in Hells Canyon. Under the Species of Concern subcategory "Undetermined Status Species," they listed the fringed myotis *(Myotis thysanodes),* western pipistrelle *(Pipistrellus hesperus)*, and spotted bat *(Euderma maculatum)*. There is also an Idaho Conservation Data Center and Rare Animal List that operates in concert with the Natural Heritage Network. It is the central repository for information concerning the state's rare plant and animal populations, and its aim is to provide accurate, comprehensive, and timely information on Idaho's rare species to decision makers at the earliest stages of land-management planning. The Idaho Fish and Game Department published its first list of "Species of Special Concern" in its 1981–1985 Nongame Management Plan. The list ranks ten of the fourteen species of bats in the state as rare as of April 2000.

Montana

The Montana Fish, Wildlife and Parks (http://www.fwp.state.mt.us/) nongame program relies on donations from the state's Watchable Wildlife Program income

tax checkoff. They have developed a Bat Education Trunk (www.fwp.state.mt.us/
educat/trunkeddt.htm#BatEducation) in concert with the Natural Resource Conservation Education Program and in cooperation with Bat Conservation International. The educational trunk aims at dispelling bat-related myths and fostering
respect for bats and includes videos, slides, displays, field tools, and a curricular
package. The target grade levels are third through eighth grade. The cost of using
the trunk is free if it is picked up at USFS; otherwise, patrons must pay the cost of
return shipping. Montana's *Fish, Wildlife and Parks News* has published several
articles on bats and their conservation.

New Mexico

New Mexico's Bat Population Database (BPD) is a work in progress. It is a
compilation of information that relates primarily to colony-size estimates or similar data for bats in the United States and Territories. The main objectives of the
BPD will be to test the usefulness of existing data as a framework for estimating
trends in bat populations and to allow researchers and resource managers access
to local historic information that may help in planning new studies on bat population trends. Those interested in macrobiogeographic and other analyses that
involve bat colony sizes, roost types, and so forth may also find this database
useful. It also is a source of bibliographic information related to bat populations.
The BPD is not intended to be a database of species distribution records, although information included may be of use in this regard (www.mesc.usgs.gov/
products/data/bpd/).

Utah

The Utah Department of Natural Resources (http://www.nr.state.ut.us/) published
an article in its newsletter *Utah Weekly Wildlife News* (http://yeehaw.state.ut.us/
yeehaw?DB=state&T=eutah&Query=bats) on October 23, 1998, titled "Abandoned Mines Reclamation Program Provides Misunderstood Bats Needed Protection." It describes how researchers have been tracking usage of three mines in
the Silver Reef District of southern Utah and have found that two of the mines are
being used by bats on their Sensitive Species list. One of the mines is used year-
round. The DNR also published *Utah's Southern Mammal Species,* featuring
species accounts of bats, which can be found at (http://yeehaw.state.ut.us/
yeehaw?DB=state&T=eutah&Query=bats).

Wyoming

The Wyoming Game and Fish Department web site is at http://gf.state.wy.us/.
Conservation efforts are directed through the Wyoming Natural Diversity Database (WYNDD) at http://uwadmnweb.uwyo.edu/wyndd/default.htm. Data in the
files at WYNDD are gathered, synthesized, and stored in the computerized Bio-

logical and Conservation Data System (BCDS). Information on the biology, location, and status of native plant and animal species and of natural communities is provided for management decisions in key resource areas. WYNDD distributes information to individuals and organizations involved with the conservation, management, and development of the state's natural resources. Because information in the database comes from a variety of sources, WYNDD provides as complete a picture of Wyoming's rare native biological diversity as possible. Information is gathered from on-the-ground surveys, published literature, unpublished reports, collections in museums and herbaria, and biologists and other knowledgeable individuals. Information in the files is updated constantly with new data. As more information becomes available, the status of each species or community is re-evaluated, and any necessary changes are made in the database. Information can be retrieved quickly and reported through data requests to WYNDD. Database searches are tailored to respond to individual requests.

Information available concerns species conservation and management status from the U.S. Fish and Wildlife Service, U.S. Forest Service, Bureau of Land Management, Wyoming Game and Fish Department, and Natural Heritage Network rankings. Information on the status of bat species in the state can be found at this web page, where searches can be carried out by species or by county.

RANKINGS BY NATURAL HERITAGE PROGRAMS: IMPERILED BAT SPECIES

Listings by The Nature Conservancy's Natural Heritage Program (http://www.natureserve.org) reflect a risk status for animals and plants that is independent from that of government agencies. However, some state and local agencies use these rankings to construct their own lists. The system combines the numbers 1–5 (with 1 being the most critically imperiled and 5 being the most secure) with the letters G (indicating Global Status: G1, etc.) and S (indicating State Status: S1, etc.). Thereby each species is ranked in terms of its overall global footing as well as its regional standing, which may differ significantly from one another depending on local population numbers and risks that particular species face.

INTERNATIONAL CONSERVATION EFFORTS FOR BATS

In 1999 the North American Bat Conservation Partnership (NABCP, www.batcon.org/nabcp/newsite/index.html) was established. The mission of the NABCP is to integrate and plan conservation efforts for bats on a continental scale. It is an alliance of working groups, bat researchers, nongovernmental organizations, and state and federal agencies from all three countries. The partnership has created a Strategic Plan that identifies conservation priorities. Through a vital communication network, information and resources are provided to aid local bat research, conservation, and education initiatives. In addition, the North American Symposium on Bat Research (NASBR, www.nasbr.com/) has been integral to bat research and conservation in North America for more than thirty years. It is an organization dedicated to the promotion and development of the scientific study of bats in all its branches, including conservation and public education. The group holds an annual meeting, usually in October, of professional bat researchers from throughout North America, with occasional attendees from Europe, Asia, Africa, and Central and South America.

COALITION OF NORTH AMERICAN BAT WORKING GROUPS

Several grassroots not-for-profit groups concerned about bat conservation exist in North America. At the largest scale are the Bat Working Groups. Currently, there are four such groups in North America: Western Bat Working Group, Mexican Bat Working Group, Northeast Bat Working Group, and Southeast Bat Diversity Network (Map A1.1). Visit the following web page for information on each group: http://www.batworkinggroups.org/.

Western Bat Working Group

The Western Bat Working Group, or WBWG, is made up of agencies, organizations, and individuals from thirteen western U.S. states and British Columbia, Yukon, and Alberta who are interested in bat research, management, and conservation. The WBWG grew from an effort in 1994–1996 to develop a rangewide conservation strategy for Townsend's big-eared bat *(Corynorhinus townsendii)*. The first informal meeting to discuss formation of the WBWG occurred in January 1996 as part of the Four Corners Regional Bat Conference sponsored by the Colorado Bat Society, Boulder (www.coloradobats.org). The first formal meeting of the WBWG was in February 1998 in Reno, Nevada, and the group currently works in an area encompassing ten ecoregions (Map A1.2), seven of which are in the Rocky Mountain region relative to this book.

Mission Statement

The goals of the WBWG are:

- to facilitate communication among interested parties and reduce risks of species decline or extinction;
- to provide a mechanism by which current information regarding bat ecology, distribution, and research techniques can be readily accessed;
- to develop a forum in which conservation strategies can be discussed, technical assistance provided, and education programs encouraged.

Organizational Structure

The WBWG is composed of a Steering Committee, state coordinators (for thirteen states total), and special committees to address specific bat conservation issues.

Map A1.1. Map of North American Bat Working Group boundaries (from Western Bat Working Group web page)

Priority Matrix for Western Bats

The Western Bat Working Group has derived a Regional Priority Matrix constructed at a workshop held in Reno, Nevada, in 1998. The matrix is intended to provide states, provinces, federal land-management agencies, and interested organizations and individuals a better understanding of the overall status of bat species inhabiting western North America. Color descriptors are used and designate conservation priority: **Red, or High,** ranking indicates that these species should be the highest priority for funding, planning, and conservation actions. Information about status and threats to most species could result in effective conservation actions being implemented should a commitment to management exist. These species are imperiled or are at high risk of imperilment. **Yellow,**

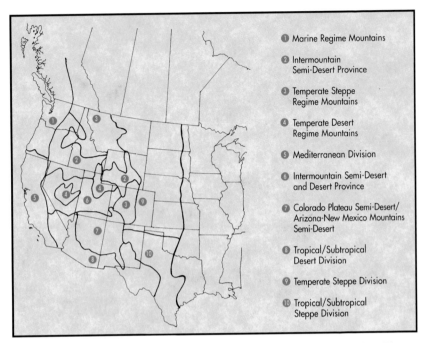

Map A1.2. Map of ecoregions used in assessing western bat conservation needs (from Western Bat Working Group web page)

or Medium, indicates a level of concern that should warrant closer evaluation, more research, and conservation efforts targeted at both preserving the species and reducing possible threats. A lack of meaningful information is a major obstacle in adequately assessing these species' status. **Green, or Low,** indicates that most of the existing data support stability for populations of the species and that the potential for major change in status in the near future is unlikely. There may be localized concerns, but the overall status of the species is believed to be secure. Conservation actions would still apply for these bats, but limited resources are best used on red or yellow species. Cells of the matrix are shaded gray to indicate "multiple habitat species," green indicates "tree-roosting species," olive codes for "cliff-roosting species," and orange indicates "cave-roosting species."

Mexican Bat Working Group

With approximately 140 bat species, Mexico has one of the richest bat faunas of the world. To protect its incredible bat diversity, many of the country's leading conservation authorities met in Monterrey in July 1999 to form the Mexican Bat Working Group (MBWG). As an active member of the North American Bat Conservation Partnership, the Mexican Bat Working Group (MBWG) plays a key role in protecting North America's bats.

Table A1.3. Western Bat Working Group Priority Matrix

Species	Region 1	Region 2	Regions 3, 4, 9, 10	Region 5	Region 6	Regions 7 & 8
Myotis auriculus	X	X	X	X	X	Yellow
Myotis californicus	Green	Yellow	Green	Green	Yellow	Green
Myotis ciliolabrum	Yellow	Yellow	Green	Yellow	Yellow	Yellow
Myotis evotis	Yellow	Yellow	Green	Yellow	Yellow	Yellow
Myotis lucifugus	Green	Green	Green	Yellow	Yellow	Yellow
Myotis occultus	X	X	X	X	X	Yellow
Myotis septentrionalis	X	X	Green	X	X	X
Myotis thysanodes	Red	Red	Yellow	Red	Red	Yellow
Myotis volans	Yellow	Yellow	Green	Red	Green	Yellow
Myotis yumanensis	Green	Yellow	Green	Green	Yellow	Green
Eptesicus fuscus	Green	Green	Green	Green	Green	Green
Idionycteris phyllotis	X	X	X	X	Red	Red
Antrozous pallidus	Red	Yellow	Green	Red	Yellow	Green
Tadarida brasiliensis	Green	X	Green	Green	Yellow	Green
Lasiurus blossevillii	X	X	X	Red	Red	Red
Lasiurus borealis	X	X	Green	X	X	X
Lasiurus cinereus	Yellow	Yellow	Yellow	Yellow	Yellow	Yellow
Lasiurus xanthinus	X	X	X	Red	X	Red
Lasionycteris noctivagans	Yellow	Yellow	Yellow	Yellow	Yellow	Yellow
Pipistrellus hesperus	P	Green	Green	Green	Yellow	Green
Euderma maculatum	P	Red	Yellow	Red	Red	Yellow
Nyctinomops femorosaccus	X	X	X	Yellow	X	Yellow
Nyctinomops macrotis	X	X	Green	Yellow	Red	Yellow
Eumops perotis	X	X	X	Red	Red	Yellow
Eumops underwoodi	X	X	X	X	X	Yellow
Mormoops megalophylla	X	X	X	X	X	Yellow
Macrotus californicus	X	X	X	Red	X	Red
Choeronycteris mexicana	X	X	X	Yellow	X	Red
Leptonycteris curasoae	X	X	X	X	X	Red
Myotis velifer	X	X	Green	X	X	Yellow
Corynorhinus townsendii	Red	Red	Red	Red	Red	Red

The MBWG has identified three groups of focal species:

- the priority species for conservation,
- the flagship species (those whose strong influence in ecosystems, attractive morphology, or otherwise important biology make them useful and give them high potential as tools to create and raise awareness in the public about bats), and
- the rainforest species, a large group that shares many threats and that if included in the priority species would swamp the other species there. Rainforest species would be saved if the rainforest is protected.

Organizational Structure

The leader of the Mexican Bat Working Group is Héctor Arita, and the Mexican scientist serving on the NABCP Executive Steering Committee is Rodrigo Medellín W.

ROCKY MOUNTAIN STATE WORKING GROUPS AND OTHER REGIONAL NONPROFITS

In addition to the larger Bat Working Groups, there are smaller local grassroots groups providing an arena in which the public can become involved in bat conservation efforts in their home area.

The **Utah Bat Working Group** (www.batworkinggroups.org/states/utah.htm) is currently in the process of preparing a statewide strategic plan for conservation and management of bats and their habitat.

Similarly, the **Colorado Bat Working Group** (www.batworkinggroups.org/states/colorado.htm) is currently in the process of completing a statewide conservation plan for bats.

The **Colorado Bat Society** (CBS; www.coloradobats.org) priorities are educational outreach and conservation. Its mission is to foster educational materials about bats and to work toward the conservation of bats and their habitats in Colorado. Currently, CBS is working with the Colorado Bat Working Group on a conservation strategy for bats in the state. CBS provides educational trunks, outreach and educational talks, and monitoring and research funds and also publishes a quarterly newsletter, *The Chiropteran,* for its membership.

The **Arizona Bat Resource Group** (www.batworkinggroups.org/states/arizona.htm) is in the process of compiling an Arizona Bat Conservation Strategic Plan.

The **Wyoming Bat Working Group** has begun work on the Burt House at Fort Laramie National Historical Site. This project is to relocate thousands of little brown myotis (*Myotis lucifugus*) from this historic building where they have roosted for more than one hundred years to artificial roosts built by the Park Service. The colonies are so large that there is concern that bat guano will begin to damage the building and artifacts.

Appendix 2
Agency Reports
by State

This appendix is a compilation of literature that may not be readily available to people involved with the conservation of bats. This literature appears as internal government publications and reports that, in many cases, like bats, rarely see the light of day. The list was generated using literature cited in sources that include databases and publications of government agencies and conservation groups, as well as electronic versions of literature citations gathered by many of those listed herein. I have arranged the citations by state and have updated the references to the best of my ability. Personal contacts are provided where available for each publication.

ARIZONA

Agyagos, J. D., D. Lutch, L. Bizios, and W. Michael Ross. 1994. Tonto Rim bat inventory and Cave Creek bat survey. U.S. Forest Service, Tonto National Forest, Payson Ranger District.

Arizona Game and Fish Department. 1991. Bats of the Tonto National Forest. Arizona Game and Fish Department, Nongame Branch, Phoenix.

Arizona Game and Fish Department. 1994. *Choeronycteris mexicana*. Unpublished abstracts compiled and edited by the Heritage Data Management System, Phoenix.

Arizona Game and Fish Department. In press. Wildlife of special concern in Arizona. Nongame and Endangered Wildlife Program, Phoenix.

Arizona Game and Fish Department. Nongame and Endangered Wildlife Program Technical Report 155. Phoenix.

Bain, J. R. 1988. Management recommendations for a nursery colony of Townsend's big-eared bat, *Plecotus townsendii*, in the Last Chance Mine, Horseshoe Mesa, Grand Canyon National Park. Arizona report to National Park Service, Grand Canyon National Park, and Arizona Game and Fish Department, Phoenix.

Bain, J. R., and H. Bodenhauser. 1986. Status of a nursery colony of Townsend's big-eared bat, *Plecotus townsendii*, in Stanton's Cave, Marble Canyon, Arizona. Unpublished report, National Park Service, Grand Canyon National Park, and Arizona Fish and Game Department, Phoenix.

Bogan, M. A. and C. A. Ramotnik. 1995. Baseline surveys for mammals in four riparian areas in Glen Canyon National Recreation Area. Unpublished report, Glen Canyon National Recreation Area, Page, Arizona.

Brown, P. E. 1995. Bat survey of Bill Williams River. Final report, Arizona Game and Fish Department, Phoenix.

———. 1996. Bat survey of the Bill Williams River, fiscal years 1994–1996. Unpublished report, Bureau of Land Management, Havasu Resource Area, Lake Havasu City.

———. 1997a. Bat survey of mines near Swansea town site, Mojave County, Arizona. Unpublished report, Bureau of Land Management, Havasu Resource Area, Lake Havasu City.

———. 1997b. Bat survey of mines near Planet Ranch on the Bill Williams River. Unpublished report, Bureau of Land Management, Havasu Resource Area, Lake Havasu City.

Burger, W. P. 2002. Region 6 bat inventory, monitoring, and management 1996–2001. Region 6, Field Operations Division and Nongame and Endangered Wildlife Program Technical Report 204. Arizona Game and Fish Department, Phoenix.

Burger, W. P., T. D. Hildebrandt, and S. D. Harris. 2001. Arizona Game and Fish Department Region 6 Wildlife Areas Nongame Inventories. Nongame and Endangered Wildlife Program Technical Report 196. Arizona Game and Fish Department, Phoenix.

Castner, S. V., T. K. Snow, and A. T. Holycross. 1996. Bat inventory of the Wet Beaver Creek Wilderness Area (Coconino County, Arizona). Nongame and Endangered Wildlife Program Technical Report 106. Arizona Game and Fish Department, Phoenix.

Castner, S. V., T. K. Snow, and D. C. Noel. 1993a. Bat inventory and monitoring in Arizona. Nongame and Endangered Wildlife Program Technical Report. Arizona Game and Fish Department, Phoenix.

———. 1993b. Bat inventory of the U.S. Army Yuma Proving Ground. Nongame and Endangered Wildlife Program Technical Report. Arizona Game and Fish Department, Phoenix.

———. 1994. Bat inventory and monitoring in Arizona, 1992–1994. Nongame and Endangered Wildlife Program Technical Report 54. Arizona Game and Fish Department, Phoenix.

———. 1995a. Bat inventory of the Imperial National Wildlife Refuge. Nongame and Endangered Wildlife Program Technical Report 70. Arizona Game and Fish Department, Phoenix.

———. 1995b. Bat inventory of the U.S. Army Yuma Proving Ground, Arizona: 1995. Nongame and Endangered Wildlife Program Technical Report 90. Arizona Game and Fish Department, Phoenix.

Cryan, P. M., and M. A. Bogan. 2000. Recurrence of the Mexican long-tongued bat (*Choeronycteris mexicana*) at historical sites in Arizona and New Mexico. Final report, U.S. Geological Survey Species at Risk Program.

Dalton, V. M., and D. C. Dalton. 1993. Assessment of impacts of low-level military aircraft on *Leptonycteris curasoae,* an endangered bat, at Organ Pipe Cactus National Monument, Arizona. Final report, Organ Pipe Cactus National Monument, Ajo and Luke AFB.

———. 1994. Roosting use of Agua Caliente Cave by the big-eared bat (*Plecotus townsendii*) and California leaf-nosed bat (*Macrotus californicus*). Unpublished report, Arizona Department of Game and Fish, Phoenix.

Dalton, V. M., D. C. Dalton, and S. L. Schmidt. 1994. Roosting and foraging use of a proposed military training site by the long-nosed bat, *Leptonycteris curasoae.* Final report, Luke Air Force Base Natural Res. Prog., Luke AFB.

Herder, M. J. 1997. Northern Arizona bat roost inventory. Arizona Fish and Game Department, Phoenix.

Kolazar, J. G., and T. K. Snow. 1999. Subalpine grassland bat survey on the Apache Sitgreaves National Forest. Nongame and Endangered Wildlife Program Technical Report 145. Arizona Game and Fish Department, Phoenix.

Lutch, D. J. 1996a. 1995 bat survey report for the Payson and Pleasant Valley Ranger Districts of the Tonto National Forest. U.S. Forest Service, Tonto National Forest, Payson Ranger District.

———. 1996b. 1996 bat survey report for the Payson and Pleasant Valley Ranger Districts of the Tonto National Forest. U.S. Forest Service, Tonto National Forest, Payson Ranger District.

O'Farrell, M. J. 1996. Development of vocal signatures as a method for accurate identification of free-flying bats in northern Arizona. O'Farrell Biol. Consult., Las Vegas, NV. Unpublished report, Arizona Game and Fish Department, Phoenix.

———. 1997. Summer bat survey—lower Virgin River Corridor. O'Farrell Biol. Consult., Las Vegas, NV.

Peachey, W. D., 1994. Nectar-feeding Mexican long-tongued bats (*Choeronycteris mexicana*) use of Soil Piping "Caves" in Cienega Creek Preserve, Pima County, Arizona. Unpublished report, Pima County Parks and Recreation.

Rabe, M. J., and H. Greene. 1997. Bat roost survey: Grassland habitat. Arizona Game and Fish Department, Phoenix.

Schmidt, S. L., and V. M. Dalton. 1995. Bat/mine survey, Dragoon and Chiricahua Mountains. Final report, Arizona Game and Fish Heritage Fund, Phoenix.

Schmidt, S. L., and S. DeStefano. 1997. Bat survey of San Bernardino and Leslie Canyon National Wildlife Refuges, Cochise County, Arizona. Final report, U.S. Fish and Wildlife Service Cooperative, Albuquerque.

Siders, M. S., and R. Steffensen. 1998. Spotted and western mastiff bat roost study of the North Kaibab Ranger District (Coconino County, Arizona). Kaibab National Forest, Fredonia, AZ. Final report, Arizona Game and Fish Department, Phoenix.

Sidner, R. and R. Davis. 1994a. Bat inventory of riparian areas of Fort Huachuca Military Reservation. Final report, Arizona Game and Fish Department, Phoenix.

———. 1994b. Bat survey of riparian areas in Rincon Mountains. Final report, Arizona Game and Fish Department, Phoenix.

————. 1994c. Bat inventory of the Buenos Aires Wildlife Refuge. Final report, Arizona Fish and Game Department, Phoenix.

Snow, T. K. 1998. Bat inventory of the Kofa National Wildlife Refuge. Nongame and Endangered Wildlife Program Technical Report. Arizona Game and Fish Department, Phoenix.

Snow, T. K., S. V. Castner, and A. T. Holycross. 1996. Bat management review 1995–1996. Nongame and Endangered Wildlife Program Technical Report 109. Arizona Game and Fish Department, Phoenix.

Snow, T. K., S. V. Castner, S. R. MacVean, C. R. Miller, and D. C. Noel. 1996. Spotted bat survey of the North Kaibab Ranger District (Coconino County, Arizona). Nongame and Endangered Wildlife Program Technical Report 102. Arizona Game and Fish Department, Phoenix.

Snow, T. K., S. V. Castner, and D. C. Noel. 1994a. Bat survey of Roaring Springs Cave (Coconino County, Arizona). Nongame and Endangered Wildlife Program Technical Report 58. Arizona Game and Fish Department, Phoenix.

————. 1994b. Bat survey of the Prescott National Forest (Yavampia County, Arizona). Nongame and Endangered Wildlife Program Technical Report. Arizona Game and Fish Department, Phoenix.

————. 1995a. Bat inventory and monitoring in Arizona: June–December 1994. Nongame and Endangered Wildlife Program Technical Report 77. Arizona Game and Fish Department, Phoenix.

————. 1995b. Bat survey of the Prescott National Forest (Yavapai County, Arizona). Nongame and Endangered Wildlife Program Technical Report 63. Arizona Game and Fish Department, Phoenix.

————. 1996. Bat inventory of abandoned mines: Bureau of Land Management-Tucson Resource Area (Pima County, Arizona). Nongame and Endangered Wildlife Program Technical Report 104. Arizona Game and Fish Department, Phoenix.

Snow, T. K. and J. G. Koloszar. 2000. Lesser long-nosed bat (*Leptonycteris curasoae*) surveys on various Bureau of Land Management properties in southeastern Arizona: 1997–1999. Arizona Game and Fish Department, Phoenix.

————. 2001a. Lesser long-nosed bat (*Leptonycteris curasoae*) surveys on the Bureau of Land Management properties in southern Arizona, 1997–1999. Nongame and Endangered Wildlife Program Technical Report 155. Arizona Game and Fish Department, Phoenix.

————. 2001b. ANABAT survey on Arizona Army National Guard properties, 1997–1999. Nongame and Endangered Wildlife Program Technical Report 156. Arizona Game and Fish Department, Phoenix.

COLORADO

Adams, R. A. 1989. Population status of Brazilian free-tailed bats at the Orient Mine. Processed report, Colorado Division of Wildlife, Denver, 15 pp.

————. 1990. Bat species abundance and distribution at Colorado National Monument. Processed report, Colorado National Monument Association Report, Fruita.

————. 1993. Report: Follow-up study of bat species presence and abundance at Colorado National Monument. Colorado National Monument Association Report, Fruita.

———. 1995. Boulder County bats: A one-year census. City of Boulder Open Space Department Report, Boulder.

———. 1996. Patterns of water use by Boulder bats. City of Boulder Open Space Department Report, Boulder.

———. 1997. Survey of Boulder County bats: A study in biodiversity and community ecology. City of Boulder Open Space Department Report, Boulder.

———. 1998. Survey of Boulder County bats: A study in roost site distribution and community ecology. City of Boulder Open Space Department Report, Boulder.

———. 2000. Location and distribution of diurnal roosts, roost site parameters, and the use of water resources by Boulder County bats. City of Boulder Open Space Department Report, Boulder.

———. 2001. Location and distribution of diurnal roosts, roost site parameters, and the use of water resources by Boulder County bats. City of Boulder Open Space Department Report, Boulder.

———. 2002. 2002 Final report: Census and radio telemetry of bats at Heil Valley Ranch. Boulder County Parks and Open Space Department, Boulder.

Adams, R. A., and J. Freeman. 1993. Status of Townsend's big-eared bats at historic cave sites in Colorado. Processed report, Colorado Division of Wildlife.

Adams, R. A., and K. M. Thibault. 1999. Roosting and foraging ecology of Boulder County bats. City of Boulder Open Space Department Report, Boulder.

Armstrong, D. M., and J. Freeman, eds. 1982. Mammals of the Boulder Mountain Parks. Unpublished report, City of Boulder Department of Parks and Recreation, Boulder.

Burghardt, J. E. 1996. Effective management of radiological hazards at abandoned radioactive mine and mill sites. Unpublished report, National Park Service, Denver. (http://www2.nature.nps.gov/grd/distland/amlindex.html#technicalreports)

———. 1997. Bat-compatible closures of abandoned underground mines in National Park system units. Abstract, 1997 National Meeting of the American Society of Surface Mining and Reclamation, Austin.

———. 2000. Bat-compatible closures of abandoned underground mines in National Park system. Office of Surface Mining Technical Interactive Forum on Bat Conservation and Mining, St. Louis. (http://www2.nature.nps.gov/grd/distland/amlindex.html#technicalreports)

Everette, A. L., T. J. O'Shea, and L. A. Stone. 1997. Bats of the Rocky Mountain Arsenal National Wildlife Area: Status and potential impacts of contaminants. Fiscal Year 1997 Progress Report to U.S. Fish and Wildlife Service.

Finch, D. M. 1992. Threatened, endangered and vulnerable species of terrestrial vertebrates in the Rocky Mountain Region. Rocky Mountain Forest and Range Experimental Station, Fort Collins.

Freeman, J., and R. A. Adams. 1992. Project report: Conservation of Colorado's bat fauna; the effects of gating inactive mines on bat activity. Processed report, Colorado Division of Wildlife, Denver.

Graul, W., J. Freeman, and L. Wunder. 1981. Statewide bat distribution study. Unpublished report, Colorado Division of Wildlife, Denver.

Navo, K. W. 1990. Spotted bat (*Euderma maculatum*) surveys on the Green River, Dinosaur National Monument. Processed report, Colorado Division of Wildlife, Denver.

————. 1993. Mesa Verde National Park spotted bat (*Euderma maculatum*) survey. Processed report, Colorado Division of Wildlife, Denver.

————. 1994. Guidelines for the survey of caves and abandoned mines for bats in Colorado. Colorado Division of Wildlife, Denver.

Navo, K. W., and T. Ingersoll. 1992. Bats/Inactive Mines Project Report. Processed report, Colorado Division of Wildlife, Denver.

————. 1993. Bats/Inactive Mines Project Report: 1991–1993 Summary. Processed report, Colorado Division of Wildlife.

————. 1994. Bats/Inactive Mines Project Report. Processed report, Colorado Division of Wildlife, Denver.

————. 1995. Bats/Inactive Mines Project Report. Processed report, Colorado Division of Wildlife, Denver.

————. 1995. Tenderfoot Mesa bats/abandoned mines survey report. Processed report, Colorado Division of Wildlife.

————. 1996. Bats/Inactive Mines Project Report. Processed report, Colorado Division of Wildlife, Denver.

————. 1997. Bureau of Land Management 1997 bat/mine evaluations. Processed report, Colorado Division of Wildlife, Denver.

————. 1997. Colorado bats/inactive mines project B/IMP 1997 project summary. Processed report, Colorado Division of Wildlife, Denver.

Navo, K. W., T. E. Ingersoll., and C. E. Wilkey. 1996. BLM bat/abandoned mines summary report. Processed report, Colorado Division of Wildlife, Denver.

Navo, K. W., and C. Knapp. 1991. Bats/Inactive Mines Project Report. Processed report, Colorado Division of Wildlife, Denver.

Navo, K. W., and A. J. Piaggio. 1996. Final report: Colorado Bats/Inactive Mine Project. Bat evaluations on Dillon Ranger District. Processed report, Colorado Division of Wildlife, Denver.

Navo, K. W., and C. E. Wilkey. 1997. Pike/San Isabel National Forest 1997 bat/mine evaluations. Processed report, Colorado Division of Wildlife, Denver.

O'Shea, T. J., and M. A. Bogan, eds. 2000. Interim report of the Workshop on Monitoring Trends in U.S. Bat Populations: Problems and Prospects. [On-line interim report]. U.S. Geological Survey, Midcontinent Ecological Science Center, Fort Collins. http://www.mesc.usgs.gov/BPD/ireport.htm

Somers, P. 1978. Faunal inventory: San Miguel Project. Final report, Bureau of Reclamation, Durango.

IDAHO

Arthur, W. J., J. W. Connelly, D. K. Halford, and T. D. Reynolds. 1984. Vertebrates of the Idaho National Engineering Laboratory, DOE/Id–12099. U.S. Department of Energy, Idaho Falls.

Bohn, K., and B. L. Keller. 1997a. Forest dwelling bat populations in the Crystal Creek Area, Pocatello Ranger District, Caribou National Forest. Caribou National Forest, Pocatello.

————. 1997b. Forest dwelling bat populations in the Crystal Creek Area, Pocatello Ranger District, Caribou National Forest. Caribou National Forest: Second Year. Caribou National Forest, Pocatello.

Cassirer, E. F. 1995. Wildlife inventory, Craig Mountain, Idaho. Idaho Department of Fish and Game, Nongame and Endangered Wildlife Program, Boise.

Clark, T., T. Campbell, B. Keller, and F. R. Rose. 1980. Inventory of threatened, endangered, and sensitive mammal species in the Burley BLM District. Final report, Western Environmental Research Associates, Pocatello.

Dalke, P. D. 1973. A partial bibliography of Idaho wildlife. Wildlife Bulletin No. 6–1973, Idaho Fish and Game Department, Boise.

Doering, R. W., and B. L. Keller. 1996. A survey of bat species of the Bruneau-Jarbidge River area of southwestern Idaho with special reference to the occurrence of the spotted bat (*Euderma maculatum*). Draft Technical Bulletin, Idaho Bureau of Land Management, Boise.

Fenton, M. B., D. C. Tennant, and J. Wyszecki. 1983. A survey of the distribution of *Euderma maculatum* (Chiroptera: Vespertilionidae) throughout its known range in the United States and Canada by monitoring its audible echolocation calls. Unpublished report, U.S. Fish and Wildlife Service, Boise.

Groves, C. R. 1987. A bibliography of Idaho mammalogy (1940–1987). Idaho Natural Heritage Program, Idaho Department of Fish and Game, Boise.

Groves, C. R., B. Butterfield, A. Lippincott, B. Csuti, and J. M. Scott. 1997. Atlas of Idaho's wildlife: Integrating gap analysis and natural heritage information. Idaho Department of Fish and Game, Nongame and Endangered Wildlife Program, Boise.

Gunnell, F., and T. A. Phillips. 1972. Wildlife analysis of the White Cloud, Boulder and Pioneer Mountains. USDA Forest Service, Intermountain Region, Ogden.

Hanna, P. 1978. Bighorn sheep: Surveys and inventories. Unpublished report, Idaho Department of Fish and Game.

Howard, P. E., and D. Hintzman. 1964. Zortman Cave survey project. Unpublished U.S. Forest Service Memo 2300 (2800), Lewis and Clark National Forest, Boise.

Idaho State Conservation Effort. 1995. Habitat conservation assessment and conservation strategy for the Townsend's big-eared bat. Draft Unpublished Report No. 1, Boise.

Keller, B. L. 1980. Spotted bat, pygmy rabbit, sagebrush vole. In *Inventory of threatened, endangered and sensitive mammal species in the Burley BLM District,* pp. 36–51. Final report, Western Environmental Research Associates, Pocatello.

———. 1981. The status of the spotted bat in Cassia County, Idaho. In *Inventory of threatened, endangered and sensitive mammal species in the Burley BLM District,* pp. 29–38. Final report, Western Environmental Research Associates, Pocatello.

———. 1987. Analysis of the bat species present in Idaho, with special attention to the spotted bat, *Euderma maculatum*. Final report, Department of Biological Sciences, Idaho State University, Pocatello.

———. 1992. The status of bat populations at selected localities in Owyhee County, Idaho. Unpublished report, Science Applications International, Boise.

———. 1994. The status of bat populations in the Craig Mountain area, Nez Perce County, Idaho. Cooperative Challenge Cost-Share Project, Idaho Department of Fish and Game, Boise.

———. 1995. The status of bat populations in selected mines in the Silver Valley, Kootenai and Shoshone Counties and the Clark Fork area, Bonner County, Idaho. Final report, Idaho Department of Fish and Game, Conservation Data Center, and Bureau of Land Management Coeur d'Alene, Cooperative Challenge Cost-Share Project, Boise.

————. 1996. The status of selected mines as bat habitat in the greater Coeur d'Alene mining region, Kootenai and Shoshone Counties, Idaho, with special reference to mines near Clark Fork, Bonner County, Idaho: Research Year 2. Draft Challenge Cost-Share Report, Bureau of Land Management, Coeur d'Alene.

————. 1997a. An analysis of bat occupancy of selected inactive mines located adjacent to the shore of Lake Pend Oreille, Bonner County, and the Bethlehem and Montgomery Mine, Boundary County, Idaho. Idaho Panhandle National Forests, Bonners Ferry Ranger District, Bonners Ferry.

————. 1997b. An analysis of selected mines as bat habitat in the greater Coeur d'Alene mining region, Shoshone County, Idaho, with special reference to mines near Clark Fork, Bonner County, Idaho: Summary and Research Year 3. Bureau of Land Management, Coeur d'Alene.

Keller, B. L., W. R. Bosworth, and R. W. Doering. 1993. Bat habitat research. Final Technical Report, Idaho State University, Pocatello.

————. 1994. The status of bat populations in and adjacent to the C. J. Strike Reservoir Area, Owyhee County, Idaho. Idaho Power Corporation, Boise.

Keller, B. L., and R. W. Doering. 1994. The status of bat populations in the Idaho Panhandle National Forests, Coeur d'Alene.

————. 1995. The status of bat populations in the Idaho Panhandle National Forest. Idaho Panhandle National Forests Contract No 53–0281–8–51, Coeur d'Alene.

Keller, B. L., and R. T. Saathoff. 1995. A survey of day roosting by *Plecotus townsendii* in lava-tube caves at Craters of the Moon National Monument, Butte County, ID. National Park Service, Craters of the Moon National Monument, Arco.

————. 1996. A netting survey of water and cave areas used by bats at Craters of the Moon National Monument, Butte County, Idaho. National Park Service, Craters of the Moon National Monument, Arco.

Klott, J. 1996. Sensitive animals of the Jarbidge Resource Area, Idaho. Idaho Bureau of Land Management Technical Bulletin 96–10.

Lengas, B. J. 1993a. A survey of the American Phosphate Corporation mine (Montpelier Canyon), Parts 1–10. USDA Forest Service, Caribou National Forest, Pocatello.

Lengas, B. J. 1993b. A survey of the bats of the Minnetonka Cave and four nearby adits. USDA Forest Service, Caribou National Forest, Montpelier.

Lengas, B. J. 1993c. Unpublished reports, Caribou National Forest Supervisors Office, Pocatello.

Lengas, B. J. 1994. Unpublished reports, Caribou National Forest Supervisors Office, Pocatello.

Lengas, B. J. 1995a. A summer bat survey of the caves and abandoned mines on the Montpelier Ranger District of the Caribou National Forest. USDA Forest Service, Caribou National Forest, Pocatello.

Lengas, B. J. 1995b. Unpublished reports, Caribou National Forest Supervisors Office, Pocatello.

Lengas, B. J. 1996a. Spring and summer bat surveys of the caves and abandoned mines on the Wasatch-Cache National Forest, administered by the Caribou National Forest. USDA Forest Service, Caribou National Forest, Pocatello.

Lengas, B. J. 1996b. A winter bat survey of the caves and abandoned mines on the Montpelier Ranger District of the Caribou National Forest. USDA Forest Service, Caribou National Forest, Pocatello.

Lengas, B. J. 1996c. Winter bat surveys of the abandoned mines in Elkhorn Canyon, on the Malad Ranger District of the Caribou National Forest. USDA Forest Service, Caribou National Forest, Pocatello.

Lewis, L. 1994. Assessment of bat inventory and monitoring data in the Shoshone District BLM. BLM report, Shoshone District, Pocatello.

Lewis, L., and M. Wackenhut. 1996. 1995 Idaho bat status survey report. Reports of the Idaho State Conservation Effort, Report 6, Pocatello.

Lewis, L., G. Wright, and P. Perletti. 1996. Hibernating bat inventory and monitoring data in lava-tube caves, southern Idaho. Bureau of Land Management, Unpublished survey report, Shoshone.

Markham, O. D. 1987. Summaries of the Idaho National Engineering Laboratory Radio-ecology and Ecology Program Research Projects. U.S. Department of Energy, Idaho Operations Office DOE/Id–12111, Idaho Falls.

Perkins, J. M., and J. R. Peterson. 1997. Bat distribution in the juniper woodlands of the Idaho Owyhee Mountains: Summer 1996. Idaho Bureau of Land Management Technical Bulletin 97–4, Shoshone.

Pierson, E. D., M. C. Altenbach, P. Bradley, P. Call, D. L. Genter, C. E. Harris, B. L. Keller, B. Lengas, L. Lewis, B. Luce, K. W. Navo, J. M. Perkins, S. Smith, and L. Welch. 1999. Species conservation assessment and strategy for Townsend's big-eared bat (*Corynorhinus townsendii townsendii* and *Corynorhinus townsendii pallescens*). Idaho Conservation Effort, Idaho Department of Fish and Game, Boise.

Reynolds, T. D., R. C. Morris, and O. D. Markham, eds. 1995. Environmental science and research foundation annual technical report [on the Idaho National Engineering Laboratory]: April 11–December 31, 1994. Environmental Science and Research Foundation ESRF-007, Idaho Falls.

Vullo, C., et al. 1997. 1996 Idaho bat status survey report. Idaho State Conservation Effort, Report 9, Boise.

Wackenhut, M. C., and M. McGraw. 1996. Idaho's bats: Description, habitats and conservation. Nongame Leaflet 11. Idaho Department of Fish and Game, Boise.

Wilson, L. O. 1975. Distribution, season of use, and habitat of the mammals, birds, reptiles, amphibians, and fishes of Idaho. Bureau of Land Management, State Office, Boise.

MONTANA

Butts, T. W. 1993a. A preliminary survey of the bats of the Deerlodge National Forest, Montana, 1991. Montana National Heritage Program, Helena.

Butts, T. W. 1993b. A preliminary survey of the bats of the Deerlodge National Forest, Montana, 1992. Montana National Heritage Program, Helena.

Butts, T. W. 1993c. A survey of the bats of the Townsend Ranger District, Helena National Forest, Montana. Montana National Heritage Program, Helena.

Butts, T. W. 1995. Bat surveys, Indian Creek Canyon, Elkhorn Mountains, Montana, 1995. Continental Divide Wildlife Consulting, Helena.

DuBois, K. 1999. Region 4 bat surveys: 1998 Progress Report, Montana Fish, Wildlife and Parks, Region 4 Headquarters, Great Falls.

Feigley, H. P., M. Brown, S. Martínez, and K. Schletz. 1997. Assessment of mines for importance to bat species of concern, southwestern Montana. A progress report to USGS, Midcontinent Ecological Science Center. Montana Heritage Program, Helena.

Genter, D. L., and K. A. Jurist. 1996. Bats of Montana. Montana Natural Heritage Program, Helena.

Hendricks, P. 1997. Mine assessment for bat activity, Garnet Resource Area, BLM. Report to USDI, Bureau of Land Management, Montana Natural Heritage Program, Helena.

———. 1998. Bat surveys of Azure Cave and the Little Rocky Mountains: 1997–1998. Montana National Heritage Program, Helena.

———. 1999a. Effects of gate installation on continued use by bats of four abandoned mine workings in western Montana. Montana National Heritage Program, Helena.

———. 1999b. Mine assessment for bat activity, Helena National Forest: 1999. Montana National Heritage Program, Helena.

———. 2000a. Assessment of abandoned mines for bat use on Bureau of Land Management lands in the Phillipsburg area. Montana National Heritage Program, Helena.

———. 2000b. Preliminary bat inventory of caves and abandoned mines on BLM lands, Judith Mountains, Montana. Montana Natural Heritage Program, Helena.

Hendricks, P., and J. C. Carlson. 2001. Assessment of abandoned mines in the Pryor Mountains for use by bats. Technical Report, Montana Department of Environmental Quality, Mine Waste Cleanup Bureau. Montana Natural Heritage Program, Helena.

Hendricks, P., and D. L. Genter. 1997. Bat surveys of Azure Cave and the Little Rocky Mountains: 1996. Montana Natural Heritage Program, Helena.

Hendricks, P., K. A. Jurist, D. L. Genter, and J. D. Reichel. 1995. Bat survey of the Sioux District, Custer National Forest: 1994. Montana Natural Heritage Program, Helena.

———. 1996. Bats of the Kootenai National Forest, Montana. Montana Natural Heritage Program, Helena.

Hendricks, P., and D. Kampwerth. 2001. Roost environments for bats using abandoned mines in southwestern Montana: A preliminary assessment. Report, U.S. Bureau of Land Management, Montana National Heritage Program, Helena.

Hendricks, P., D. Kampwerth, and M. Brown. 1999. Assessment of abandoned mines for bat use on Bureau of Land Management lands in southwestern Montana: 1997–1998. Report, Montana National Heritage Program, Helena.

Montana Natural Heritage Program. 1992. *Biological data system, 1992 edition.* Arlington, Va.: The Nature Conservancy.

Roemer, D. M. 1994. Results of field surveys for bats on the Kootenai National Forest and Lolo National Forest of western Montana, 1993. Montana Natural Heritage Program, Helena.

Worthington, D. J. 1991. Abundance and distribution of bats in the Pryor Mountains of south-central Montana and northeastern Wyoming. Montana Natural Heritage Program, Helena.

NEW MEXICO

Bogan, M. A., T. J. O'Shea, P. M. Cryan, A. M. Ditto, W. H. Shaedla, and L. Ellison. 1997. Status and trends of bat populations at Los Alamos National Laboratory and Bandelier National Monument, Jemez Mountains, New Mexico. Annual report, Los Alamos National Laboratory and Bandelier National Monument, Los Alamos.

Bogan, M. A., T. J. O'Shea, P. M. Cryan, A. M. Ditto, W. H. Shaedla, E. W. Valdez, and K. T. Castle. 1998. A study of bat populations at Los Alamos National Laboratory and Bandelier National Monument, Jemez Mountains, New Mexico. Annual report, Los Alamos National Laboratory, Los Alamos.

Bogan, M. A., T. J. O'Shea, P. M. Cryan, A. M. Ditto, W. H. Shaedla, E. W. Valdez, K. T. Castle, and L. Ellison. 1998. A study of bat populations at Los Alamos National Laboratory and Bandelier National Monument, Jemez Mountains, New Mexico. Report FY95–97, Los Alamos National Laboratory and Bandelier National Monument, Los Alamos.

Bogan, M. A., T. J. O'Shea, E. W. Valdez, A. M. Ditto, and K. T. Castle. 1998. Continued studies of bat species of concern in the Jemez Mountains, New Mexico. Annual report, Los Alamos National Laboratory and Bandelier National Monument.

Castner, S. V., T. K. Snow, and D. C. Noel. 1994. Bat inventory and monitoring in Arizona 1992–1994. Nongame and Endangered Wildlife Program Technical Report 54. Arizona Game and Fish Department, Phoenix.

Cryan, P. M., and M. A. Bogan. 2000. Recurrence of the Mexican long-tongued bat (*Choeronycteris mexicana*) at historical sites in Arizona and New Mexico. Final report, U.S. Geological Survey Species at Risk Program.

Geluso, K. N., J. S. Altenbach, and R. C. Kerbo. 1987. Bats of Carlsbad Caverns National Park. Carlsbad Caverns Natural History Association, Carlsbad.

Hensley, S., and C. Scott. 1993. Ozark big-eared bat, *Plecotus townsendii ingens* (Hadley), revised recovery plan. U.S. Fish and Wildlife Service Region 2, Albuquerque.

Perry, T., M. A. Bogan, and S. R. Davenport. 1995. Habitat use analysis and needs assessment for bat species on the Lincoln National Forest, Sacramento Mountains, New Mexico. Annual report, Lincoln National Forest, Alamogordo.

UTAH

AGEISS Environmental Inc. 1996. Bat survey report. U.S. Army Dugway Proving Ground, Dugway, Utah. Unpublished report, Dugway Proving Ground Directorate of Environmental Programs, Dugway.

Day, K. S., and L. C. Peterson. 1999a. 1998 baseline inventory of bat species in Grand Staircase-Escalante National Monument, Utah. Unpublished report, Bureau of Land Management, Grand Staircase-Escalante National Monument, Kanab.

———. 1999b. A bat survey of selected locations on Cedar City and Pine Valley Ranger Districts of Dixie National Forest, Utah. Unpublished report, U.S. Forest Service, Dixie National Forest, Cedar City.

Hallows, G. O. 1982. Mammals of Bryce Canyon National Park, Unpublished report, Bryce Canyon Natural History Association, Bryce Canyon.

Jackson, J. G., and M. J. Herder. 1997. Baseline bat inventory of southern Utah using mist nets and ultrasonic detectors. Publication No. 97–10, Utah Division of Wildlife Resources, Cedar City.

Lengas, B. J. 1994a. BLM summer 1994 bat survey. Unpublished report, Bureau of Land Management, Utah State Office, Salt Lake City.

———. 1994b. Summer 1993 bat survey of the Ashley National Forest. Unpublished report, Ashley National Forest, Vernal.

——— 1994c. Summer 1994 bat survey of the Dixie National Forest. Unpublished report, Dixie National Forest, Cedar City.

————. 1994d. A survey of the bat fauna of the caves and mines of Logan Canyon (Cache Co.) and Bat Cave (Weber Co.). Unpublished report, Ogden Ranger District of the Wasatch-Cache National Forest, Ogden.

Lengas, B. J. 1996a. An evaluation of abandoned underground hard rock mines as bat roosting habitat on the Bullion Canyon mining district, Piute County, Utah. Unpublished report, Utah Abandoned Mine Reclamation Program Office, District of Oil, Gas & Mining, Salt Lake City.

Lengas, B. J. 1996b. An evaluation of abandoned underground hard rock mines as bat roosting habitat on the Silver Reef mining district, Washington County, Utah. Unpublished report, Utah Abandoned Mine Reclamation Program Office, District of Oil, Gas & Mining, Salt Lake City.

Lengas, B. J. 1996c. An evaluation of four abandoned shafts as bat roosting habitat on the Flaming Gorge Ranger District of the Ashley National Forest, Uintah County, Utah. Unpublished report, Flaming Gorge Ranger District, Ashley National Forest, Manila.

Lengas, B. J. 1996d. An evaluation of nine abandoned underground hard rock mines as bat roosting habitat in the area of Upper Lathrop Canyon and Airport Tower, Canyonlands National Park, San Juan County, Utah. Unpublished report, Utah Abandoned Mine Reclamation Program Office, Division of Oil, Gas & Mining, Salt Lake City.

Lengas, B. J. 1996e. An evaluation of three abandoned underground hard rock mines as bat roosting habitat in the areas of Shafer Trail and Musselman Arch, Canyonlands National Park, San Juan County, Utah. Unpublished report, Utah Abandoned Mine Reclamation Program Office, Division of Oil, Gas & Mining, Salt Lake City.

Lengas, B. J. 1996f. Results of mist netting for bats over beaver ponds on the Yellowstone Creek, in the High Uinta Wilderness Area of the Ashley National Forest. Unpublished report, Roosevelt Ranger District of the Ashley National Forest, Roosevelt.

Lengas, B. J. 1996g. A survey of the bat fauna from three sites on the Dutch John Privatization Area, Flaming Gorge Ranger District, Ashley National Forest. Unpublished report, Flaming Gorge Ranger District, Ashley National Forest, Manila.

Lengas, B. J. 1997a. An evaluation of abandoned underground hard rock mines as bat roosting habitat in the West Dip abandoned mine project area, Tooele County, Utah. Unpublished report, Utah Abandoned Mine Reclamation Program Office, Division of Oil, Gas & Mining, Salt Lake City.

Lengas, B. J. 1997b. An evaluation of abandoned underground hard rock mines as bat roosting habitat in the Whitehorse abandoned mine project area, Piute and Sevier Counties, Utah. Unpublished report, Utah Abandoned Mine Reclamation Program Office, Division of Oil, Gas & Mining, Salt Lake City.

Lengas, B. J. 1997c. A spring survey for bats within Sheep Creek Cave, Flaming Gorge Ranger District, Ashley National Forest. Unpublished report, Flaming Gorge Ranger District of the Ashley National Forest, Manila.

Lengas, B. J., and J. A. MacMahon. 1996. Summer and winter roost selection in abandoned hard rock mines by Townsend's big-eared bat (*Corynorhinus townsendii*). Abstract, Four Corners Regional Bat Conference, Durango.

Mesch, M., and B. J. Lengas. 1996. Identification and protection of bat habitat at a Utah abandoned mine land site: The Silver Reef Mining District. Abstract, 18th Annual Meeting of the Association of Abandoned Mine Land Programs, Kalispell.

Mollhagen, T. R., and M. A. Bogan. 1995. Baseline surveys for mammals in the Henry Mountains, Utah. Unpublished report, Bureau of Land Management, Henry Mountain Resource Area, Hanksville.

———. 1996. Baseline surveys for mammals in the Henry Mountains, Utah. Unpublished report, Bureau of Land Management, Henry Mountain Resource Area, Hanksville.

Oliver, G. V. 1997. Bats of Utah: Status summaries. Unpublished report, Utah Division of Wildlife, Salt Lake City.

Perkins, J. M. 1996. Results of the survey for bats and other species of concern at the King Edward and Avalanche Mines, San Juan County, Utah, 1995–1996. Unpublished report, Utah Division of Wildlife, Salt Lake City.

Perkins, J. M., and J. R. Petersen. 1997. Bat survey for the Sufco Mine, Emery County, Utah: September 1997. Unpublished report. Utah Division of Wildlife, Salt Lake City.

Poché, R. M. 1981. Ecology of the spotted bat (*Euderma maculatum*) in southwest Utah. Published Report No. 81, Utah Division of Wildlife Resources, Salt Lake City.

Rogers, D. S. 1997. Spotted bat survey (*Euderma maculatum*) in southern Utah. Unpublished report, Bureau of Land Management, Utah State Office, Salt Lake City.

Sherwin, R. E. 1996a. An evaluation of abandoned underground hard rock mines as bat roosting habitat in the Ridgetop abandoned mine project area, Wasatch and Utah Counties, Utah. Unpublished report, Utah Abandoned Mine Reclamation Program Office, Division of Oil, Gas & Mining, Salt Lake City.

Sherwin, R. E. 1996b. Roost site selection by the Townsend's big-eared bat in Northern Utah. Unpublished report, Pleasant Grove Ranger District, Uinta National Forest, Pleasant Grove.

Sherwin, R. E. 1997a. Bat conservation in Utah. Where are we now? Abstract, Annual Meeting of the Utah Wildlife Society, Provo.

Sherwin, R. E. 1997b. Bat survey results of Sheep Creek Cave and Sheep Creek Canyon, Utah. Unpublished report, Flaming Gorge.

Sherwin, R. E. 1997c. Bat survey results of Whiterocks Cave, Ashley National Forest, Utah. Unpublished report, Vernal Ranger District, Vernal.

Sherwin, R. E., and C. Burch. 1995. Surveys of habitat and analysis of success of gating project for C2 bat species in Utah. Unpublished report, Pleasant Grove Ranger District, Uinta National Forest, Pleasant Grove.

Sherwin, R. E., and D. S. Rogers. 1996. Evaluation of bat diversity in Snow Canyon and Coral Pink Sand Dunes State Parks. Unpublished report, SWCA Environmental Consultants, Salt Lake City.

———. 1997. A survey of abandoned mines in the Northern Utah ecoregion: Quantification of their habitat values to bats, and recommendations for methods of closure: Interim report. Unpublished report, Pleasant Grove Ranger District, Uinta National Forest, Pleasant Grove.

Sherwin, R. E., D. S. Rogers, and C. A. Johansson. 1997a. Spotted bat (*Euderma maculatum*) and Townsend's big-eared bat (*Corynorhinus townsendii*) surveys for the LBA 11 Lease Area. Unpublished report, Manti-La Sal National Forest, Emery County.

Sherwin, R. E., D. S. Rogers, and C. A. Johansson. 1997b. Spotted bat (*Euderma maculatum*) and Townsend's big-eared bat (*Corynorhinus townsendii*) surveys of the Cottonwood Canyon Lease Area. Unpublished report, Manti-La Sal National Forest, Emery County.

Sherwin, R. E., D. S. Rogers, and C. A. Johansson. 1997c. Spotted bat (*Euderma maculatum*) and Townsend's big-eared bat (*Corynorhinus townsendii*) surveys of the North Rilda Lease Area. Unpublished report, Manti-La Sal National Forest, Emery County.

Toone, R. A. 1991. General inventory for spotted bats (*Euderma maculatum*) on Abajo Mountain, Monticello RD, Manti-La Sal National Forest, Utah. Unpublished report, Utah Department of Natural Resources, Utah Natural Heritage Program, Salt Lake City.

———. 1992. General inventory for spotted bats (*Euderma maculatum)* on the Wasatch Plateau and Thousand Lakes Mountain, Fishlake National Forest, Unpublished report, United States Forest Service.

———. 1993. General inventory for spotted bats (*Euderma maculatum*) on Wasatch Plateau, Manti-La Sal National Forest, Old Woman Plateau and Thousand Lakes Mountain, Fishlake National Forest, Unpublished report, United States Forest Service.

———. 1994. General inventory for bats in the Abajo Mountains and La Sal Mountains, Manti-La Sal National Forest, Utah, with emphasis on the spotted bat (*Euderma maculatum)* and the Townsend's big-eared bat *(Plecotus townsendii),* Unpublished report, United States Forest Service.

WYOMING

Anonymous. Species profile: Little brown bat. Wyoming Fish and Game Department, Cheyenne.

Armstrong, D. M., and R. A. Adams. 1988. The vertebrates at Fort Laramie National Historical Site: An historical and ecological perspective. Unpublished report, Fort Laramie National Historical Site and National Park Service.

Bogan, M. A., and K. Geluso. 1999. Bat roosts and historical structures on National Park Service lands in the Rocky Mountain Region (Wyoming). Final report, National Park Service, Denver.

Garber, C. S. 1991. A survey for Townsend's big-eared bat and the spotted bat on Bridger Teton and Targhee National Forests in Wyoming. Wyoming Natural Diversity Database, Laramie.

Greenhall, A. M. 1982. Bat house management. Resource Publication, 143. U.S. Fish and Wildlife Service, Laramie.

Haraden, T. 1996. Bat observations, 1995–96, Grand Teton National Park and Teton County, Wyoming. Grand Teton National Park, Moose.

———. 1997. Bat observations, 1996–97, Grand Teton National Park and Teton County, Wyoming. Grand Teton National Park, Moose.

Priday, J., and B. Luce. 1995. Inventory of bats and bat habitat associated with caves and abandoned mines in Wyoming. In *Endangered and nongame bird and mammal investigations—Annual completion report,* pp. 72–131. Cheyenne: Nongame Program, Wyoming Game and Fish Department.

Priday, J., and B. Luce. 1996. Inventory of bats and bat habitat associated with caves and abandoned mines in Wyoming. In *Endangered and nongame bird and mammal investigations—Annual completion report,* pp. 67–116. Cheyenne: Nongame Program, Wyoming Game and Fish Department.

Glossary

adaptation: in evolutionary biology, a behavior, physiology, or structure that makes an organism a better survivor in its environment.

adipose tissue: a type of connective tissue whose cells readily store fat.

altricial: born at a relatively undeveloped and helpless stage of development. Compare *precocial*.

arboreal: tree-dwelling.

bachelor colony: a group of male bats that roosts separately from females, usually during the reproductive period.

bat detector: electronic device sensitive to ultrasonic and audible sounds produced by bats.

bilaterally symmetrical: an arrangement of body axis such that mirror images of an organism result from a single cut passing longitudinally along its midline.

bioamplification: the exponential accumulation and increase in toxins in organisms eating at higher levels of food webs.

biodiversity: all the varieties of life; usually refers to the number and richness of species that make up a community.

biological species: a taxonomic category of interbreeding populations that are reproductively isolated from other such groups.

boreal: northern.

breeding season: the period beginning with courtship and ending with weaning of young.

calcar: a cartilaginous and sometimes partly calcified process of the calcaneus (ankle) bone that contributes to the support of the tail membrane in bats.

carnivory: the habit of eating meat (e.g., insects, fish, amphibians, reptiles, birds, and mammals).

CF: constant frequency (pure tone); a component of ultrasonic pulses produced by some echolocating bats, used in flight for ranging and for judging the speed and direction of prey movements.

Chiroptera: a taxonomic order of mammals that categorizes bats.

coevolution: evolutionary change in which an adaptation in one species acts as a selective force on a second species that in turn acts as a selective force on the first species in a positive-feedback loop.

colony: an aggregation of individuals of a species that interact together.

competitive exclusion principle: the concept that populations of two species cannot coexist in a community if their niches are nearly identical.

copulation: sexual intercourse.

derived characters: features that have changed from the ancestral conditions that are unique to an evolutionary lineage.

dispersal: refers to the geographic movement of an individual away from its place of birth or origin.

dorsal or dorsum: pertaining to the back of a bilaterally symmetrical organism. See *ventral*.

echolocation: the use of echoes of sounds produced by an animal for orientation and prey capture.

ecology: the study of interactions between organisms and their environments, including both living and nonliving components.

ecomorphology: the study of morphological correlates of ecological patterns.

ecotone: a transition zone between adjacent ecosystems.

ectotherm: an animal that warms itself mainly by absorbing heat from its surroundings.

elevational gradient: a predictable change in environmental conditions and relative flora/fauna with elevation.

emergence: the exodus of a bat colony from its roost.

endotherm: an animal that derives most of its body heat from its own metabolism.

ephemeral: fleeting, short-lived.

fauna: the animal life of an ecosystem.

feeding buzz: a rapid series of vocal pulses made by an echolocating bat in its final approach to a prey item.

flora: the plant life of an ecosystem.

FM: frequency modulated pulses produced by some echolocating bats and used mostly for discriminating the size and shape of objects.

foraging: the act of seeking food.

frugivory: the habit of eating fruit.

genus: a taxonomic category within which related species are grouped; plural is *genera*.

gestation: the length of time from fertilization to parturition.

gleaning: a foraging tactic used by some bats whereby prey items are taken from a surface.

guano: the fecal and urinary waste that accumulates within or below a bat roost.

habitat: a place where organisms live.

heterogeneous habitat: a habitat having many plant species and a three-dimensional structure (e.g., piñon-juniper woodlands). See *homogeneous habitat*.

heterotherm: an animal capable of maintaining a constant and regulated body temperature, but also having the ability to survive, without injury or death, temperatures that vary substantially over a wide range.

hibernaculum: a roost used by temperate zone bats in winter (e.g., caves, mines, buildings) for hibernation; plural is *hibernacula*.

hibernation: the assumption of a state of greatly reduced core body temperature for prolonged periods of time during the cold season by a heterothermic animal.

homeotherm: an animal that maintains a constant and tightly regulated body temperature.

homing: the ability of an animal to return to its place of birth or origin if displaced.

homogeneous habitat: a habitat having few numbers of plant species and only a two-dimensional structure (e.g., grasslands). See *heterogeneous habitat*.

Insectivora: a taxonomic order of mammals that includes shrews and moles.

insectivory: the habit of eating insects.

juvenile: an animal that has not reached reproductive age or adult physical dimensions.

kilohertz (kHz): a measure of sound frequency in units of 1,000 cycles per second.

mammalian radiation: an increase in number of species of mammals over a short period of geologic time (i.e., a few million years).

maternity colony: an aggregation of female bats during pregnancy and lactation.

maternity roost: a site used by females during pregnancy and lactation.

mating: the act of pairing between males and females during courtship.

Megachiroptera: one of two suborders of bats; it is composed of a single family, the Pteropodidae. See *Microchiroptera.*

megafauna: large-bodied animals.

mesic: refers to a relatively wet habitat. See *xeric.*

Microchiroptera: one of two suborders of bats; it includes seventeen families of mostly insectivorous and frugivorous bats. See *Megachiroptera.*

migration: the regular and predictable seasonal movements of individuals or populations.

natural selection: the mechanism of evolution proposed by Charles Darwin and Alfred Russel Wallace in 1859 based on differential reproductive success of individuals exhibiting adaptive traits in populations.

nectarivory: the habit of feeding on nectar.

neonate: newborn young.

Neotropics: New World tropical habitats.

night roost: a roost site used by bats at night for various activities, such as consuming and digesting prey and behavioral interactions, usually located under an open-air overhang made by a rock or human-made structure such as a porch.

nose leaf: a fold of skin of various shapes extending mostly vertically above the nose of some bat species indicating nasal emission of echolocatory calls.

ontogeny: the process of development of an organism.

orogeny: the process of mountain building.

parturition: the process of giving birth.

patagium: the membrane that forms the wings and uropatagium of bats.

pelage: a collective term pertaining to body fur.

phylogeny: the evolutionary relationships among taxonomic groups.

physiography: the study of land forms.

pinna: the fleshy outer flap of a mammal's ear; plural is *pinnae.*

postlactating: the reproductive state of a female when lactation has ceased.

precocial: active from birth; requiring little maternal care.

propatagium: the membrane between the wrist and the body in bats.

pup: the term for a newborn bat.

raptor: a bird of prey.

roost: a site used by bats when not in flight.

shrub: a woody plant having no well-defined trunk and of relatively low height.

sonar: a method of using sound for navigation or investigating the environment.

spectrograph: a graphical depiction of sound, usually kHz plotted against time.

swarming: an activity of bats (males and females) observed around hibernacula from midsummer through early autumn that apparently involves mating.

thermoregulation: the ability to regulate body temperature either by internal or external means.

torpor: a voluntary physiological state in which a heterothermic animal's body temperature is depressed, resulting in a lowered metabolic rate and an inability to perform normal behaviors, such as locomotion.

tragus: the fleshy projection from the lower medial margin of the pinnae in most microchiropteran bats.

ultrasonic: pertains to sound frequencies above the audible range of human hearing, usually frequencies above 20 kHz.

uropatagium: the membrane extending between the tail and hind legs in bats.

ventral or ventrum: refers to the underside of a bilaterally symmetrical animal. See *dorsal*.

vertebrate: having a skull and usually a backbone.

volant: having the power of flight.

volcanism: volcanic activity.

weaning: the period when a juvenile switches from taking mother's milk to a "solid" diet.

whispering bat: a bat species that emits low-frequency echolocation pulses.

wing loading: the ratio of body mass (g) divided by wing area (cm²).

xeric: refers to an extremely dry habitat. See *mesic*.

xerification: the process of changing from a wetter to a drier habitat.`

Index